MERCEDES-BENZ
G-WAGEN

1979 to 2015

Brian Long

Other books from Veloce Publishing

1½-litre GP Racing 1961-1965 (Whitelock)
AC Two-litre Saloons & Buckland Sportscars (Archibald)
Alfa Romeo 155/156/147 Competition Touring Cars (Collins)
Alfa Romeo Giulia Coupé GT & GTA (Tipler)
Alfa Romeo Montreal – The dream car that came true (Taylor)
Alfa Romeo Montreal – The Essential Companion (Classic Reprint of 500 copies) (Taylor)
Alfa Tipo 33 (McDonough & Collins)
Alpine & Renault – The Development of the Revolutionary Turbo F1 Car 1968 to 1979 (Smith)
Alpine & Renault – The Sports Prototypes 1963 to 1969 (Smith)
Alpine & Renault – The Sports Prototypes 1973 to 1978 (Smith)
Anatomy of the Works Minis (Moylan)
Armstrong-Siddeley (Smith)
Art Deco and British Car Design (Down)
Autodrome (Collins & Ireland)
Autodrome 2 (Collins & Ireland)
Automotive A-Z, Lane's Dictionary of Automotive Terms (Lane)
Automotive Mascots (Kay & Springate)
Bahamas Speed Weeks, The (O'Neil)
Bentley Continental, Corniche and Azure (Bennett)
Bentley MkVI, Rolls-Royce Silver Wraith, Dawn & Cloud/ Bentley R & S-Series (Nutland)
Bluebird CN7 (Stevens)
BMC Competitions Department Secrets (Turner, Chambers & Browning)
BMW 5-Series (Cranswick)
BMW Z-Cars (Taylor)
BMW Boxer Twins 1970-1995 Bible, The (Falloon)
BMW Cafe Racers (Cloesen)
BMW Custom Motorcycles – Choppers, Cruisers, Bobbers, Trikes & Quads (Cloesen)
BMW – The Power of M (Vivian)
Bonjour – Is this Italy? (Turner)
British 250cc Racing Motorcycles (Pereira)
British at Indianapolis, The (Wagstaff)
British Cars, The Complete Catalogue of, 1895-1975 (Culshaw & Horrobin)
British Custom Motorcycles – The Brit Chop – choppers, cruisers, bobbers & trikes (Cloesen)
BRM – A Mechanic's Tale (Salmon)
BRM V16 (Ludvigsen)
BSA Bantam Bible, The (Henshaw)
BSA Motorcycles – the final evolution (Jones)
Bugatti Type 40 (Price)
Bugatti 46/50 Updated Edition (Price & Arbey)
Bugatti T44 & T49 (Price & Arbey)
Bugatti 57 2nd Edition (Price)
Bugatti Type 57 Grand Prix – A Celebration (Tomlinson)
Caravan, Improve & Modify Your (Porter)
Caravans, The Illustrated History 1919-1959 (Jenkinson)
Caravans, The Illustrated History From 1960 (Jenkinson)
Carrera Panamericana, La (Tipler)
Chrysler 300 – America's Most Powerful Car 2nd Edition (Ackerson)
Chrysler PT Cruiser (Ackerson)
Citroën DS (Bobbitt)
Classic British Car Electrical Systems (Astley)
Cobra – The Real Thing! (Legate)
Competition Car Aerodynamics 3rd Edition (McBeath)
Concept Cars, How to illustrate and design (Dewey)
Cortina – Ford's Bestseller (Robson)
Coventry Climax Racing Engines (Hammill)
Daily Mirror 1970 World Cup Rally 40, The (Robson)
Daimler SP250 New Edition (Long)
Datsun Fairlady Roadster to 280ZX – The Z-Car Story (Long)
Dino – The V6 Ferrari (Long)
Dodge Challenger & Plymouth Barracuda (Grist)
Dodge Charger – Enduring Thunder (Ackerson)
Dodge Dynamite! (Grist)
Dorset from the Sea – The Jurassic Coast from Lyme Regis to Old Harry Rocks photographed from its best viewpoint (Belasco)
Dorset from the Sea – The Jurassic Coast from Lyme Regis to Old Harry Rocks photographed from its best viewpoint (souvenir edition) (Belasco)
Draw & Paint Cars – How to (Gardiner)
Drive on the Wild Side, A – 20 Extreme Driving Adventures From Around the World (Weaver)
Ducati 750 Bible, The (Falloon)
Ducati 750 SS 'round-case' 1974, The Book of the (Falloon)
Ducati 860, 900 and Mille Bible, The (Falloon)
Ducati Monster Bible (New Updated & Revised Edition), The (Falloon)
Dune Buggy, Building A – The Essential Manual (Shakespeare)
Dune Buggy Files (Hale)
Dune Buggy Handbook (Hale)
East German Motor Vehicles in Pictures (Suhr/Weinreich)
Fast Ladies – Female Racing Drivers 1888 to 1970 (Bouzanquet)
Fate of the Sleeping Beauties, The (op de Weegh/ Hottendorff/op de Weegh)
Ferrari 288 GTO, The Book of the (Sackey)
Ferrari 333 SP (O'Neil)
Fiat & Abarth 124 Spider & Coupé (Tipler)
Fiat & Abarth 500 & 600 – 2nd Edition (Bobbitt)
Fiats, Great Small (Ward)
Fine Art of the Motorcycle Engine, The (Peirce)
Ford Cleveland 335-Series V8 engine 1970 to 1982 – The Essential Source Book (Hammill)
Ford F100/F150 Pick-up 1948-1996 (Ackerson)
Ford F150 Pick-up 1997-2005 (Ackerson)
Ford GT – Then, and Now (Streather)
Ford GT40 (Legate)
Ford Model Y (Roberts)
Ford Small Block V8 Racing Engines 1962-1970 – The Essential Source Book (Hammill)
Ford Thunderbird From 1954, The Book of the (Long)
Formula 5000 Motor Racing, Back then ... and back now (Lawson)
Forza Minardi! (Vigar)
France: the essential guide for car enthusiasts – 200 things for the car enthusiast to see and do (Parish)
From Crystal Palace to Red Square – A Hapless Biker's Road to Russia (Turner)
Funky Mopeds (Skelton)
Grand Prix Ferrari – The Years of Enzo Ferrari's Power, 1948-1980 (Pritchard)
Grand Prix Ford – DFV-powered Formula 1 Cars (Robson)
GT – The World's Best GT Cars 1953-73 (Dawson)
Hillclimbing & Sprinting – The Essential Manual (Short & Wilkinson)
Honda NSX (Long)
Inside the Rolls-Royce & Bentley Styling Department – 1971 to 2001 (Hull)
Intermeccanica – The Story of the Prancing Bull (McCredie & Reisner)
Italian Cafe Racers (Cloesen)
Italian Custom Motorcycles (Cloesen)
Jaguar, The Rise of (Price)
Jaguar XJ 220 – The Inside Story (Moreton)
Jaguar XJ-S, The Book of the (Long)
Jeep CJ (Ackerson)
Jeep Wrangler (Ackerson)
Karmann-Ghia Coupé & Convertible (Bobbitt)
Kawasaki Triples Bible, The (Walker)
Kawasaki Z1 Story, The (Sheehan)
Kris Meeke – Intercontinental Rally Challenge Champion (McBride)
Lamborghini Miura Bible, The (Sackey)
Lamborghini Urraco, The Book of the (Landsem)
Lambretta Bible, The (Davies)
Lancia 037 (Collins)
Lancia Delta HF Integrale (Blaettel & Wagner)
Land Rover Series III Reborn (Porter)
Land Rover, The Half-ton Military (Cook)
Laverda Twins & Triples Bible 1968-1986 (Falloon)
Lea-Francis Story, The (Price)
Le Mans Panoramic (Ireland)
Lexus Story, The (Long)
Little book of microcars, the (Quellin)
Little book of smart, the – New Edition (Jackson)
Little book of trikes, the (Quellin)
Lola – The Illustrated History (1957-1977) (Starkey)
Lola – All the Sports Racing & Single-seater Racing Cars 1978-1997 (Starkey)
Lola T70 – The Racing History & Individual Chassis Record – 4th Edition (Starkey)
Lotus 49 (Oliver)
Marketingmobiles, The Wonderful Wacky World of (Hale)
Maserati 250F In Focus (Pritchard)
Mazda MX-5/Miata 1.6 Enthusiast's Workshop Manual (Grainger & Shoemark)
Mazda MX-5/Miata 1.8 Enthusiast's Workshop Manual (Grainger & Shoemark)
The book of the Mazda MX-5 Miata – The 'Mk1' NA-series 1988 to 1997 (Long)
Mazda MX-5 Miata Roadster (Long)
Maximum Mini (Booij)
Meet the English (Bowie)
Mercedes-Benz SL – R230 series 2001 to 2011 (Long)
Mercedes-Benz SL – W113-series 1963-1971 (Long)
Mercedes-Benz SL & SLC – 107-series 1971-1989 (Long)
Mercedes-Benz SLK – R170 series 1996-2004 (Long)
Mercedes-Benz SLK – R171 series 2004-2011 (Long)
Mercedes-Benz W123-series – All models 1976 to 1986 (Long)
MGA (Price Williams)
MGB & MGB GT– Expert Guide (Auto-doc Series) (Williams)
MGB Electrical Systems Updated & Revised Edition (Astley)
Micro Caravans (Jenkinson)
Micro Trucks (Mort)
Microcars at Large! (Quellin)
Mini Cooper – The Real Thing! (Tipler)
Mini Minor to Asia Minor (West)
Mitsubishi Lancer Evo, The Road Car & WRC Story (Long)
Montlhéry, The Story of the Paris Autodrome (Boddy)
Morgan Maverick (Lawrence)
Morgan 3 Wheeler – back to the future!, The (Dron)
Morris Minor, 60 Years on the Road (Newell)
Moto Guzzi Sport & Le Mans Bible, The (Falloon)
Motor Movies – The Posters! (Veysey)
Motor Racing – Reflections of a Lost Era (Carter)
Motor Racing – The Pursuit of Victory 1930-1962 (Carter)
Motor Racing – The Pursuit of Victory 1963-1972 (Wyatt/ Sears)
Motor Racing Heroes – The Stories of 100 Greats (Newman)
Motorcycle Apprentice (Cakebread)
Motorcycle GP Racing in the 1960s (Pereira)
Motorcycle Road & Racing Chassis Designs (Noakes)
Motorhomes, The Illustrated History (Jenkinson)
Motorsport In colour, 1950s (Wainwright)
MV Agusta Fours, The book of the classic (Falloon)
N.A.R.T. – A concise history of the North American Racing Team 1957 to 1983 (O'Neil)
Nissan 300ZX & 350Z – The Z-Car Story (Long)
Nissan GT-R Supercar: Born to race (Gorodji)
Northeast American Sports Car Races 1950-1959 (O'Neil)
Nothing Runs – Misadventures in the Classic, Collectable & Exotic Car Biz (Slutsky)
Off-Road Giants! (Volume 1) – Heroes of 1960s Motorcycle Sport (Westlake)
Off-Road Giants! (Volume 2) – Heroes of 1960s Motorcycle Sport (Westlake)
Off-Road Giants! (volume 3) – Heroes of 1960s Motorcycle Sport (Westlake)
Pass the Theory and Practical Driving Tests (Gibson & Hoole)
Peking to Paris 2007 (Young)
Pontiac Firebird (Cranswick)
Porsche Boxster (Long)
Porsche 356 (2nd Edition) (Long)
Porsche 908 (Födisch, Neßhöver, Roßbach, Schwarz & Roßbach)
Porsche 911 Carrera – The Last of the Evolution (Corlett)
Porsche 911R, RS & RSR, 4th Edition (Starkey)
Porsche 911, The Book of the (Long)
Porsche 911SC 'Super Carrera' – The Essential Companion (Streather)
Porsche 914 & 914-6: The Definitive History of the Road & Competition Cars (Long)
Porsche 924 (Long)
The Porsche 924 Carreras – evolution to excellence (Smith)
Porsche 928 (Long)
Porsche 944 (Long)
Porsche 964, 993 & 996 Data Plate Code Breaker (Streather)
Porsche 993 'King Of Porsche' – The Essential Companion (Streather)
Porsche 996 'Supreme Porsche' – The Essential Companion (Streather)
Porsche Racing Cars – 1953 to 1975 (Long)
Porsche Racing Cars – 1976 to 2005 (Long)
Porsche – The Rally Story (Meredith)
Porsche: Three Generations of Genius (Meredith)
Preston Tucker & Others (Linde)
RAC Rally Action! (Gardiner)
RACING COLOURS – MOTOR RACING COMPOSITIONS 1908-2009 (Newman)
Racing Line – British motorcycle racing in the golden age of the big single (Guntrip)
Rallye Sport Fords: The Inside Story (Moreton)
Renewable Energy Home Handbook, The (Porter)
Roads with a View – England's greatest views and how to find them by road (Corfield)
Rolls-Royce Silver Shadow/Bentley T Series Corniche & Camargue – Revised & Enlarged Edition (Bobbitt)
Rolls-Royce Silver Spirit, Silver Spur & Bentley Mulsanne 2nd Edition (Bobbitt)
Runways & Racers (O'Neil)
Russian Motor Vehicles – Soviet Limousines 1930-2003 (Kelly)
Russian Motor Vehicles – The Czarist Period 1784 to 1917 (Kelly)
RX-7 – Mazda's Rotary Engine Sportscar (Updated & Revised New Edition) (Long)
Scooters & Microcars, The A-Z of Popular (Dan)
Scooter Lifestyle (Grainger)
SCOOTER MANIA! – Recollections of the Isle of Man International Scooter Rally (Jackson)
Singer Story: Cars, Commercial Vehicles, Bicycles & Motorcycle (Atkinson)
Sleeping Beauties USA – abandoned classic cars & trucks (Marek)
SM – Citroën's Maserati-engined Supercar (Long & Claverol)
Speedway – Auto racing's ghost tracks (Collins & Ireland)
Sprite Caravans, The Story of (Jenkinson)
Standard Motor Company, The Book of the
Subaru Impreza: The Road Car And WRC Story (Long)
Supercar, How to Build your own (Thompson)
Tales from the Toolbox (Oliver)
Tatra – The Legacy of Hans Ledwinka, Updated & Enlarged Collector's Edition of 1500 copies (Margolius & Henry)
Taxi! The Story of the 'London' Taxicab (Bobbitt)
Toleman Story, The (Hilton)
Toyota Celica & Supra, The Book of Toyota's Sports Coupés (Long)
Toyota MR2 Coupés & Spyders (Long)
Triumph Bonneville Bible (59-83) (Henshaw)
Triumph Bonneville!, Save the – The inside story of the Meriden Workers' Co-op (Rosamond)
Triumph Motorcycles & the Meriden Factory (Hancox)
Triumph Speed Twin & Thunderbird Bible (Woolridge)
Triumph Tiger Cub Bible (Estall)
Triumph Trophy Bible (Woolridge)
Triumph TR6 (Kimberley)
TT Talking – The TT's most exciting era – As seen by Manx Radio TT's lead commentator 2004-2012 (Lambert)
Two Summers – The Mercedes-Benz W196R Racing Car (Ackerson)
TWR Story, The – Group A (Hughes & Scott)
Unraced (Collins)
Velocette Motorcycles – MSS to Thruxton – New Third Edition (Burris)
Vespa – The Story of a Cult Classic in Pictures (Uhlig)
Volkswagen Bus Book, The (Bobbitt)
Volkswagen Bus or Van to Camper, How to Convert (Porter)
Volkswagens of the World (Glen)
VW Beetle Cabriolet – The full story of the convertible Beetle (Bobbitt)
VW Beetle – The Car of the 20th Century (Copping)
VW Bus – 40 Years of Splitties, Bays & Wedges (Copping)
VW Bus Book, The (Bobbitt)
VW Golf: Five Generations of Fun (Copping & Cservenka)
VW – The Air-cooled Era (Copping)
VW T5 Camper Conversion Manual (Porter)
VW Campers (Copping)
You & Your Jaguar XK8/XKR – Buying, Enjoying, Maintaining, Modifying – New Edition (Thorley)
Which Oil? – Choosing the right oils & greases for your antique, vintage, veteran, classic or collector car (Michell)
Works Minis, The Last (Purves & Brenchley)
Works Rally Mechanic (Moylan)

www.veloce.co.uk

Published in May 2016 by Veloce Publishing Limited, Veloce House, Parkway Farm Business Park, Middle Farm Way, Poundbury, Dorchester DT1 3AR, England. Fax 01305 268864 / e-mail info@veloce.co.uk / web www.veloce.co.uk or www.velocebooks.com.
ISBN: 978-1-845847-77-7. UPC: 6-36847-04777-1 Readers with ideas for automotive books, or books on other transport or related hobby subjects, are invited to write to the editorial director of Veloce Publishing at the above address.
British Library Cataloging in Publication Data – A catalogue record for this book is available from the British Library. Typesetting, design and page make-up all by Veloce Publishing Ltd on Apple Mac.
Printed in India by Replika Press.

For post publication news, updates and amendments relating to this book please visit www.veloce.co.uk/books/V4777

MERCEDES-BENZ
G-WAGEN

1979 to 2015

Brian Long

Contents

Introduction and acknowledgements

The author has been following the development of the Mercedes-Benz marque since childhood, but even I was surprised by the massive number of variants fielded under the iconic G-Wagen name during the last 35 years or so – not just in military and specialist working machine lines, where one can expect to come across a few surprises, but in the road car offerings as well. I have to say that I'd totally underestimated the number of avenues requiring research, although the new knowledge that came about as a result of this project – often resorting to handwritten notes on huge sheets of paper to make sense of things over such a long period of time – was actually quite refreshing.

Just as refreshing, in an era where all cars are starting to look and drive much alike, is the chance to write about something that flies in the face of convention. As the US journalist Daniel Pund said in 2001, the Mercedes-Benz G-Wagen is "built like a brick scheisshaus in the age of modern plumbing."

Indeed, just about every aspect of the car breaks the unwritten rules of the motor trade. Early sales, at around 6000-6500 units a year, were hardly worth bothering with for a company the size of Daimler-Benz, but the Stuttgart giant continued to support the G-Wagen, and widened its appeal as a road car via the 463-series. Eventually, the US market was conquered as the popularity of SUVs soared, and now, despite the boxy shape staying a constant throughout the life of the model (the retention of a basic body design would normally send sales in a downward spiral in a lesser vehicle line), demand for the G-Wagen is at record levels, justifying the launch of a new generation in 2015. It's also nice to report that at the same time as a revised line-up is being introduced, as many as eight out of every ten vehicles built beforehand are still on the road – a true testament to the quality of the materials used, and the original design work, which has stood the test of time remarkably well given the way in which technology has progressed and the demands of motorists changed during the last three or four decades.

Mention should be made at this stage that the book centres on the mainstream production cars, venturing into the wilderness every now and again to briefly cover things like rivals, top-flight competition, military machines and tuning to put things into perspective and give the reader an idea of what was available. I trust people will understand this stance, as virtually every car going down the line at Graz is unique – there are so many variations of the regular models to cover as it is, while a true record of the vehicles built for the armed forces and professional users would each run to several thousand pages, assuming we left out the contemporary showroom models!

In addition, this book takes the story up to the introduction of the 2016 Model Year face-lift only, which took place in the middle of 2015, and has only been covered lightly to allow more space for the cars built beforehand. There's already a lot happened since, but we have to decide on a suitable cut-off point somewhere along the line, and this seemed like the ideal spot. I'm sure there will be plenty to talk about further into the future, too.

Anyway, for now, I sincerely hope that past owners, present owners, those thinking of ownership, or simply followers of Mercedes-Benz lore, will all enjoy tracking the steady evolution of the Mercedes-Benz and Puch G-Wagen through these pages, and perhaps gain the same appreciation for this old warrior as I have during my months and months of research. Don't be surprised if you happen to spot a pre-loved G500 with wood and leather trim in my driveway by the time this book goes into its second edition ...

Acknowledgements

As always, because of the use of contemporary photography as a matter of policy, these books cannot possibly be done without a great deal of help from the factory. As with the author's earlier Mercedes books, I would particularly like to record my sincere appreciation for the services of Gerhard Heidbrink at Daimler AG in Stuttgart – a more helpful chap would be hard to find, and this book simply wouldn't have been possible without his kind co-operation.

I should also like to thank Nils Beckmann and Joerg Rupp in Stuttgart for managing to drag me into the 21st century on the parts book front, Kenichi Kobayashi at Miki Press, Richard Kaan, the extensive research facilities at the Japan Motor Industry Federation (JMIF) in Tokyo, Scott Worden, Ana Topolic, Alexandra Reisinger of Magna Steyr AG, Rob Halloway at Mercedes-Benz UK, and Robert Moran and Christian Bokich of Mercedes-Benz USA. There have been many, many others, but to list them all would take another book! You know who you are, and I will not forget you ...

Brian Long
Chiba City, Japan

1

The three-pointed star

There can be few trademarks so readily recognisable in all corners of the globe as the Mercedes-Benz three-pointed star. The three arms signify the land, sea and air, and the Stuttgart company the star has come to represent has indeed conquered each in its own inimitable way over the years. The story behind the star, though, is a long and complicated one, so this chapter briefly outlines the brand's history to set the scene before the arrival of the first G-Wagen models.

The story starts with two men – pioneers in the motor industry – Gottlieb Daimler, and Carl Benz. Amazingly, given the pre-eminence of the pair in a fledgling trade, not to mention their closeness geographically, the two never actually met, but the coming together of their names is the important thing here.

In 1882, Gottlieb Daimler established a small workshop at the back of his villa in Cannstatt, on the outskirts of Stuttgart, about 12 miles (20km) west of his birthplace, with Wilhelm Maybach working alongside him. A number of single-cylinder, air-cooled petrol engines were duly developed, and used to power the world's first motorcycle in 1885, along with a four-wheeled horseless carriage, which made its initial runs during the

Daimler Wagon from the mid-1890s, an era when automobiles really were still little more than horseless carriages.

An early version of the Benz Motorwagen, which quickly evolved into the Benz Patent – the world's first series-production car to be powered by a petrol engine.

autumn of 1886. Within a short space of time, the engines were finding various applications on land, on water, and even in the air. By 1890, the products emanating from the Daimler Motoren Gesellschaft had caught the imagination of the engineering world.

Meanwhile, about 55 miles (90km) north in Mannheim, Carl Benz was busy working on his two-stroke petrol engines,

Founding fathers of the brand

Gottlieb Daimler

Daimler was born in Schorndorf in March 1834, and after serving an apprenticeship as a gunsmith, promptly moved into the field of engineering, gaining experience in France and Britain before returning to his homeland.

He was appointed Technical Manager of the Deutz Gas Engine Works (founded by Nikolaus August Otto, credited as the father of the four-stroke, or 'Otto-cycle' engine) in 1872, with Wilhelm Maybach as his right-hand man. However, Daimler's overwhelming interest in faster-running, more powerful petrol engines created a rift in the Cologne-based firm, and ultimately a decision was made to form an independent company dealing with this new technology.

After building a second car, this time powered by a water-cooled V-twin, in 1889, it was obvious that Daimler and Maybach were on the right track. The Daimler Motoren Gesellschaft (DMG) was registered in November 1890 to manufacture and market these two-cylinder units, which were a revelation at the time. As such, Daimler was successful in selling patents to many concerns. One of the first to sign up was Panhard & Levassor in France, who duly provided engines for a number of makers, and became a highly successful car manufacturer in its own right.

Daimler and Maybach remained close friends even after the latter was forced to leave the Cannstatt company due to a clash of policy with its new investors. Meanwhile, Daimler's health was failing. Internal conflict with members of the Board probably didn't help, and he ultimately resigned from the company he'd founded at one point in 1894.

Daimler and Maybach joined forces again, this time with Daimler's son, Paul, and between them they designed a four-cylinder engine equipped with Maybach's innovative spray-nozzle carburettor. Known as the Phönix, it signified the rebirth of a fine team in both name and nature, and, following some political manoeuvring from Frederick Simms (a key figure in the Daimler Motor Co. Limited in England), the pair was asked to return to the DMG on new, far more favourable terms.

Gottlieb Daimler died in March 1900, although Maybach continued his work before ultimately making aero-engines for the famous Zeppelin airships. After the Great War, Maybach built a series of luxury cars until the Second World War put an end to production. Recently, the name was revived as a Mercedes-Benz flagship saloon.

Carl Benz

The son of a train driver, Carl Benz was born in November 1844. After moving around a number of concerns, some involved in the building of iron structures, such as bridges, Benz finally established his own engineering shop in Mannheim in 1871. This was not successful, and Benz turned his attention to two-stroke engines in 1877, with the first unit running successfully two years later.

By 1882, the Benz engine had attracted investors, and Gasmotorenfabrik Mannheim was established, although Benz left the company soon after when the shareholders tried to influence designs. Notwithstanding, in October 1883, 'Benz & Co Rheinische Gasmotorenfabrik, Mannheim' was formed with the help of two local businessmen, and by 1886 the world's first, purpose-built vehicle to be powered by a petrol engine – the three-wheeled Benz Patent Motorwagon – had made its debut.

Four-wheeled cars were produced in 1891, and Benz continued to innovate, designing steering systems and developing the horizontally-opposed (boxer) engine amongst other things. The commercial success of the company can be gauged by the fact that Benz & Cie AG was registered in May 1899. However, by early 1903, Benz became disillusioned with the people running the firm and resigned, although he did retain a position on the Supervisory Board until his death.

Meanwhile, Benz formed a new company with his son Eugen in 1906, called C Benz Söhne, which turned to car production after a spell in the field of gas engines. This business, based in Ladenburg, to the east of Mannheim, was duly handed over to Eugen and his younger brother, Richard, in 1912. This particular firm officially stopped building cars in 1923.

Incidentally, for many years, it was assumed and accepted that Benz's forename was Karl, in the German tradition, but the correct spelling is in fact Carl. He died in April 1929, but at least he was able to witness motoring evolve from a sport for the well-heeled into an essential part of daily life.

Gottlieb Daimler.　　　　Carl Benz.

while the companies bearing their names fought in the showrooms and on the race tracks of Europe. The battle for the hearts of the rich and famous, and the silverware that comes with victory in competition, was never as fierce as it was in the years leading up to the First World War.

At Daimler, rapid expansion led to the purchase of a large site in Untertürkheim on the eastern edge of Stuttgart in August 1900, which would duly become the spiritual home of Mercedes-Benz.

The Mercedes moniker was first adopted by Emil Jellinek, an Austrian who, among other things, sold Daimlers to wealthy clients in the south of France. Jellinek was a clever businessman, and he proposed a number of changes that he knew would appeal to his customers and his own sporting nature, such as a lower body and longer wheelbase in order to cope with the greater power outputs he outlined.

Jellinek promised to take a large number of these vehicles (at least by the standards of the day) in return for distribution rights in France, Belgium, the Austro-Hungarian Empire, and America, but also requested that they carry the 'Mercédès' badge – the name of his daughter, and the pseudonym he used during his various racing exploits.

A 4/8hp Paul Daimler-Wagen, built between 1901 and 1902. It was the DMG's celebrated Mercédès model that captured the headlines, however.

as patents covering four-stroke power-units had already been filed by the Deutz concern, the company Daimler worked for. Eventually, Benz also opted for Otto-cycle engines, putting a single-cylinder unit in a purpose-built frame to produce the world's first petrol-driven car, patented in January 1886. By 1890, Benz & Co was Germany's second largest engine manufacturer, and as the century drew to a close, one of the world's most prolific automobile makers, with almost 600 cars built in 1899 alone.

A healthy rivalry

At the end of the day, Daimler and Benz were rival inventors,

The Mercédès 14/35hp limousine from before the Great War. Although most cars were typically staid, like this one with factory-built coachwork, it should be noted that both the Mercédès and Benz marques were very active in motorsport at this time, not only in Europe, but America, too. Both made some beautiful two-seaters reflecting this.

The 12/14hp Benz Parsifal from 1903. This popular shaft-driven series made its debut at the Paris Salon in December 1902.

A deal was struck, and Wilhelm Maybach (1846-1929) set about designing the first Mercédès in conjunction with Paul Daimler. The end result, a racing car which appeared at the end of 1900, provided the foundation stone for the modern automobile, with a low, pressed steel chassis frame playing host to a 5.9-litre, 35hp engine cooled by a honeycomb radiator, and a gate for the gearchange.

The Mercédès was raced with a great deal of success, and many variations were produced for regular use, from an 8/11hp version all the way up to a 9.2-litre 60hp model. The Mercédès set the standard for the day in the high-class car market, and was built under licence – or often simply copied – by numerous manufacturers, although it should be said that by this time, Daimler in Coventry, England, had long since found its own direction in terms of design and manufacturing.

Six-cylinder engines followed in 1906, and there was a limited run of Knight sleeve-valve models just before the First World War. A few years after the conflict, when technology, metallurgy and production techniques made great strides, the first supercharged Mercédès made its debut, and in April 1923, Ferdinand Porsche was drafted from Austro-Daimler to become Chief Engineer, bringing overhead camshafts and front-wheel brakes to the marque in a series of exceptionally elegant supercharged models.

Meanwhile, Benz & Cie also made giant steps forward at the turn of the century, albeit against the wishes of Carl Benz, modernising the range with conventional two- and four-cylinder cars designed by a Frenchman, Marius Barbarou. Internal conflict ultimately led to Benz giving up his post as Chief Engineer, although he remained on the Board until his death, and also formed another company with his sons to allow himself more freedom on design policy. The latter business was short-lived, however, building cars from 1906 to 1923.

Benz & Cie continued to follow a safe path with its vehicles thereafter, with Hans Nibel in charge of design from 1910. However, Nibel's love of racing spawned a number of interesting competition cars (he had even been involved with the machine that formed the basis for the streamlined Blitzen Benz record breaker), and the Benz marque duly found favour with a wealthy clientele. One of the most ardent supporters of the brand was Prince Henry of Prussia – the brother of Kaiser Wilhelm II.

Benz introduced its first six-cylinder engine in 1914, and

A Benz 14/30hp saloon of 1912 vintage.

Stylish artwork released soon after the merger of two of the greatest names in the German car industry, if not the world.

stuck almost exclusively to straight-sixes following the conflict. By this time, the company had produced some magnificent aero-engines, including a supercharged V12, and was also a leading light in the field of diesel technology.

In the background, however, the wheels of finance were turning, and, for a number of reasons, a huge amount of shares in both firms came to be held by the Deutsche Bank. An agreement of mutual interest was signed on 1 May 1924, with a syndicate being formed in order to save production costs in an era of high inflation, and then, on 28 June 1926, a full merger took place, giving birth to Daimler-Benz AG.

A new star is born

Although the company was known as Daimler-Benz, the cars were marketed using the Mercedes-Benz name, with Mercedes officially losing the accents along the way. Only two Benz models made it into the Mercedes-Benz passenger car programme, and both were gone by 1927.

There were straight-eights from October 1928, and the marque went into the mid-1930s with some magnificent creations, with the SS and SSK giving way to the 500K and 540K.

The supercharged six-cylinder SS (27/140/200hp) seen here with a magnificent touring body – the epitome of vintage era glamour.

By this time, the company was producing a range of vehicles that went from modest 1.3-litre saloons, with its NA four at the rear, all the way up to 7.7-litre supercharged eights with their glamorous coachbuilt bodies.

1938 –
ein neues Rekordjahr der Siege!

Rennen	Erster	Zweiter	Dritter
Großer Preis von Pau	—	Lang-Caracciola	—
Großer Preis von Tripolis	Lang	v. Brauchitsch	Caracciola
Großer Preis von Frankreich	v. Brauchitsch	Caracciola	Lang
Großer Preis von Deutschland	Seaman	Lang-Caracciola	—
Coppa Ciano	Lang	—	—
Coppa Acerbo	Caracciola	—	—
Großer Preis der Schweiz	Caracciola	Seaman	v. Brauchitsch
Großer Preis von Italien	—	—	Caracciola-v. Brauchitsch
Großer Preis von Donington	—	Lang	Seaman

Rudolf Caracciola zum dritten Mal Europameister

MERCEDES-BENZ

Advertising from 1938, by which time the Silver Arrows legend had already been firmly established by the Mercedes-Benz and Auto Union concerns.

The 170V (W136) four-door saloon. This extensive range of four-cylinder models, with various body options, was revived after the conflict.

Meanwhile, 1934 had witnessed the debut of the first of the Silver Arrows – the W25 Grand Prix car. This was followed by a string of successful models that put Germany at the forefront of the motorsport scene until the outbreak of the Second World War. Record breakers were also built, based on the GP cars, and brought the new Autobahn network into use in a rather unexpected fashion – the straight, level roads were perfect for the challenge to find the fastest man on Earth.

Then, of course, 1939 brought with it conflict, first in Europe, and then on a global scale. Virtually all of the historic Untertürkheim factory was destroyed during an Allied bombing run in September 1944, so it was difficult for Daimler-Benz to bounce back once hostilities ended in 1945.

Like so many manufacturers, Daimler-Benz warmed-over some of its prewar designs as part of the rebuilding process, releasing its first postwar car (ignoring utilitarian versions and commercial vehicles) – the 1.7-litre 170V four-door sedan – in July 1947. Two new 170-series variants joined this in May 1949, and production continued until 1955, by which time the 180 had been introduced as a stablemate.

1951 saw the revival of six-cylinder engines with the launch of the 2.2-litre 220 series (W187) and the 3-litre 300 (W186 II) models in April that year. The sporting two-door 300S made its debut at the 1951 Paris Salon, and shortly after, a deal was signed with Max Hoffman, securing a good sales outlet in America. Hoffman also handled Porsche imports for the US, incidentally, as well as other top European brands.

The start of the modern era can be tracked back to two cars – the 300SL racer of 1952 that duly served as the basis for the legendary Gullwing series, and the Ponton line. Arriving in September of 1953, the slab-sided Ponton series gave the styling cue for a whole new generation of Mercedes-Benz models. It was launched in 1.8-litre four-cylinder guise (W120), but a

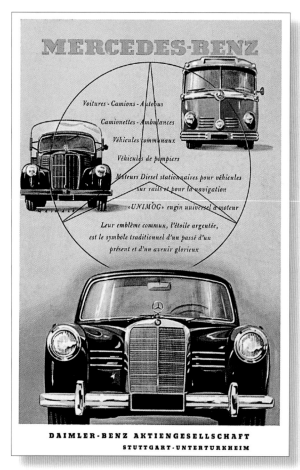

French advertising featuring Mercedes cars, trucks and buses, as well as specialised motors and vehicles, including the Unimog. Looking at the model mix, this piece would date from around 1953, when the Ponton 180 (W120) was introduced.

New models were coming thick and fast, and moves were made to secure a stronger sales organisation in the States, ultimately leading to the foundation of Mercedes-Benz of North America Inc (MBNA). With annual production up to around 100,000 units (as well as 55,000 commercials) by the end of the 1950s, it's fair to say that Daimler-Benz had made a full recovery from the dark days of 1945.

Resurgence

The 1959 Frankfurt Show heralded a new era for Daimler-Benz, with the first of the Fintail series models lining up alongside a revised four-cylinder Ponton line. These original Fintail cars (W111) were six-cylinder saloons, replacing the Ponton sixes, although by 1961, two-door fixed head and drophead models had been launched (with disc brakes and an automatic transmission adding technical appeal), as well as a new W110 four-cylinder range, bringing the Ponton era to an end, and a flagship W112 3-litre model. The Fintail variants were a perfect blend of modernity and tradition, and allowed Mercedes to make huge steps forward in the field of safety – the introduction of crumple zones being a case in point.

The 300SL (right) brought the Stuttgart company a great deal of publicity, cementing its image for fielding products featuring top-class engineering.

2.2-litre six-cylinder version (W180) had joined the line-up by the following spring as a replacement for the W187.

The company made its long-awaited return to Grand Prix racing in 1954, with the straight-eight W196 quickly dominating the GP scene in 1954 and 1955 in much the same way as the prewar Silver Arrows had, while the 300SLR offshoot made a real impression in sports car racing. However, prompted by a bad accident at Le Mans, the motorsport programme was brought to an end in October 1955, with only long-distance rallies being tackled to any extent – the tough events proving to be an ideal way of mixing publicity with research and development.

The Fintail series, seen here in W110 four-cylinder guise, set the tone for the Mercedes brand during the 1960s, with reliability and safety being key selling points.

Production at Sindelfingen in the early 1970s, with an R107 SL vastly outnumbered by W116 S-Class models.

The SL range was also brought up-to-date during 1963, when the 230SL (W113) replaced the 190SL and 300SL, bridging the gap between the two in many ways, but the modern styling was

another sign that the Mercedes-Benz brand had moved on a generation. Similar lines were chosen for the upmarket 1964 V8-engined 600 – a stately vehicle available as a 5/6-seater or 7/8-seater on an extended wheelbase.

Things moved forward again in September 1965, when the W108 and W109 models replaced the Fintail six-cylinder saloons, although the two-door models and four-cylinder W110 line continued for a while longer, duly joined by the 250SL before augmenting the 280SL and a new range of '/8' machines that took the place of the 'Fintail' fours at the start of 1968. These W114 and W115 cars were a thoroughly modern interpretation of traditional Mercedes thinking, overseen by Dr Hans Scherenberg, who took over the responsibility for product development following the retirement of Professor Fritz Nallinger at the end of 1965. As 1968 continued, the 300SEL 6.3 broke cover, along with an attractive W114 coupe body, which eventually went into production the following year.

The 3.5-litre V8 engine made its debut at the 1969 Frankfurt Show, powering 300SEL 3.5 (W109) and two-door W111 variants, although the event was probably best remembered for the world premiere of the Wankel-engined C111. This magnificent creation was perhaps too far ahead of its time, although it's a shame that more wasn't done with the rotary engine – after a few more C111 prototypes, as with so many companies that had paid NSU for patent rights, the RE adventure came to an end.

The Hanomag truck concern became a wholly-owned subsidiary of the Stuttgart giant in December 1970 – the tractor side of the business was separated and sold to Massey Ferguson.

Meanwhile, the 280SE 3.5 and 280SEL 3.5 saloons were added to the W108 series in early 1971, although it was the R107 SL that stole the limelight. Introduced in April, the two-seater V8 roadster was joined by a slightly longer tin-top version (the C107, or SLC) at the end of the year. Not long after, a new batch of W114 models joined the range, giving Mercedes-Benz a particularly sporting ambience in time to compliment the luxury W116 S-Class, announced at the 1972 Paris Salon. Eventually, 4.5-litre V8 engines were added to the S-Class and SL line-up, as well as long-wheelbase variants on the big saloons.

Mercedes-Benz UK Ltd was formed as 1974 dawned, the same year in which the SL line gained a six-cylinder engine

The big hit of the mid-1970s was the 123-series, seen here in coupe, saloon and estate guise. With sports and luxury cars also featuring strongly in the Mercedes line-up, as well as a huge range of commercials, the only thing missing was an SUV ...

option, while 1975 saw the launch of the 450SEL 6.9 – a true wolf in sheep's clothing. With a workforce of roughly 150,000 at this time, annual production during 1975 stood at 350,098 cars and 229,302 trucks.

After years of running countless model variations alongside each other – some, like the W111 two-door models, lasting six years beyond their four-door counterparts – the introduction of the W123-series saloons in January 1976 brought with them a sense of calm. Although a few of their '/8' predecessors were allowed to continue for a little while longer, compared with other model changeovers, it was a clean progression this time around. From now on, the W123s would take up the mid-range (as what would become known as the E-Class), the saloon, coupe, and estate models augmenting the S-Class saloons at the top of the line, and the SL/SLC sports cars.

While Dr Joachim Zahn was still the Chairman of the Board of Management (a position he'd held since the summer of 1971), Dr Wilfried Guth was at the helm of the Supervisory Board by now, and one of his first decisions to make the new

estate version of the W123 at the Bremen plant – first established by Borgward in 1938, but inherited by Daimler-Benz after the Hanomag takeover. This gradual move from commercial vehicle to passenger car production would duly become significant for fans of Mercedes sports cars at the end of the 1980s.

At the end of 1977, an all-alloy V8 was introduced on the 450SLC 5.0, while at the other end of the scale, a turbo-diesel engine was launched for the 300SD saloon. On 14 October that year, the 5,000,000th postwar passenger car left the line at Sindelfingen. Interestingly, the first million cars built after the conflict had taken 16 years to complete, whilst this last batch of a million had taken just two years. A few weeks later, Hans Scherenberg retired, leaving Werner Breitschwerdt in charge of product development.

Many companies, young and old, talk of having pedigree. However, with so many landmark machines to its name and a rich history created by some of the biggest names in the industry, it's fair to say that few can match the bloodlines behind the Mercedes-Benz brand ...

Birth of the G-Wagen

In today's marketplace, for a major car manufacturer not to have an SUV (or sport utility vehicle) in its line-up is unthinkable, with even the likes of Porsche, Maserati, Jaguar and Bentley – makers of pure sporting and luxury machines – getting in on the act nowadays. It wasn't always that way, though ...

For the current generation, it's taken for granted that an SUV is a standard vehicle type, rather than something specialised, aimed at a market niche. Indeed, when the author was looking for one in Japan a couple of years ago, several books and magazines devoted purely to SUVs were available to guide me through the multitude of offerings from all over the world. The mud-plugging image of the past has slowly but surely given way to smooth sophistication – the modern sport utility vehicle is a car for all seasons that will probably never go off-road for its entire life. Indeed, some of the latest offerings are simply cashing in on an upswing in the SUV's popularity, styled to look like one, yet possessing none of the attributes that would endow it with good off-road performance.

Before looking at the development of the G-Wagen (or Geländewagen), it's worth a couple of pages to discover the roots of the SUV, for unlike the majority of car or body types still on sale in today's showrooms, this one, like the people mover (or MPV), is actually a relatively new breed. Even after its introduction, it seems odd – particularly with so many on the road nowadays, and something of an SUV boom before the Lehman Brothers crisis made people tighten their purse-strings – that it took some time to become accepted as a mainstream product, and even longer to become fashionable ...

The new Mercedes-Benz SUV in the terrain it was built for.

Emergence of the SUV

To trace the birth of the SUV one need look no further than the Jeep, a robust four-wheel drive machine forged in the heat of battle. Indeed, had America not been drawn into the Second World War, it's unlikely it would have ever seen the light of day. With the cessation of hostilities, Willys-Overland created a series of 'CJ' models (or Civilian Jeeps) based on the wartime icon, and even produced an estate version in 1946. By the end of the 1947 season, the Willys range was quite extensive, although it was the Jeep that provided the basis for the entire line-up.

The quaint Woody wagons that sprang up all over America during the late-1940s hurt Jeep sales, but Willys-Overland moved 63,000 Jeeps in 1948, and almost 32,000 in the following year, despite difficulties with strikes at a number of suppliers. Some liked the rugged looks, others the practical benefits offered by the go-anywhere chassis and drivetrain, and features like a power take-off (PTO) allowed farmers and maintenance crews to operate machinery without having to drag a stationary motor into the wilds.

Still in the States, Crosley introduced the Farm-O-Road as a smaller alternative to the Jeep in 1950, and station wagons became ever more popular in suburbia, but it was still the Jeep that led the way, even after the Kaiser concern took-over the Willys business. In fact, the Jeep even earned itself a face-lift in the mid-1950s, with the CJ5 and lwb CJ6 keeping the Jeep name alive for decades after, helped by improvements in tyre technology seen in the likes of the Firestone Town & Country line-up. However, it was probably the Rover company on the other side of the Atlantic

Early postwar advertising for the Willys-Overland CJ-type Jeep, produced for the civilian market.

Sir Winston Churchill pictured with his Series I Land Rover.

that pushed the SUV's evolutionary envelope to the next stage with its groundbreaking Land Rover model.

Maurice Wilks, the Chief Engineer at Rover in England, had bought an ex-army Jeep after the war. Inspired by its simplicity and usefulness, Wilks set about designing a British version of the Jeep in April 1947. By March 1948, the first Series I Land Rover had rolled off the line, with doors and a canvas roof classed as options, although by 1950, it had already taken on its more familiar appearance. Ironically, the 4x4 model was outselling the regular Rovers, and, as well as finding favour as a workhorse in both military and civilian fields, attracted many famous owners, including the Royal Family, and Sir Winston Churchill, Britain's fabled Prime Minister.

The standard wheelbase, taken from the old Jeep dimension, was lengthened in 1953, and the short chassis car was duly joined by a lwb version not long after. Further increases to allow for a four-door model came in 1956, and a diesel engine option was added before the Series II cars were introduced in 1958.

The Land Rover kept evolving, with updated powertrains and subtle styling changes. By the mid-1960s, over half-a-million had been built, with record sales being recorded as the swinging sixties came to an end. The Land Rover was obviously here to stay, and thoughts now turned toward enhancing the line's appeal. Initial work on the Range Rover – an upmarket version of the Land Rover with superior on-road performance –

The Ford Bronco of 1966 vintage.

began in 1966, while those looking for something smaller and cheaper could opt for the Mini Moke.

America duly caught up on Land Rover's lead with the likes of the International Scout of 1960 and Jeep Wagoneer of 1962, which were a lot more refined than the original Jeep, and not simply working tools. Ford then brought out the 1966 Model Year Bronco, which was the first SUV to come from one of the more mainstream – ie Big Three – American automobile manufacturers. Naturally, once the breed became established, General Motors (GM) reacted with its own truck-based SUV, the Chevrolet Blazer, although some will class the earlier Suburban as a sport utility vehicle, too – it certainly leaned further and further away from pure estate car as the generations passed. As it happens, Chrysler joined the game late, eventually fielding the Dodge Ramcharger and Plymouth Trailduster in the mid-1970s, but the company was nonetheless determined not to get left behind, and found itself in a strong position by the time the SUV boom started. Ultimately, Chrysler later consolidated its position by claiming the Jeep nameplate in March 1987, following the take-over of AMC – the relatively short-lived company that had bought the Jeep brand from Kaiser Industries in 1970.

In the meantime, while the folks in Solihull probably couldn't believe their luck in finding so many willing Land Rover buyers, somewhat surprisingly, mainland Europe was not so fast to pick up on the fact that cornering a niche market could lead to big sales. Indeed, other than the air-cooled Steyr-Puch Haflinger and its more specialised Pinzgauer stablemate, having been developed from the West German army's Type 181 (and the slightly more civilised Type 182 spawned from it, sold as the 'Thing' in the States, which just about says it all), Volkswagen's Iltis from the late-1970s stands out as something almost unique prior to the G-Wagen, and although it was launched as a road car at the 1979 Amsterdam Show, it seems it was done more for publicity than any real attempt at wooing customers – the spartan machine was basically a capable military vehicle to take the place of the DKW Munga, and nothing more. It was also far too expensive to be taken seriously as a competitor in the showroom category, although it would ultimately go on to steal German military sales from the G-Wagen's creators.

At least Japan had its own ideas for the SUV. Toyota had been asked to build the Jeep by the US military for use in the Korean War, and for several years after the conflict, Toyota built Jeeps to sell to regular customers off the street, utility companies and the various military and public service organisations.

The Toyota J40-series represented the birth of the Land Cruiser as we know it, arriving in 1960. It sold in huge numbers

A Toyota Land Cruiser dating from 1969.

One of the first press pictures announcing the arrival of the iconic Range Rover.

until its replacement was launched in the mid-1980s, and was even built abroad under licence. Mitsubishi was also involved with SUVs, building Jeep variants before the first Pajero prototype made its debut at the 1973 Tokyo Show – it was still very much a Jeep-type vehicle at this stage, though, looking much like the Toyota Marine Cruiser concept across the hall. In reality, the Daihatsu Taft of 1974 was much closer to being a true SUV, but the Pajero II from the late-1970s hit the mark, and ultimately, after one more prototype, led to the production model of 1982 vintage. By this time, the Nissan Patrol had moved away from its spartan Jeep and Land Rover roots, and the tiny Suzuki Jimny had carved out a market for itself, too.

But Land Rover had another card up its sleeve, extending market reach via the more luxurious Range Rover – a "car that offered a new dimension in motoring" according to the advertising blurb, and, for all intents and purposes, the original SUV as we know it today. Overseen by Spen King, the three-door hatchback Range Rover was launched in June 1970, featuring full-time four-wheel drive, a coil spring suspension, and a 3.5-litre V8 under the bonnet. Not long after, the Series III Land Rovers were released, bringing greater refinement to the base models as well, although the five-door Range Rover remained a prototype due to the first fuel crisis and a lack of funds within BLMC (later British Leyland) – the holding company that looked after the Rover name, along with that of Jaguar, Austin, Triumph, MG, and so on.

Introduced at a fraction under £2000 in the UK, the Range Rover wasn't cheap: a Mini was £600, and the average weekly wage was less than £35. Perhaps unsurprisingly, then, only 5510 units were sold in 1972, but the 10,000 cars per annum barrier was broken in 1975, and stayed constant at around that level throughout the rest of the 1970s, actually increasing to around 12,000 units as the 1980s progressed, when the normal sales trend would be downward a few years after launch. Granted, they were hardly huge numbers (the Land Rover continued to be far more popular), but the relatively expensive SUV was a profitable product, and the market was definitely there ...

The G-Wagen project

Stuttgart's answer to the Land Rover and Range Rover line-up was born in a somewhat roundabout fashion, with none of the familiar figures at the Daimler-Benz factory taking a leading role in its development. Indeed, the majority of the design and R&D work was done outside, in conjunction with the Steyr-Daimler-Puch concern – a company with a long and proud history in the motor industry, and vaguely linked to Daimler-Benz through the Austro-Daimler connection from prewar days.

This may seem a strange situation for those that know a little about Mercedes history, for off-road vehicles have been associated with the brand for over a century, firstly through the 4WD Dernburg-Wagen; a sidestep via imposing six-wheelers used by dignitaries in the twenties and thirties, and then military machines like the 170VG and G5 developed in readiness for WWII, which duly evolved into the Unimog line after the conflict. However, it's fair to say that four-wheel drive experience was fairly limited, and the company's Unimog brand quickly became associated with commercial machines rather than road cars.

I suppose one also has to wonder why Hanomag was not chosen to take on some of the responsibility in creating the new SUV, as the company had been taken over by Daimler-Benz at the end of 1970 after all, and had a great deal of experience in all-wheel drive systems. In reality, though, the tractor side of the business had already been split off, and Hanomag's famous half-track models from the Second World War were not quite in line with the design brief!

As such, with the joint manufacture of buses already in hand, and a replacement for the long-running Haflinger already on the cards, one can readily see why the Steyr-Daimler-Puch concern was the Stuttgart company's preferred

ally for this project, with the small Haflinger Allrad Getriebene Geländewagen models providing something much closer to the G-Wagen concept than anything built in-house for many years – decades, in fact.

The Mercedes-Benz G4 touring car in action in the mid-1930s. Trucks were built along similar lines during the same period.

The Mercedes G5 failed to impress the German military, which ordered the vehicle in relatively small numbers. In order to recover some of its development costs, from 1938, the 4WD machine was also sold as an attractive open tourer for civilian use, and in 'colonial and hunting car' guise, as seen here.

Unimog and MB-Trac machines from 1974, showing how far the Unimog brand had moved away from roadworthy machines by the time the G-Wagen project was mooted.

Early Unimog models being demonstrated at the Sauberg test centre.

The Steyr-Daimler-Puch story

The Steyr element of this conglomerate can be traced back to 1864 and the foundation of a weapons factory in Steyr in northern Austria (halfway between Salzburg and Vienna) by Josef Werndl, although the company had diversified into the bicycle trade by 1894, building British Swift bikes under licence.

A car department was eventually established in 1916, with the legendary Hans Ledwinka being named as Chief Engineer in the following year. This led to the creation of the 12/40hp Steyr Waffenauto six, but Ledwinka's tenure was to be short-lived. By the time Steyr-Werke AG had been registered in February 1926, the company's automobiles were already well-respected, and the firm's commitment to cars was further strengthened with the appointment of Ferdinand Porsche as Chief Engineer in 1929, following his stint at the Mercedes (DMG) works in Stuttgart. However,

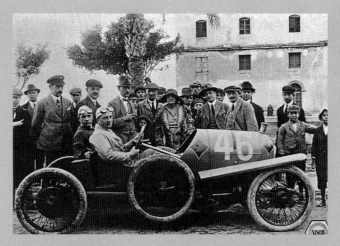

An Austro-Daimler 'Sascha' competing in the 1922 Targa Florio. Professor Porsche can be seen standing just beyond the car's race number. The legendary Mercedes race team boss, Alfred Neubauer, is at the wheel.

The Steyr-Puch Haflinger featured on an Austrian postage stamp.

The famous Steyr logo.

the loss of Porsche's flair in 1930 and the depression caused by the Wall Street Crash took their toll, and a merger with Austro-Daimler and Puch was approved at a shareholders' meeting in October 1934.

The Austro-Daimler concern was established by Eduard Bierenz in Austria's Wiener Neustadt in 1899. A close friend of Gottlieb Daimler, Bierenz started producing Daimler vehicles under licence in the following year, but soon began fielding original designs thanks to input from Paul Daimler, and had even produced a four-wheel drive machine by 1905.

Interestingly, Ferdinand Porsche became Chief Engineer in 1906, and Emil Jellinek (of Mercédès fame) started buying up licences to expand his business interests abroad. Thanks to cars like the Prince Henry model, the company eventually shook free of its Stuttgart roots, with the Daimler head office selling the last of its shares in its Austrian namesake in 1912. Despite the success of the 'Sascha' racers (one of Porsche's last designs for the company), the postwar years were not kind to Austro-Daimler, though. Links were formed with local arms manufacturer Skoda, Italy's Fiat (via Austro-Fiat), and the Puch firm.

The Puch story is an interesting one. Johann Puch (1862-1914) was born in today's Slovenia, close to the current Austrian border. When he was a child, he carried the name of Janez Puh, but adopted the German-style spelling (as was the norm in the Styria region at the time) when he was baptised. Puch studied metalworking and engineering from a young age, and after military service, he eventually moved a few miles north to Graz, the area's capital in what is now Austria, to put his experience as a mechanic to greater use.

The Puch marque was, for a long time, better known for its two-wheelers than its cars.

Finding favour with those in the local cycle industry, Puch had established his own workshop by the time the 1890s rolled along, importing Humbers from England and building his own bikes, badged as 'Styria' models. The path to success was rocky due to overstretched budgets and so on, but eventually, in September 1899, the foundation of the Puch works was set in motion. Motorcycles were duly built as a natural evolution of the bicycle trade, and cars and aero-engines were also produced in the first decade of the new millennium. Just before his death, the factory bearing his name was turning out no fewer than 16,000 bicycles, 300 motorbikes and 300 cars a year.

Without Puch's leadership and the difficult trading conditions caused by the break-up of the Austro-Hungarian Empire following the end of the Great War, Puchwerke AG, as it was now known, was beginning to struggle. Car production ceased in 1923, but a successful motorcycle – reliable and cheap to run – kept the company afloat long enough for it to merge with Austro-Daimler in May 1928. However, the Wall Street Crash prompted another merger with Steyr and the creation of Steyr-Daimler-Puch AG in 1934 – Steyr would concentrate on car production, Puch on two-wheeled machines, and the Austrian Daimler business was effectively dissolved.

Austria was declared part of the German Reich in 1938, and the various factories were duly classed as armament makers soon after. Postwar revival came thanks to the production of bicycles and motorbikes, and eventually the Puch 500 (a Fiat 500 built under licence) was launched in 1957. This unlikely vehicle actually provided Steyr-Puch with the foundation of its four-wheel drive expertise, as a 4WD version of it, christened the Puch 700 AP (or 'Haflinger,' designed by Erich Ledwinka), was developed at the end of the 1950s, ultimately leading to the four- and six-wheeled Pinzgauer line of 1971 vintage.

If nothing else, we have established the roots of the Steyr-Daimler-Puch (SDP) business, and where it gained its necessary experience in both the motor trade and 4WD systems, the latter proven in the harsh spotlight of the world's armed forces. This was probably the overwhelming reason that Daimler-Benz approached SDP as a business partner ...

The go-anywhere Steyr-Puch Haflinger, which was sold in a number of guises, from pure utility versions to vehicles that were far more suited to road use, at least for unfettered types.

Having made a few discreet enquiries within the trade, the original decision to kick off the new Benz 4WD SUV as a joint-project was taken in 1972, leading to an agreement of co-operation drawn up in May 1973 and the formation of a new company known as Gelände-fahrzeug Gesellschaft mbH (which basically translates into the Off-Road Vehicle Co, but was often shortened to GfG in internal documents) – a 50/50 venture between Steyr-Daimler-Puch and Daimler-Benz to design, develop and build cross-country machines suitable for both military, utilitarian and civilian use. With the new concern finally registered in February 1977, it made sense for both parties at the time, bringing about an extension of the SDP factory on the southern side of Graz, in the south-eastern corner of Austria. With the foundation stone for the huge new building laid a few days later, on 11 March, by the Austrian Chancellor, Bruno Kreisky, it was hoped that the investment of DM 100 million would provide 800 extra jobs (through body and frame manufacture, as well as final assembly) and allow around 9000 cars a year to be built, or up to 11,000 if a second shift was added. For the Daimler-Benz side, there was expert design input in unfamiliar territory, the constant supply of components, an expansion of production facilities without having to try and find the necessary land in Stuttgart, which was already bursting at the seams, and reduced financial risk.

The groundbreaking ceremony for the plant extension at Graz, with Dr Bruno Kreisky (right) doing the honours. Kreisky was the long-serving Austrian Chancellor, holding the post from 1970 to 1983. Two near-production prototypes used for testing were at the event, one badged as a Mercedes, the other as a Puch.

Zur Erinnerung an die Grundsteinlegung dieser Fertigungsstätte durch Bundeskanzler Dr. Bruno Kreisky am 11. März 1977

The new G-Wagen facility pictured in May 1977, and again in June 1978, close to completion.

With the earliest concept requiring both military and civilian usage, the Type W460 G-Wagen (or Geländewagen) design brief called for something that would be equally at home on normal paved roads or off the beaten track, with greater emphasis placed on the latter. But with expectations that nine out of ten vehicles would be sold with a three-pointed star on the nose (a Puch badge was used in Austria, Switzerland, and Eastern Bloc countries), buyers had a right to expect the quality, comfort, safety and driving dynamics of a typical Mercedes-Benz saloon, in addition to an off-road level of prowess that would allow the new model to compete with existing bench mark SUVs – the Range Rover, in particular, as that was considered the leader of the all-rounder pack by quite some margin at the time. As well as good on- and off-road performance, a third prong was added to the brief, calling for simplicity, both in terms of manufacture (to allow CKD production in the future) and in servicing and repair – the need for strength and reliability were taken as read.

By the way, the rather hopeful figure quoted in the initial sales targets can partly be explained by the interest shown in the G-Wagen by the German army (which opted to buy the VW Iltis in the end) and HIM the Shah of Iran for military use.

Whilst owning a substantial number of shares in Daimler-Benz (the Shah, Mohammad Reza Pahlavi, is believed to have held around $1 billion in stock at one point after the families that had previously been the dominant shareholders began breaking up their investments in the early part of 1975), he had placed a tentative order for 20,000 units of the proposed off-roader for the Iranian military, although the post-revolution government formed in the wake of the Shah fleeing Iran on 16 January 1979 – in addition to abolishing the monarchy – quickly cancelled the contract, and the GfG partnership was left holding something of a hot potato, or, at the very least, found itself facing a future that was a lot less assured.

However, the market research carried out in the early-1970s that pointed towards an upsurge in interest in 4WD vehicles was solid enough, with the SUV market expanding by as much as five to ten per cent globally at the time. In addition, recouping costs through a multitude of variations on a theme was something Daimler-Benz was very good at – one only needs to think of the numerous 123-series models based on the W123 saloon, as well as their predecessors in the mid-size lines. While very little could be done at this late stage in the proceedings, as a result of these unfortunate and unexpected game-changing developments, at least the two partners in the G-Wagen project knew that more emphasis would have to be put on the road car side sooner or later; preferably sooner ...

Design & development

Initial design work was based on the replacement for the Steyr-Puch Haflinger – the so-called H2 version, which was being lined up to take the place of the original car that had entered series-production way back in 1959. Kurt Klötzl had been responsible for keeping the Haflinger alive, with almost 17,000 having been made before its run came to an end in 1974. Sales were down to minuscule amounts by the early-1970s, and the final nail in its coffin was basically its inability to cope with a new, more powerful engine – without a huge amount of modifications, the transmission, chassis and brakes simply couldn't cope with the extra horses. Thus, the H2 project was put in motion, with thoughts focusing on it to be built alongside the Pinzgauer.

For good, all-round off-road performance, the designers opted for an exceptionally strong ladder frame chassis with rigid beam axles front and rear, as was the accepted norm at the time for true SUV models. As it happens, the Steyr-Puch Pinzgauer had an independent suspension, but the Austrian firm admitted this arrangement ultimately added needless complexity into the equation for hardly any gain in real terms, and often hampered ground clearance. The separate chassis also allowed different bodies to be mounted with ease, as well as variations in wheelbase lengths, giving the marketing people more room to manoeuvre.

The big difference for the W460 project compared to the H2 was, of course, the choice of drivetrain and suspension components, for while the second generation Haflinger was

Early design work that ultimately led to the presentation of a small wooden model to the Board at Daimler-Benz in April 1974.

The first G-Wagen steel prototype, built in September 1974. The very sharp edges and simple shutlines were to allow production in poorer countries that didn't have access to expensive pressing tools. However, this train of thought was duly abandoned as development continued. Back in the 1970s, it was hoped that the G-Wagen's shape could remain current for at least ten years.

A later prototype soft top model. As can be seen from the pictures, a folding windscreen developed for a 1977 military prototype had been envisaged for the cabriolet, but the added expense incurred by the need for different tooling ruled this out. Note also the 'Explorer' badging and abandoned fuel filler position.

aimed at a more utilitarian audience (albeit one that was expected to hold creature comforts a lot dearer than that of a decade earlier), with Daimler-Benz involved, things went upmarket in a hurry. But while this immediately implied a higher selling price than the one envisaged for the H2, at least by employing what amounted to proprietary engines, transmission units (modified to mate up to a selectable – rather than full-time – four-wheel drive system), and numerous chassis pieces from the Stuttgart side of the partnership, a great deal of development time was saved, and the necessary funding required for such things could be slashed from the start-up budget.

Having taken the decision to offer two wheelbase lengths initially, basic styling was adjusted to suit, allowing a line of two- and four-door variants to cover most work and/or leisure scenarios. The design work hinted at the rugged simplicity of the Haflinger and Pinzgauer, and the intended military application and practical considerations left no room for flirtation – the flat, boxy panelwork was easy to build, and more importantly, easy to repair in a hurry.

As can be seen from the pictures, the prototypes were actually even simpler than the showroom models, although the sharp edges on these earliest cars were far from ideal. In the end, it was decided to invest in costlier tooling to give less aggravation on the production line, and add strength via subtle curves and creases. By attaching a rubber-insulated steel frame to the parallel box-section chassis rails (braced by transverse tubular pieces, sealed and then duly given a zinc primer and PVC coating to protect the main chassis members), this allowed each of the major panels to be readily removed and replaced without affecting structural rigidity, as well as speeding up repairs, and reducing the cost of them as a result.

The author would usually spend quite some time talking about styling, pointing out subtle lines and continuity, but there is very little one can say about the G-Wagen in this respect! The front mask consisted of an upright, oblong-shaped grille made up of black horizontal slats, with only a silver three-pointed star offering any relief. To the sides of this were matt black housings to take and protect the traditional round headlight units, angled

The main body section used for the G-Wagen, this shell being that of a four-door estate built after 1981.

The Geländewagen's chassis frame, with the engine showing this to be a 230G model. The body was mounted on the chassis as a separate entity, insulated by rubber bushes where the chassis and bodyshell met.

the HVAC system) and the windscreen frame-cum-bulkhead, which carried the conventional windscreen wipers and a guard moulding above the screen. Like the rest of the front-end, the bumper blade was simplicity itself, with a flat centre section that bent backwards a touch at both ends once the chassis rails had been cleared; although the number plate often hid it, there was a removable towing attachment in the centre of the matt black bumper blade.

From the side, the straight-edge styling that was very much en vogue at the time was taken to extremes. The wheelarch profiles had flat top surfaces and sharply angled leading and trailing edges, with only the slightest curve at the points where the three lines joined. The harshness of these cut-outs left the onlooker with little doubt that this was nothing more than a purely functional machine.

The starkness continued in the flat roofline, which had only a subtle slope at the leading edge to improve the bricklike aerodynamics, the angle being roughly the same as that employed on the bonnet. The screen rake was minimal, with a panel shutline continuing from the A-post down to the front wheelarch (butting up to the bolt-on front wings), but other than the bumper corners, a guard moulding on the sill, another rubbing strip at waist height in line with the door handle and

inwards at the lower outside edges to follow the wing profiles, while the separate indicators were attached to the top of the wings above them, placed on the flat surface created by the way the bonnet tapered from full-width at the bulkhead to being level with the grille at the front, à la Land Rover fashion. Unless the optional foglights or a winch were fitted, apart from the bumper, the only other things one could see from the front were a hint of wheelarch, the leading edge of the bonnet (which featured a central power bulge and a black vent at the rear to feed

Four of the five body variants available in 1979, with a cabriolet (left) and two-door (short-wheelbase) station wagon nearest the camera, and a four-door (long-wheelbase) estate and lwb van in the background. The missing member in the line-up was the swb van, of which very few press photographs exist.

the drip rail on the roof, this was about the only notable feature to break up the sides at first glance. However, closer inspection revealed some subtle creaselines between the wheelarches and continuing to the back light units, as well as a pair above and below the waistline moulding.

One or two workmanlike doors were employed depending on the wheelbase and body type, with a hefty mirror and model grade badge on each front door, and a repeater indicator just ahead of it. When fitted, the radio aerial was mounted just above the offside repeater lens, incidentally.

(Above and opposite) This series of shots showing an early four-door station wagon clearly illustrate the door format (short-wheelbase models had the same front doors, while the rearmost pair were the same on swb estates and similar on vans), the interior design of a petrol-engined car with front and rear diff locks, and the standard seating arrangements; there was cloth upholstery for the seats (seen here), with perforated vinyl trim available for those of a more practical disposition. While one would have expected the use of W123 parts, as it happens, a lot of the interior components were sourced from the contemporary Mercedes light commercial range on the earliest cars.

31

Picture from the August 1979 catalogue showing the rear tailgate arrangement on the cabriolet model. As it happens, while a pair of doors was the norm on lwb cars, a left-hinged one-piece rear door (with window) was available as an option on long-wheelbase vehicles.

It was the bodywork aft of the B-post that gave the model variations. On the two-door short chassis, with a 2400mm (94.5in) wheelbase, there was firstly a van, with crease lines in the rear panel, but no window – only an air extraction vent on the C-post. Then there was the same basic vehicle but with the window in place ahead of the vent to give an estate, and a third vehicle with a heavier B-post that supported a cross-brace (or a Targa bar, if you want to call it that) to add rigidity to the open body, which was made weatherproof by a canvas top with side windows and a rear screen. On the longer chassis, featuring a 2850mm (112.2in) wheelbase, there was the van body again, with two doors and an elongated version of the rear side panel, and an estate, with a pair of rear doors added, and a shorter window above the rear wheels. This gave customers a total of five bodies to choose from.

Around the back, the kink at the trailing edge of the drip rail on the roof allowed a pair of tall, narrow doors to be fitted on the vans and estates. Like the side panels, the vans had impressions where the windows were on the estates, but they were physically the same shape and size, supported by a pair of strong hinges on the C-post on each side. Although the wide pillars at the back had a pleasant curve to break up the 90-degree bend in the metalwork, the shutlines on the doors were as straight as a die! The subtle creases found in the side panels continued

around the tail to visually break up the panels and add strength, while simple light units with separate reflectors were added on the bottom of each C-post. Above these, there was a foglight on the left (when specified) and a fuel filler cap on the right. The left-hand door carried the door handle and lit registration plate housing on lhd cars, while the right-hand one was usually covered by the optional swing-out spare wheel carrier. Below the doors were split bumper blades, as simple in design as the one upfront (as well as painted matt black to match), with the gap between them allowing a towbar to be fitted with ease; the exhaust pipe exited below the offside bumper section, tucked up tight to it, while square-cut mudflaps allowed the bodywork to stay high off the ground and offer motorists following behind a modicum of protection from rain, flying stones and so on.

The tail of the soft top model (or cabriolet, which sounds a lot better than pick-up – a term some press members insisted on using) was quite different, with the metalwork finishing on the uppermost creaseline that ran below the side windows to give an open rear section. Although the bottom half of the C-posts was the same as the closed vehicles, the upper edge was dressed with a matt black guide rail that ran forwards to the B-post in order to the accept the removable steel framework that supported the canvas top whenever the latter was required. The guide also carried the hood fasteners and ran along the top of the rear door, too, which, in the case of the soft top car, was a single tailgate hinged at the bottom and fitted with a central door handle. The lighting, registration plate, fuel filler and spare wheel arrangements were all the same as the other G-Wagens, though.

In conjunction with careful drivetrain design and positioning, the simple body gave the new Mercedes exceptional clearance figures for serious off-road users, including an approach and departure angle of roughly 40 degrees (with the option of a hefty plate protecting the engine and cooling components, running from underneath the bumper back towards the front axle), and a massive 215mm (8.5in) of ground clearance. At the same time, its narrow proportions allowed the G-Wagen to travel down small forest tracks with ease – something the makers of many of today's heavyweight SUVs have forgotten is a positive boon, even in urban traffic and tight parking spaces.

It's fair to say the functional interior was as free of styling gimmicks as the bodywork – it was designed around the needs of the driver in a number of envisaged scenarios for such a vehicle and nothing more. There was a very narrow moulded top roll that played host to a separate instrument binnacle (containing a speedometer and combination gauge for the fuel level and coolant temperature, tell-tale warning lights, plus the option of a tachometer on petrol-engined machines), central air vents for the heater, a speaker grille and passenger grab handle for when the going got rough. Below that, there was a central moulded section carrying the radio slot, minor switchgear (including the hazard warning lights), an ashtray and cigarette lighter, the HVAC controls, and a quartz clock, which was actually classed as an option on the earliest cars.

As it happens, the metal framework on which the top roll and instrument binnacle was mounted was pressed in one piece to allow two deep side sections to drop down either side of the centre console. Eyeball vents for the heater were placed at either end, with a hole for the steering column dressing pieces placed ahead of the driver (which also housed the ignition barrel and master light switch) and the glovebox at the other end. The exposed metalwork beneath the top roll was finished in black, or sometimes body colour to break up the expanse of black plastics and painted surfaces. A simple two-spoke steering wheel was fitted, with a multi-function wand beyond it, looking after indicators, wipers and the horn; the screen washer was looked after by a foot-operated pump on the earliest cars.

There was a footrest to the left of the pedal set, with the footwells lined with a tough plastic that was protected by moulded rubber floormats. The door panels were lined and featured door pockets for maps and suchlike, along with armrests, while the console between the lightweight bucket seats carried the various transmission levers and handbrake. The rear doors on the four-door models carried armrests and ashtrays, and provided access to the rear bench seat. Regardless of the wheelbase, this rear seat could be ordered in foldable guise, which could then be tilted forward to allow more to be carried in the luggage area. Another option was a pair of longitudinally-mounted occasional seats that could turn the short-wheelbase G-Wagen into a seven-seater, or the long-wheelbase version into a nine-seater; heater

Leading dimensions
This sidebar shows the leading dimensions for the first G-Wagen in 280GE station wagon guise (the pair of two-door vans and swb soft top version, launched at the same time as the station wagons, used the same wheelbase measurements), along with those for the contemporary three-door Range Rover for comparison. Considering the Range Rover was the industry bench mark in this category, it should prove useful. The overall width, incidentally, does not include outside mirrors, or the optional spare wheel on the German cars; the latter added 200mm (7.9in) to the figures quoted with the swivel carrier. Note that with regard to the fuel tank capacity, gallons are UK (Imperial) gallons.

	Mercedes-Benz G-Wagen 2dr	Mercedes-Benz G-Wagen 4dr	Range Rover (1979 MY)
Wheelbase	2400mm (94.5in)	2850mm (112.2in)	2540mm (100.0in)
Track (front)	1425mm (56.1in)	1425mm (56.1in)	1486mm (58.5in)
Track (rear)	1425mm (56.1in)	1425mm (56.1in)	1486mm (58.5in)
Overall length	3955mm (155.7in)	4405mm (173.4in)	4470mm (176.0in)
Overall width	1700mm (66.9in)	1700mm (66.9in)	1778mm (70.0in)
Overall height	1925mm (75.8in)	1920mm (75.6in)	1778mm (70.0in)
Clearance (min)	215mm (8.5in)	215mm (8.5in)	190mm (7.5in)
Weight (unladen)	1830kg (4026lb)	1935kg (4257lb)	1727kg (3800lb)
Max payload	670kg (1474lb)	865kg (1903lb)	780kg (1716lb)
Max trailer load	2500kg (5500lb)	2500kg (5500lb)	2000kg (4400lb)
Fuel capacity	68-l (15.0 gallons)	68-l (15.0 gallons)	82-l (18.1 gallons)

vents in the rear compartment made life more comfortable for those in the back.

Despite the basic, almost spartan interior, the car's kerb weight was much heavier than that of its British rivals, largely because the latter employed aluminium alloy panelwork on a steel frame in most areas, rather than the all-steel body construction chosen by the GfG partnership. In reality, the burden of additional weight could be offset by practical issues (such as ease of repair and the cost of replacement panels), but

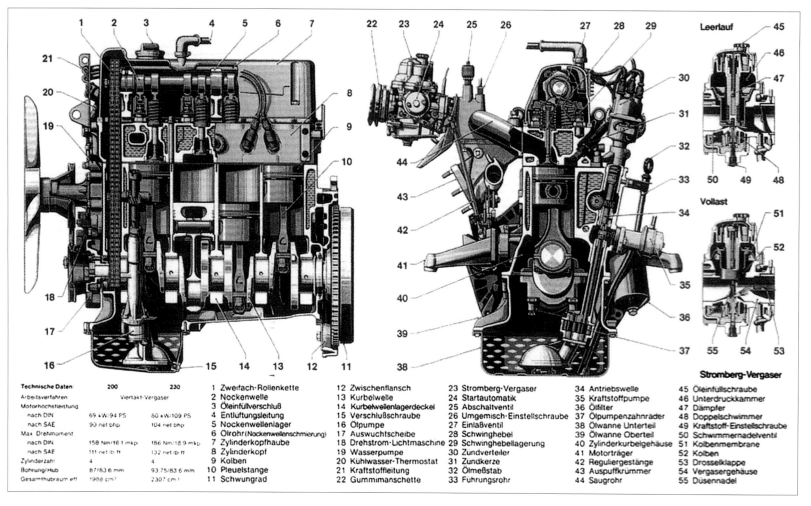

The M115 four-cylinder petrol engine.

Technische Daten:	200	230
Arbeitsverfahren	Viertakt-Vergaser	
Motorhochstleitung		
nach DIN	69 kW/94 PS	80 kW/109 PS
nach SAE	90 net bhp	104 net bhp
Max. Drehmoment		
nach DIN	158 Nm/16.1 mkp	186 Nm/18.9 mkp
nach SAE	111 net lb ft	132 net lb ft
Zylinderzahl	4	4
Bohrung/Hub	87/83.6 mm	93.75/83.6 mm
Gesamthubraum eff	1988 cm³	2307 cm³

1 Zweifach-Rollenkette
2 Nockenwelle
3 Öleinfüllverschluß
4 Entlüftungsleitung
5 Nockenwellenlager
6 Ölrohr (Nockenwellenschmierung)
7 Zylinderkopfhaube
8 Zylinderkopf
9 Kolben
10 Pleuelstange
11 Schwungrad

12 Zwischenflansch
13 Kurbelwelle
14 Kurbelwellenlagerdeckel
15 Verschlußschraube
16 Ölpumpe
17 Auswuchtscheibe
18 Drehstrom-Lichtmaschine
19 Wasserpumpe
20 Kühlwasser-Thermostat
21 Kraftstoffleitung
22 Gummimanschette

23 Stromberg-Vergaser
24 Startautomatik
25 Abschaltventil
26 Umgemisch-Einstellschraube
27 Einlaßventil
28 Schwinghebel
29 Schwinghebellagerung
30 Zündverteiler
31 Zündkerze
32 Ölmeßstab
33 Führungsrohr

34 Antriebswelle
35 Kraftstoffpumpe
36 Ölfilter
37 Ölpumpenzahnräder
38 Ölwanne Unterteil
39 Ölwanne Oberteil
40 Zylinderkurbelgehäuse
41 Motorträger
42 Reguliergestänge
43 Auspuffkrümmer
44 Saugrohr

45 Öleinfüllschraube
46 Unterdruckkammer
47 Dämpfer
48 Doppelschwimmer
49 Kraftstoff-Einstellschraube
50 Schwimmernadelventil
51 Kolbenmembrane
52 Kolben
53 Drosselklappe
54 Vergasergehäuse
55 Düsennadel

Leerlauf

Vollast

Stromberg-Vergaser

the G-Wagen's extra bulk is something that was pointed out in a number of contemporary reports, so must be mentioned here.

Falling back on its tried-and-tested modular system, the engine line-up would have been familiar to anyone following the Mercedes-Benz passenger car range, with W123-series units employed, one of which – the 2.8-litre straight-six petrol engine – was also used in the W116 S-Class saloons and the contemporary SL/SLC range. Four powerplants were chosen for the G-Wagen application, including the M115 V23 and M110 E28 petrol engines, and the OM616 D24 and OM617 D30 diesels, which had the advantage of reaching peak torque lower down the rev-range.

The M115 four-cylinder petrol engine had a single-overhead camshaft in an alloy head, and a cast iron block. The 93.8 x 83.6mm bore and stroke gave a cubic capacity of 2307cc, and a single Stromberg carburettor combined with a 9.0:1 compression ratio endowed the unit with 102bhp (75kW) DIN and 127lbft of torque, which was a fair bit less than the output listed against the equivalent W123 unit; a low-compression version was also available, with an 8.0:1 c/r reducing output to 90bhp (66kW) and 123lbft, but it was a sensible move to offer this variant given the poor fuel quality in a number of countries outside Europe.

The M110 six-cylinder petrol unit had a dohc arrangement in its alloy head, and a seven-bearing cast iron block. With

The M110 fuel-injected straight-six used in the 280GE.

Transmission layout on a manual pre-production G-Wagen with left-hand drive. Although the arrows on the differential locks are a little unclear (showroom models had levers that needed pulling up for diff lock selection and a transverse slot allowing the knobs to be pushed back to regain differential action), this is a useful illustration nonetheless, as the gate for the transfer box is not the easiest thing to explain. Automatic cars were similar, but a selector lever replaced the gearshift seen here in the background.

The OM617 five-cylinder diesel engine, which was basically an OM616 unit with a fifth cylinder added. Like the M110 image, this picture shows a motor show display engine, this example having an automatic gearbox attached.

Bosch K-Jetronic fuel-injection, an 86.0 x 78.8mm bore and stroke (giving 2746cc), and an 8.0:1 c/r (significantly lower than the 9.0:1 used in the W123 models to allow the unit to operate properly on regular petrol), it delivered 156bhp (115kW) DIN and 167lbft of torque.

The OM616 four-cylinder diesel lump was cast iron throughout, with a single-overhead camshaft. With Bosch injection and a 21.0:1 c/r, this 2399cc unit gave the same 72bhp (53kW) as the equivalent W123 powerplant, along with 101lbft of torque. The OM617 was basically the same engine with an extra cylinder tacked onto the end. Sharing the same 90.9 x 92.4mm bore and stroke, the fifth pot took the displacement up to 2998cc, and output up to 80bhp (59kW) DIN and 127lbft – again, the same as the figures quoted for the contemporary W123 models, although September 1979 saw power increase to 88bhp (65kW). In reality, most 3-litre G-Wagens would have the beefier 88bhp engine under their bonnet.

All four of the front-mounted, north-south engines were linked to a four-speed manual transmission as standard, although a four-speed automatic gearbox could be specified as an option

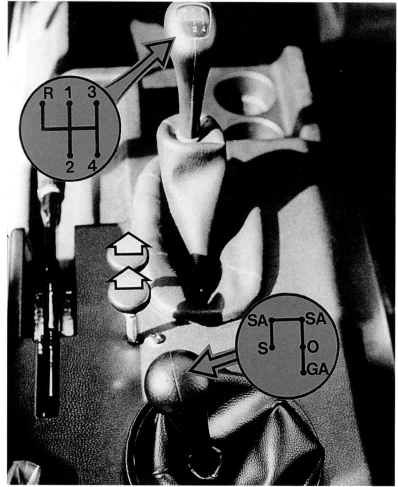

on the five- and six-cylinder cars. Drive from the engine was taken through the gearbox (the 4MT unit with a single dry-plate clutch, the 4AT unit with a torque converter) to a separate, centrally-mounted SDP-made VG80 transfer box via a short propshaft, which then fed power to two more propshafts running fore (at an offset angle) and aft to allow the driver to select rear-wheel drive only, or high or low ratio four-wheel drive.

A full-time four-wheel drive system is more acceptable for a road car that goes off-roading occasionally, as it's far more refined, but the G-Wagen concept called for superior off-road performance first and foremost. As such, the 4WD system was a manually selectable (or part-time) one, giving the driver the ultimate level of control in difficult conditions. Of course, nowadays, computers and hydraulic trickery can look after almost any situation to allow the driver to concentrate on steering and pedal input, but back in the 1970s, things were a whole lot more analogue.

The driver was given a regular gearshift, depending on whether the 4MT or 4AT was fitted, and a second gearlever further back that looked after drive selection. Left and back gave rear-wheel drive only to save fuel and reduce noise, while pushing the stubby lever forward brought about the 4WD high (or direct) mode. If one moved the lever across to the right from there, nothing changed, but it did allow the driver to select neutral if the gearknob was moved one notch back, and moving it all the way gave the 4WD low ratio mode, with a 2.14:1 reduction on the drive emanating from the alloy transfer casing. The ratios chosen for the hypoid front and rear axles (5.33:1 on the fours, and 4.86:1 on the larger-engined machines) reflected the car's purpose – it was simply not designed for fast road work!

A huge advantage for G-Wagen users, though, was the use of synchromesh gears in the transfer box, allowing the person at the wheel to change drive modes on the move with ease just by declutching (or selecting neutral on AT cars) – something that couldn't be said for a lot of the competition, and that statement holds true to this day, with quite complicated sequences still being called for on certain cars. Like the Pinzgauer, there were hydraulic controls for the transfer case, as well as the locks for the front and rear differentials when this option was specified. The differential locks effectively held the left- and right-hand

driveshafts rigidly together via a dog-clutch to stop a wheel that was spinning from taking drive away from one with traction. For the serious off-roader, it was an ideal scenario, and one that even Land Rover or Range Rover drivers could only dream of at the time.

In exchange for the relevant amount of money, the buyer could specify locking differentials for the front only, the rear only, or both axles. Again, differential mode selection could be made on the move, this time via one or two small levers that sat between the main transmission gearshift and the drive mode selector, while a tell-tale light on the dashboard told the driver what the situation was. There was also a power take-off (PTO) facility at both ends of the vehicle, allowing the use of all manner of accessories and specialist machinery, from simple winches to farming equipment.

The front suspension, located by longitudinal control arms and a Panhard rod arrangement, was made up of a rigid beam axle suspended on long-travel coil springs, telescopic dampers that were mounted aft of the springs, and an unusual transverse torsion bar stabiliser that was shackled to the radius arms. The rear suspension actually looked very similar, only in reverse, so that trailing arms were employed to keep the beam axle in

The front axle, with a clear view of the suspension and braking systems, as well as the offset drive arrangement.

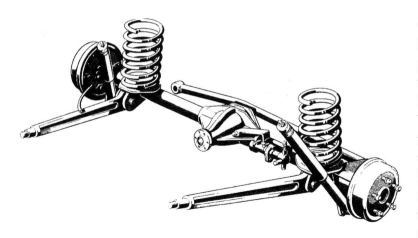

The rear axle, with drum brakes and the drive in line with the gearbox.

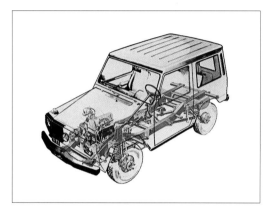

This cutaway drawing perfectly illustrates the substantial chassis frame used for the W460-series cars, as well as the suspension and drivetrain layout.

place, and the Panhard rod used for lateral location was aft of the axle line rather than in front of it. Separate coil springs and shock absorbers were used once more for ease of replacement, with variable rate springs to better cope with vehicle load and the dampers angled quite sharply forwards in this case, although there was no anti-roll bar at the rear. The self-levelling suspension found on cars like the Range Rover was not applied at this stage, as it was felt the variable rate rear springs could deal with most situations without the added cost and complexity commanded by such a system; it was, however, offered as an option on lwb cars.

Not surprisingly, given that Daimler-Benz had stuck with it for so long, steering was via the recirculating-ball system, with power-assistance (PAS) available as an option – something that

was recommended by most testers. The brakes, which were heavily shrouded to keep them as free of dirt and water as possible, were a combination of discs up front and drums at the rear, the latter allowing a good handbrake set-up. The dual hydraulic circuits were given a front/rear split for added safety. There was also a ride-height detector built into the rear suspension to allow the pressure limiting device built into the rear brakes to work more efficiently according to vehicle load, providing less braking pressure when luggage or towing loads were light, and more whenever heavier weights were being carried. According to early press material, the brakes were covered by 5.5J x 16 steel wheels shod with 6.50 R16 crossplies or 205 R16 radials depending on the grade, although radial rubber was adopted across the board by the time the first catalogue was released in August 1979.

Incidentally, testing of the new Geländewagen had begun as early as 1974, in areas as contrasting and far afield as the frozen wastes of the Arctic Circle, the gravel tracks of the Atlas Mountains, and the endless sand and salt lakes of the Sahara Desert, as well as places closer to home, like abandoned open coalmines and heavily forested areas in Europe's heartland. Production was given a preliminary green light in 1975, leading to more testing, including a lot of highway work to fine-tune the balance between off-road ability and on-road handling and comfort, and a final stamp of approval was granted in 1978, after the Daimler-Benz and SDP management gathered at the Schöckl proving ground (a short distance to the north of Graz) on the 1 June that year for a demonstration of the vehicle.

Making waves

The first batch of G-Wagen production models was announced at a week-long press event in Toulon in the south of France during the first week of February 1979. As well as track sessions on the Paul Ricard circuit, a special course was set aside to give journalists the chance to sample the new car on rough, rocky and slippery inclines.

Putting pen to paper after the launch, veteran writer Bernard Cahier could hardly contain himself after trying the G-Wagen: "Two of the most striking impressions were the ease of driving and the high degree of comfort on even the roughest terrain –

not to mention how easily the car could overcome the most challenging steep ramps and obstacles."

After noting the good visibility, the equally good ergonomics – from seating to heating and ventilation through to the layout and operation of the controls – and how roomy the new Mercedes was, Cahier concluded: "It must be said that the new cross-country Mercedes is a truly sensational machine offering a wealth of positive features and qualities applicable to both normal driving and off-road use. What Mercedes has done with this new vehicle is amazing, and its success should be immediate."

Motor's Tony Curtis noted something similar following his first encounter with the SUV, stating: "How does the new

The catalogue issued in January 1979, which had a different cover to the one seen in showrooms at the end of the year.

A very early 230G cabriolet fitted with a winch up front. This is the same car that was pictured flying through the air in one of the most memorable press images from the era.

39

Geländewagen measure up? Briefly, the answer is that it will almost certainly prove to be one of the world's finest small off-road vehicles, and even in its cheapest forms is markedly superior to the Land Rover in comfort and refinement. But the most expensive version, the 280GE, is in my view significantly less refined than the Range Rover."

He was definitely inspired, though, with user-friendly handling on paved surfaces, and real off-road ability: "Even if, out of consideration for the [off-road] inexperience of many of the journalists, the course had not been made exacting, the performance of the G-Wagen was nonetheless extremely impressive. It rode over the most savage humps and dips with total aplomb and took the steepest hills without effort. With the low-range bottom gear to call upon, even the least powerful 240GD version, though distinctly sluggish on the road, proved capable of storming up the most precipitous of slopes. The ability to lock the differential or select four-wheel drive or low-range on the move in anticipation of obstacles is invaluable."

Curtis described the G-Wagen's interior as "practical without being austere," and noted: "At low-to-moderate speeds, it is impressively refined, with low levels of engine and transmission noise, surprisingly good road noise insulation, and a ride which is radically superior to the Land Rover's and at least as good as the Range Rover's."

The short-wheelbase 280GE estate, or station wagon.

An early 3-litre diesel version of the long-wheelbase estate.

Racing through the desert with a swb station wagon.

In all fairness, however, at speed – if that's the right word, as the Mercedes SUVs were hardly fast, and *Autocar* felt the 240GD with automatic transmission was almost painfully slow, explaining why the 4AT wasn't offered to the public on the four-cylinder models – there was a lot more engine noise generated and a good deal of humming from the all-weather tyres, as well as some flapping noises from the hood on soft top models.

Like so many before, *Car & Driver* fell under the spell of Mercedes' thoroughness: "The G-Wagen never seems to take an awkward step and always seems to have all its tyres planted firmly on the ground, no matter how rough the terrain ... Lightness, low mass, and soft, ultra-long travel springs seem to be at the source of all this goodness – along with the cost-is-no-object approach to development."

An initial road car line-up of four engines and five body variations (including a convertible on the short-wheelbase model), covered most of the many Land Rover and Range Rover sales territory, allowing the Gelände-fahrzeug Gesellschaft mbH partnership to compete with its British rival almost straight away.

Actually, there was an interesting comment made in *Autocar* of February 1979: "Bearing in mind the existing competition, it has been interesting to see how Daimler-Benz would attack the market. Would they aim for a refined, land-going estate car like the American Jeep Cherokee and British Range Rover, or would

they aim more for the utilitarian sector dominated by the Land Rover? In the event, they have come out fairly midway between these two with a vehicle that is compact, appreciably smaller even than the Land Rover and yet which is well-trimmed and equipped, and offers a good standard of creature comforts."

The final line in Curtis' *Motor* report said it all, though: "Daimler-Benz is hardly likely to remain satisfied with first attempts, so watch out Range Rover, the Geländewagen is coming to get you!"

Suave sophistication was also part of the marketing plan, with the G-Wagen aiming to muscle in on Range Rover territory as well as take sales from Land Rover dealers.

The off-road ability of the G-Wagen was unquestionable, as this selection of early publicity photography featuring a pair of cabriolets clearly shows.

The swb (background) and lwb vans.

As implied in the *Car & Driver* comment, the launch timing was certainly good, as the SUV had begun to get a foothold in the marketplace, even in Britain, where one only has an image of Land Rovers and Range Rovers roaming the streets. At the end of 1979, when the first G-Wagen deliveries had already started filtering through to several EU countries, buyers could choose from the Suzuki Jimny LJ80 at the entry-level, which looked like a small G-Wagen (even more so in updated SJ30/SJ40 guise) but cost only £3088, the Lada Niva and Daihatsu F20 at around £4200, one of the Land Rover variants (starting at £4952), the Jeep Cherokee, the Chevy Blazer, and the £11,815 Range Rover at the top end.

Interestingly, as the SUV market developed into three distinct areas – one with pure utilitarian work in mind (dominated by cars such as the Land Rover), another for leisure pursuits (like the Chevy Blazer), and road cars with occasional excursions off-road being a necessity (personified by the Range Rover) – vehicles like the fwd Matra/Talbot Rancho were starting to filter through, which was an SUV-style machine rather than the real thing, and the little 4WD Subarus were bringing all-wheel drive to regular road cars in a far more successful way than the Jensen FF ever did, despite the latter being as beautiful as the Japanese cars were ugly.

Anyway, the first cars were badged as the 230G, 240GD, 280GE and 300GD depending on the engine under the bonnet, but there was no designation beyond that to give the body type. The swb 230Gs were the first models to be built, followed by swb 240GDs, and then the other grades followed as the summer progressed. Right-hand drive versions of the W460 Geländewagen were expected to be available in spring 1980 according to early reports. At the end of the day, though, despite the rising popularity of the breed, there were hardly any Mercedes G-Wagens straying far from mainland Europe for quite some time after the launch, due to the additional body and chassis engineering involved in producing rhd cars, and there were no plans to export the G-Wagen to North America at this stage, presumably because the GfG partners felt that markets closer to home would keep the factory running at full capacity for the foreseeable future anyway.

The GfG partners had every reason to be happy with its approach to market positioning, as it appeared to pay off if one is to judge things by contemporary press reaction. *Car & Driver* wrote in its May 1979 edition: "The new Mercedes-Benz G-series raises the ante for any manufacturer who thinks he wants to compete in the booming business of multi-purpose four-wheel drive vehicles. It has the charm and agility of a fine dirt bike, yet it goes down the highway like a passenger car. There are vehicles around that can do one or the other, but so far nothing – not even the Range Rover – measures up to the on- and off-road sophistication of the new vehicle hatched by Steyr of Austria and Daimler-Benz of West Germany."

A final pair of publicity shots taken in order to make the first catalogue, with the cabriolet again stealing the limelight. Note the lack of model grade badging on a lot of these early pictures, allowing those making up the brochures more freedom.

The early production models

With the majority of hoped for deals with a number of military forces around the world either falling through or being relatively small in production terms, the GfG partnership had to rely on road car sales to get the Geländewagen project in motion, allowing it to start and recoup some of the business' upfront investment ...

With the Shah of Iran no longer in power, leading to the cancellation of one large order, and the German army deciding the cheaper VW Iltis was exactly what it needed, despite a trial of the G-Wagen (a soft top vehicle with a fold-down windscreen and removable doors) in 1978, the management overseeing the Graz operation had one of two choices – abandon the project, or make the most of the civilian version of the car. Thankfully, with a handful of G-Wagens ordered by the German border police and the Argentine army, plus a dead cert order from Norway in the pipeline, the GfG team opted for the latter.

The original road car line-up

There's very little point in quoting the original G-Wagen prices for the domestic market from February 1979, as no-one could actually buy a machine until August, when the first catalogue was also released. Even then, those hoping to get their hands on a 280GE model would remain disappointed until the early part of 1980.

With so many engine and body variants, the price list was a long one, but for the sake of recording history, we need to make an occasional reference to pricing. This is how things looked in

The cover of the first catalogue, dated August 1979.

45

A 230G cabriolet finished in Agave Green, or Cactus Green as it was also known. Note the optional Rotzler-made winch on the front.

the summer of 1979, with the manual 230G cabriolet priced at DM 29,990, the 240GD cabriolet at DM 31,470, the 230G swb van at DM 31,640, the 230G swb estate at DM 32,883, the 240GD swb van at DM 33,109, the 240GD swb estate at DM 34,352, the 230G lwb van at DM 34,465, the 300GD cabriolet at DM 34,702, the 240GD lwb van at DM 35,934, the 280GE cabriolet at DM 36,216, the 300GD swb van at DM 36,341, the 230G lwb estate at DM 36,951, the 300GD swb estate at DM 37,584, the 280GE swb van at DM 37,855, the 240GD lwb estate at DM 38,420, the 280GE swb estate at DM 39,098, the 300GD lwb van at DM 39,166, the 280GE lwb van at DM 40,680, the 300GD lwb estate at DM 41,652, and the 280GE lwb estate at DM 43,166. To put these prices into perspective, the contemporary W123 models ranged in price from DM 21,041 for the 200 saloon up to DM 35,256 for the 280CE coupe.

Another 230G cabriolet from 1979 (top), and the interior of the same model grade. Note the perforated vinyl trim, the tachometer (indicating a petrol engine under the bonnet), and the rear diff lock lever and tell-tale light – the front lock has not been specified on this car.

A selection of shots showing the early short-wheelbase estate, or station wagon, in a number of different scenarios. The 280GE version can be seen pulling the boat.

The 300GD long-wheelbase estate doing a spot of mountain climbing.

Options included a W4B-type automatic transmission for five- and six-cylinder cars, front and/or rear differential locks, power-assisted steering, a front skid plate (or sumpguard – considered an absolute must for off-road users), a front winch, halogen headlights, a headlight washing system, halogen foglights, light guards, a work spotlight for swb cars, a rear foglight, tinted glass, a swiveling spare wheel carrier, additional fuel tanks (one or two, at 13.5 litres/3.0 imperial gallons each) in the rear wings, a locking fuel cap, a folding rear bench seat to provide extra luggage space when needed, occasional seats for the rear compartment, Webasto auxiliary heating, a clock, tachometer (for petrol-engined cars), a lock for the glovebox, and an ashtray on the front doors. Long-wheelbase cars had a few additional items listed, including a self-levelling rear suspension, a roofrack (with a 200kg/440lb limit), a one-piece rear door (with a rear wash/wipe system to suit available as an upgrade), rear glass demister, and standalone Behr air-conditioning. Audio equipment was an extra, of course, and for commercial users, there was also a power take-off (PTO) arrangement, but this was not generally offered in showrooms!

Only five standard coachwork colours were available at this time, all solid (as opposed to metallic) and including Colorado Beige (code 470), Wheat Yellow (681) and Agave Green (880) from the W123-series run, plus Cream-White (9050) and

Interior of a four-door (lwb) estate, this one trimmed in brown cloth, which was always combined with a lighter-coloured vinyl for the doors, flooring and seat edges.

Carmine Red (3535) from the van range. Interior trim came in either Black or Date Brown.

Incidentally, initially, it was expected that the open car would account for the majority of sales, although it was never all that popular after 1979. In the first year, the cabriolet did indeed claim the lion's share of production (just over half), but in 1980, the percentage dropped to around 17 per cent, and kept falling thereafter.

Military matters #1

The fact that the Geländewagen's roots lay in military khaki rather than the brightly coloured road cars released in 1979 can be proven via the first catalogue released for the model, which featured a short-wheelbase G-Wagen with an open body and folding windscreen on the cover. This A4 brochure was dated May 1977, which is only three months after the GfG concern was officially registered, and almost two years ahead of the launch of the civilian machines.

As we've already mentioned, the huge Iranian order fell through and European military trials failed to bring the expected results, so early G-Wagen sales were much slower than anticipated. Nonetheless, the military version (known as the 'Wolf' in Germany) did have its fans, with over 1000 being built in 1981, for instance. Most of these were 230Gs shipped to Argentina, although when General Leopoldo Galtieri took over the government at the end of 1981 (after Roberto Viola was ousted by military hardliners), he threw the outstanding invoice back across the Atlantic! Some were used in the Falklands War in 1982, and ultimately about 50 fell into the hands of the British army soon after, although around 900 are still thought to be in service in Argentina.

With a series of unhappy experiences dealing with military leaders in the early days of the Geländewagen story, not surprisingly, greater emphasis was put on marketing and refining the G-Wagen road cars until the VW Iltis (or 'Polecat') needed replacing.

Notwithstanding, an interesting machine – albeit carrying a Peugeot badge – did ultimately come out of the early marketing efforts. A series of trials starting in 1978, including a number of hybrids to increase the French content in the vehicles being tested, led Raymond Barre's government to choose the G-Wagen as a replacement for its ageing fleet of Hotchkiss M-201s (basically WWII Jeeps built under licence), although in the name of national interests and keeping French workers employed, the German engine was replaced by a Peugeot one, and final assembly of the so-called P4 took place at the historic Sochaux works on the French-German border, close to Switzerland.

The French army seen in action during the Gulf War in the early 1990s, with Peugeot P4s leading the column.

French military Peugeot P4s pictured recently on the way to Mali. Most P4s proudly displayed a trademark Sochaux lion on the nose, although some French-built cars now sport a Panhard badge.

The original order of 15,000 P4s was reduced to 13,500 units in 1981 due to Pierre Mauroy's budget cuts, but it was still a very significant coup, keeping the factory ticking over at a nice pace from 1982 onwards. The chassis frame, body parts and transfer box were all shipped to France from the SDP outfit in Graz, chassis components and axles were sourced from Stuttgart, and the rest was provided by Peugeot (including the welding and painting work until 1985, when Peugeot P4 production ultimately switched to the Panhard works in Paris – Panhard having been part of the PSA Group since the 1970s, and more recently linked to the Auverland concern and, later, Renault Trucks). A few P4s were exported to former French colonies, but most remained assigned to the French fighting forces, and with diesel power the norm after the first 2400 cars were built, the original petrol engines were duly replaced by diesel units to reduce logistical complications – something always welcome in the heat of battle. It should be noted that a handful of open swb Peugeot P4s were built for the civilian market in the mid-1980s, powered by a 2-litre petrol engine giving 83bhp or a 2.5-litre NA diesel lump rated at 75bhp. These were destined to be real rarities, however ...

Advertising for the new G-Wagen, which – when one takes body configurations and engine options into consideration – came with 20 model variations, or 40 if one includes transmission choices as well.

The Puch-badged version of the 230G four-door station wagon. Some of the earliest pictures show vehicles photographed in exactly the same spot as the Mercedes version. Indeed, I'm convinced the car wasn't moved on these occasions – the grille badges, hub trims and number plate were simply changed to give it a new identity. As can be seen in this picture, the chrome flashes, either side of the grille badge on the earliest Puch press images, were not used on showroom models.

Building on the foundation

On the corporate front, the supremely elegant W126 S-Class series was introduced at the 1979 Frankfurt Show, powered by 2.8-litre straight-sixes, or all-alloy 3.8- and 5.0-litre V8s. Production began on the state-of-the-art lines at Sindelfingen in December, which is when Joachim Zahn retired, allowing Dr Gerhard Prinz to become the new Chairman of the Board of Management of Daimler-Benz AG.

The Mercedes W123 and SL/SLC models inherited new engines in 1980, and the availability of ABS brakes became more widespread. Airbags and seatbelt pretension systems became listed in the following year, keeping Daimler-Benz very much at the forefront of safety innovation and technology. 1981 also saw the last of the 600s built, as well as the first of the W126 coupes – the 380SEC and 500SEC ranking as one of the author's all-time favourites from the postwar era, despite the fact that they brought about the end of the SLC series.

Meanwhile, the first 'Popemobile' was produced in time for Pope John Paul II's visit to Germany in November 1980, based on the long-wheelbase 230G station wagon with its roof removed to make way for a detachable plexiglass canopy. One of a pair built at the time, it was used by His Holiness for many years thereafter, being shipped as far afield as Australia for Papal visits, and now resides as a permanent exhibit in the Mercedes-Benz Museum in Stuttgart.

In the spring of 1981, G-Wagen prices ranged from DM 33,606 for the 230G cabriolet all the way up to DM 49,245 for the 280GE long-wheelbase station wagon. The Geländewagen could cost a lot more, though, for in addition to the growing option list tempting buyers to part with their hard-earned cash (a hardtop was made available for the cabriolet models – a very practical addition to the option list, given the cold weather in Europe and rising car crime), the tuners had started to muscle in on the act, too. Quite understandably, some cited a need

Another Mercedes-Benz 300GD lwb estate, but this one from 1980 and in more formal surroundings, despite what the tyre treads might suggest. In fact, G-Wagen buyers were offered a number of tyre patterns (four are illustrated in the first catalogue) to suit the car's most likely working environment or the time of year.

The 1980 'Popemobile,' based on the 230G lwb station wagon.

An interesting diversion into modelling, with Revell making a 230G fire engine. In fact, the G-Wagen inspired many models, from Esci kits to Matchbox diecast miniatures. Nowadays, some very high quality diecast models exist for enthusiasts.

for more power, others a desire for a more inviting interior. As always, the European tuners, especially those based in Germany, were quick to respond.

One of the earliest firms to breath on the G-Wagen was AMG – the famous company headed by ex-Mercedes man Hans-Werner Aufrecht that would soon become part of the Daimler-Benz empire as a works tuner. AMG started marketing body kits and tuned engines in 1981, and duly shoehorned a V8 under the bonnet of the four-door estate. With up to 300bhp on tap from 1986 onwards (thanks to the 5.6-litre lump) and a five-speed manual transmission, this was a seriously quick Geländewagen, being easy to recognise thanks to its huge wheel and tyre combination and discreet AMG badging. Owners were also able to specify an interior based on the contemporary S-Class.

Whilst not wanting to get bogged down in the world of one-offs and customising – personified by the likes of Luigi Colani and later on, firms such as Kleemann – of special interest, however, is the workshop of Richard Kaan in Graz, Austria. Kaan had previously worked for Steyr-Daimler-Puch, and was actually in charge of the team that built the prototype G-Wagen before setting up his own business in 1981. Kaan left the chassis and drivetrain alone, knowing that was the vehicle's strong suit, concentrating instead on upgrading the interior – by making it quieter and more luxurious – and individualising the exterior with special paintwork and carefully chosen accessories, such as BBS alloys.

With well over 5000 cars finding new homes in both 1980 and 1981, it's fair to say that the Geländewagen's popularity was on the rise amongst enthusiasts looking for an alternative to the Range Rover. It was evident, however, that despite the apparent

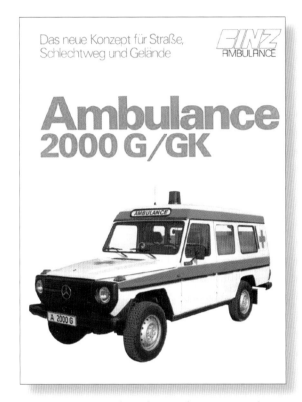

Contemporary brochures for Binz and Miesen ambulances based on the G-Wagon.

Advertising for the AMG version of the G-Wagen, with its tuned engine, huge wheel and tyre combination, bodykit, and bespoke interior. AMG was also one of the first to offer stretched versions of the off-roader – one armoured example was used by Nelson Mandela as a presidential vehicle.

A 280GE after receiving the Lorinser treatment.

A 1981 230G cabriolet – the entry-level Geländewagen, and soon to become the 230GE, making these important reference pictures.

Richard Kaan's first and second G-Wagen conversions from 1981 (one carrying the Puch badge, and the other a Mercedes one), which led to a number of commissions for luxury interior and exterior upgrades. Nowadays, Kaan specialises in the painstaking restoration of classic cars.

Advertising for the Schulz station wagon on an extended wheelbase. Binz went about creating interior space in a different way during the 1990s, extending the rear overhang on the lwb estate instead.

calm, the G-Wagen project was starting to cause rifts in the relationship between Daimler-Benz and its Austrian partners. Indeed, Daimler-Benz sold its share of the GfG business to Steyr-Daimler-Puch on the first day of October 1981, establishing a consultancy firm in Graz soon after to look after the Stuttgart concern's interests in the Geländewagen project, not only as a supplier to SDP, but also for the long-term health of the company, for Daimler-Benz promised to keep buying machines from the Austrians for a designated period and keep updating drivetrains and so on as it saw fit. Having the consultants in the middle would allow smooth transitions as engine generations changed, for instance, along with faster reaction times to the wants and needs of both parties, as well as those of the dedicated Mercedes-Benz customer. To sum things up, from now on, the Stuttgart firm became the legal manufacturer (albeit concentrating on development and marketing), while the SDP business would

focus on production, although Puch-badged models were still built alongside Mercedes ones at this stage.

Five-spoke 15-inch alloy wheels became an option at the start of the 1982 season, along with a tropical roof covering for tin-top cars in order to reduce heat build-up in hot regions, fibreglass wheelarch extensions (fender flares), and sportier Recaro seats. The 280GE also gained a larger fuel capacity from December 1981, inheriting one of the optional auxiliary tanks to take the maximum load up to 81.5 litres (18 imperial gallons).

At the same time, the folding front windscreen seen on military vehicles was also made available for civilian users in Germany, subject to special permission, while the advent of right-hand drive vehicles at the end of 1981 brought the previously optional one-piece rear door design into widespread use – all rhd closed cars (lwb and swb) came with this single side-hinged door, which was duly adopted as standard on the left-hand drive

This fascinating picture shows a Puch-badged cabriolet at the head of the production line, with more open cars following on behind in various stages of build. Production started on 1 February 1979, with Puch models accounting for around one-in-ten G-Wagen sales in the early days.

A 300GD lwb estate on display at the 1981 Frankfurt Show.

A Paris showroom photographed at the end of 1981 and containing a 500SEL (W126), a W123 saloon, and a spruced-up G-Wagen in the background.

An early 1982 Model Year lwb 280GE station wagon that was duly pressed into service for the spring 1982 face-lift image photography. Using some carefully chosen angles and reflections on the windscreen, one could hardly see the old trim and early-style towbar that are highlighted in these pictures.

equivalents by 1983. With the hinges on the nearside and the spare wheel mounted in the centre (a far neater arrangement than the swiveling carrier), this left room for a door handle on the right; all cars with the single door were offered with a rear wiper (with its own dedicated washer facility), while the rear foglight was fitted above the nearside rear combination lamp on lhd models or the space in the lower right-hand corner of the door panel on rhd cars.

With fresh competition coming from the five-door version of the Range Rover (launched in the summer of 1981 after a delay of almost a decade!) and the Isuzu Trooper (a Japanese newcomer in the SUV arena, also known as the Bighorn, launched in September 1981), the next chapter continues to track the progress of the G-Wagen, introducing the first of the right-hand drive models we've just mentioned, as well as a rather important competition car ...

Another 280GE long-wheelbase estate, in the kind of conditions made for the Geländewagen to shine. The four-door model has always been the most popular body variant amongst normal road users.

The options and accessories catalogue printed in August 1981, in time for the 1982 season, although it was reprinted several times.

A second brochure showing special equipment (SA components) for the G-Wagen, this one printed in January 1982, with the hardtop and BBS wheels being the main features.

The release of the five-door Range Rover provided some serious competition for the G-Wagen, which, if we ignore US-built cars that tend to appeal to a different clientele to buyers of European machines, had earlier been able to secure something of a niche market via the lwb estate variant.

4

Refining the breed

As Autocar had noted in 1981: "Some aspects of the car are very pleasing, making it very suitable for the tough life in which its ruggedness will be appreciated. With this, though, goes a measure of starkness reminding one that this is essentially a utilitarian vehicle." In response to remarks like this – and there were plenty of them – the spring of 1982 brought with it the first batch of changes aimed at refining the G-Wagen, making it more inviting for regular road users ...

The domestic catalogue released in April 1982 was full of subtle modifications aimed at broadening the general appeal of the Geländewagen. One of the biggest changes was the loss of the 230G in favour of a fuel-injected 230GE model. Replacing the M115 lump, the M102 E23 injection engine transplant had been adopted in the W123 saloons far earlier (in the summer of 1980, in fact), so it was well-known to followers of Mercedes lore, providing a higher level of performance, greater economy, cleaner emissions and longer service intervals.

Whilst retaining a cast iron block, angled over to keep height down to a minimum, the M102 was physically smaller than its older counterpart, and lighter thanks to this, a reduction in oil and water capacities, and things like the use of a single-row timing chain rather than a duplex one. The adoption of a crossflow head with hemispherical combustion chambers added greater efficiency into the equation as well, while the counterweighted crankshaft enhanced refinement.

With mechanically-operated Bosch K-Jetronic fuel-injection, one could be forgiven for thinking this was a scaled-down version of the M110 six, but a major difference was the use of a single overhead camshaft on the four-cylinder unit, calling for longer rocker arms to act on the camshaft, which was placed low down in the vee created by the angle of the valve stems. Visual differences compared to the M115s included the intake

The new 230GE badge.

and exhaust positions following M110 practice, breakerless transistorised ignition, a far wider, flatter rocker cover, an oil filter high up at the back of the engine (like the diesels), and a viscous-coupled cooling fan.

For the 2.3-litre engine, a larger 95.5mm bore and shorter

The M102 E23 engine in cutaway guise.

80.3mm stroke was adopted, giving a capacity of 2299cc. Retaining the 9.0:1 compression ratio of old, the fuel-injected unit gave 125bhp/92kW (less than in the saloons, but a healthy increase of 23bhp for the G-Wagen), along with 142lbft of torque. Incidentally, the extra horses allowed the engineers to adopt a taller 4.86:1 final-drive ratio on the 230GE, which was the same as that found on the 280GE and 300GD, helping to further improve fuel economy; the 240GD retained the old 5.33:1 ratio, though.

A press photograph released to coincide with the April 1982 face-lift, although few of the cars were actually face-lifted in reality.

The latest interior, with its new steering and seat trim being totally different to those found on the earlier cars. Other detail changes were made at the same time.

While all cars continued with 205 R16 reinforced radials on 5.5J steel rims, PAS was made standard on the 280GE and 300GD models (remaining optional on the 230GE and 240GD grades). Inside, the steering wheel and multi-function indicator stalk were borrowed from the W123 series, bringing the horn to the centre boss and an end to the foot-operated screen wash system, and a new handbrake was used. In addition, the saloon car light switch was brought into play, situated between the clock and heater controls, meaning the fan switch had to be moved to the opposite side of the heater sliders. There were improved central air vents (earlier versions had been criticised as too flimsy), and there was a subtle redesign of the centre console immediately beneath them.

Phased in a few months earlier, the hazard warning light was now a rocker switch, matching the other minor switchgear, dash illumination was improved, and the optional tachometer gained new, far clearer graphics. Answering the critics who complained about the comfort of the early seats over longer distances, reprofiled seat cushions were specified, covered with a new cloth trim in a Brown or Black/Grey tight check pattern. The cloth trim accent was also carried over to the door panels, reducing the starkness of the interior (although perforated vinyl was still considered the standard upholstery), while exterior paintwork options now totalled 22 colours, including metallics – a huge increase from the original five shades!

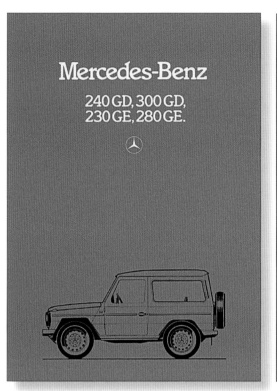

Mercedes-Benz

240 GD, 300 GD, 230 GE, 280 GE.

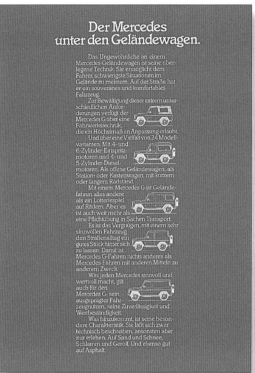

Der Mercedes unter den Geländewagen.

Das Ungewöhnliche an einem Mercedes-Geländewagen ist seine überlegene Technik. Sie ermöglicht dem Fahrer, schwierigste Situationen im Gelände zu meistern. Auf der Straße hat er ein souveränes und komfortables Fahrzeug.

Zur Bewältigung dieser extrem unterschiedlichen Anforderungen verfügt der Mercedes G über eine Fahrwerkstechnik, die ein Höchstmaß an Anpassung erlaubt. Und über eine Vielfalt von 24 Modellvarianten. Mit 4- und 6-Zylinder-Einspritzmotoren und 4- und 5-Zylinder-Dieselmotoren. Als offene Geländewagen, als Station- oder Kastenwagen, mit kurzem oder langem Radstand.

Mit einem Mercedes G ist Geländefahren alles andere als ein Lotteriespiel auf Rädern. Aber es ist auch weit mehr als eine Pflichtübung in Sachen Transport.

Es ist das Vergnügen, mit einem sehr sinnvollen Fahrzeug den Straßenalltag ein gutes Stück hinter sich zu lassen. Damit ist Mercedes G-Fahren nichts anderes als Mercedes-Fahren mit anderen Mitteln zu anderem Zweck.

Was jeden Mercedes sinnvoll und wertvoll macht, gilt auch für den Mercedes G: sein ausgeprägter Fahrzeugnutzen, seine Zuverlässigkeit und Wertbeständigkeit.

Was hinzukommt, ist seine besondere Charakteristik. Sie läßt sich zwar technisch beschreiben, ansonsten aber nur erleben. Auf Sand und Schnee, Schlamm und Geröll. Und ebenso gut auf Asphalt.

Geländefahren kann abenteuerlich sein. Ein Geländewagen sollte es nicht sein.

Wie jeder Mercedes erfüllt auch der Mercedes G ein traditionelles Bauprinzip des Hauses: Ein Mercedes fordert seinen Fahrer nicht heraus, er entlastet ihn.

Der Mercedes G imponiert nicht durch eine verwirrende Vielzahl von Hebeln und Instrumenten oder durch abenteuerlichen Anti-Komfort, der – wenn es hart auf hart geht – unnötig die Kondition des Fahrers fordert.

Er imponiert durch das genaue Gegenteil: Er ermöglicht auch im schwierigsten Gelände ein ergonomisch sinnvolles Handling des Fahrzeuges bei gleichzeitig hohem Fahrkomfort.

Damit gibt der Mercedes G dem Fahrer die Möglichkeit, seine Konzentration und Kondition dort zu investieren, wo es angebracht ist: bei der Beherrschung des Geländes. Lenkrad, Schalthebel und Handbremse sind räumlich nahe angeordnet und erlauben immer einen schnellen, sicheren Zugriff.

Zur Bewältigung von extremen Anforderungen verfügt der Mercedes G über eine überlegene Fahrwerkstechnik.

Zum komfortablen Federungs- und Dämpfungssystem des Mercedes G kommt der Komfort des Innenraumes: großzügige Abmessungen, haltgebende, körpergerecht geformte Sitze, ein aufwendiges Lüftungssystem und eine Heizung, deren Kapazität ausreicht, bei Außentemperaturen bis – 25 °C die Innentemperatur bei + 20 °C konstant zu halten.

Mercedes G-Modelle verfügen – serienmäßig oder auf Sonderwunsch – über Ausstattungs-Details, die für andere Geländewagen oft überhaupt nicht lieferbar sind:

Zur besonderen Entlastung des Fahrers trägt die beim 300 GD und 280 GE serienmäßige, für 240 GD und 230 GE auf Wunsch lieferbare Servolenkung bei. 300 GD und 280 GE können zusätzlich mit einem 4-Gang-Automatic-Getriebe ausgestattet werden – eine Erleichterung, die auch Geländeprofis zu schätzen wissen, besonders wegen des sperrbaren 1. Gangs, zur sicheren Bergabfahrt.

Der Mercedes-Geländewagen ermöglicht auch in schwierigstem Gelände ergonomisch sinnvolles Handling.

Exakt dosierte Antriebskraft durch anspruchsvolle Antriebstechnik.

Im Mercedes G kann der Fahrer während der Fahrt von Hinterrad- auf Allradantrieb umschalten, um die Antriebskraft auf alle vier Räder gleichmäßig zu verteilen.

Und wenn potenzierte Leistung gefordert wird, sorgt die während der Fahrt zuschaltbare Geländeübersetzung für eine Verdoppelung der Kraft an den Rädern bei halbierter Geschwindigkeit. Dem Fahrer stehen damit acht Vorwärtsgänge und zwei Rückwärtsgänge zur Verfügung.

Die auf Wunsch lieferbaren Differentialsperren für die Hinter- und Vorderachse halten das Fahrzeug selbst dort noch in Gang, wo der Mercedes G nur noch unter einem Rad festen Boden hat. Sie sind – während der Fahrt – einzeln zu- und abschaltbar. Dieses außergewöhnliche Antriebssystem ist ein entscheidender Vorteil der Mercedes-Geländewagen. Es ermöglicht die kraftschlüssige unterbrechungslose Leistungs-Anpassung in schwierigstem Gelände.

Ohne Zwangs-Stopps durch technische Halbheiten, die dem Fahrzeug den Schwung nehmen. So hilft die Antriebstechnik des Mercedes G seinem Fahrer, schnell und wirkungsvoll zu reagieren. Und dadurch das Gelände sicher und überlegen zu beherrschen.

Station-Wagen, langer Radstand.

Station-Wagen, kurzer Radstand.

Überlegen in jedem Gelände, souverän auf allen Straßen.

Diese einzigartige Antriebstechnik kommt dem Mercedes G nicht nur auf unwegsamem Boden zugute, sondern auch im Allroundeinsatz auf allen Straßen.

So verbessert der Allrad-Antrieb zum Beispiel generell die Spurtreue in schnell gefahrenen Kurven, bei Regen, besonders aber bei Schnee und Fahrbahnglätte. Die starren Achsen und Schraubenfedern mit extrem langem Federweg sorgen dafür, daß das Fahrzeug nicht nur im Gelände außerordentlich gut zu beherrschen ist. Auch auf der Straße ermöglicht diese Fahrwerkstechnik optimales Handling und neutrales Kurvenverhalten. Auch dann noch, wenn der Mercedes G schwer beladen ist und große Lasten ziehen muß.

Bis zu 925 kg kann ein Geländewagen von Mercedes als Zuladung aufnehmen. Und bis zu 2.800 kg zusätzlich ziehen, je nach Typ und Ausstattung. Unter besonderen Zulassungsbedingungen sogar bis zu 4.000 kg.

(This page and overleaf) The April 1982 brochure, reproduced here in full due to its limited content (the original domestic G-Wagen catalogue went to 54 pages!). Most of the cars illustrated are pre-facelift models angled to hide distinguishing features that point to earlier cars. Note the optional hardtop and fender flares shown on the one page.

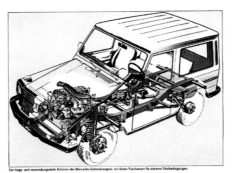

Der biege- und verwindungssteife Rahmen des Mercedes-Geländewagens: ein festes Fundament für extreme Fahrbedingungen.

Ein festes Fundament für extreme Fahrbedingungen.

Das „Rückgrat" der Geländewagen von Mercedes besteht aus zwei starken, kastenförmigen Längsträgern, die durch mehrere rohrförmige Quertraversen zu einem biege- und verwindungssteifen Rahmen gefügt sind. Der komplette Aufbau ist eine unabhängige, stabile und geschlossene Einheit, die über 8 Gummilager fest mit dem Rahmen verschraubt wird. Diese Trennbarkeit von Rahmen und Aufbau erhöht gerade im Falle eines stark strapazierten Geländewagens die Reparaturfreundlichkeit entscheidend – und macht sie preiswert.

Der steife Stahlrahmen in Verbindung mit zwei starren Achsen widersteht selbst härtesten Belastungen. Geführt werden die Achsen durch je zwei Längs- und einen Querlenker vorn und hinten. Große Schraubenfedern mit extrem langem Federweg an allen vier Rädern sorgen für Beweglichkeit und komfortab-

les Fahrverhalten sowohl im Gelände als auch auf der Straße.

In der Praxis beweist sich die Überlegenheit der Verbindung von Starrachsen und Schraubenfedern: Fährt zum Beispiel ein Rad über ein größeres Hindernis, hebt die starre Achse das Differential aus der Gefahrenzone.

Die straffe, gut gedämpfte Federung sorgt für weitgehende Geländeanpassung: Sie stabilisiert das Fahrzeug, gleicht Geländeunebenheiten aus und schützt gleichzeitig den Fahrer vor groben Erschütterungen und unangenehmen Vibrationen.

Radstand und Aufbauabmessungen ergeben große Überhangwinkel

Niedriger Fahrzeugschwerpunkt und optimale Achslastverteilung

Großer Rampenwinkel: hohe Bodenwellen sind kein Hindernis.

Große Bodenfreiheit hilft über manches hinweg

Freiheit nach Maß.

Bewegungsfreiheit im Gelände – das ist auch eine Frage der Abmessungen von Fahrgestell und Fahrzeugaufbau. Bei den Geländewagen von Mercedes setzt der Fahrzeugaufbau über dem Achsniveau an. Radstand und Aufbauabmessungen ergeben extrem kurze Überhänge vorn und hinten.

Mit Überhangwinkeln von über 40° vorn und hinten und einem Steigvermögen bis zu 80 % kann man sich mit einem Mercedes G auch in extremes Berggelände wagen. Und seine Wattiefe bis zu 60 cm sorgt dafür, daß auch Wasserläufe ohne Risiko durchquert werden können.

Der niedrige Fahrzeugschwerpunkt und die optimale Achslastverteilung bewirken, daß der Mercedes G in kritischer Schräglage nicht gleich kippt, sondern durch langsames Wegrutschen signalisiert, daß die Kipp-Grenze erreicht ist.

Härteste Erprobung auf elektronisch-hydraulischen Prüfständen.

Motor des 300 GD: 5-Zylinder-Dieselmotor mit 65 kW (88 PS).

Fahrwerk und Federung absolvieren große Fahrbahnunebenheiten.

Motor des 280 GE: 6-Zylinder-Einspritzmotor mit 115 kW (156 PS).

Zuverlässigkeit in Technik und Service.

Die wichtigsten Aggregate – Motoren, Getriebe, Achsen, Bremsen – haben in Mercedes-Personenwagen und -Nutzfahrzeugen längst ihre Unverwüstlichkeit weltweit bewiesen. Sie wurden nur noch dem Einsatz im Gelände angepaßt.

Gerade die Verwendung der bewährten, ausgereiften Technik gewährleistet nicht nur die zuverlässige Funktion, sondern auch die Nutzung des internationalen Mercedes-Benz Service – schnelle Verfügbarkeit von Original-Ersatzteilen zur sachgemäßen, kostengünstigen Wartung. In über 1.200 Stützpunkten im Inland und über 5.000 weltweit.

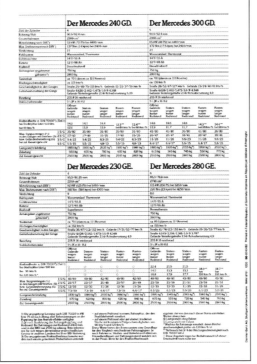

Of course, not all model year (MY) changes occur at once – one can often see new trim combined with older steering wheels, and so on, as stocks on the side of the line tend to get used up first. Indeed, while there were some very carefully chosen pictures used in the April 1982 catalogue, the press pictures released to illustrate the revised line-up had some real oddities within them due to a lack of updated vehicles being available in time for photography purposes. This is often the case, and one needs to be aware of these things, as it is something one will encounter on a regular basis, along with retouched images – older pictures being manipulated to represent later models. It's therefore fair to say that model year changes are always more a statement of intent rather than an exact science, and

(Above and overleaf) One of the first 230GE models seen in some quite different scenarios. As well as 4WD grip, the waterproofing of electrical systems was just as important for off-road vehicles. This prototype still has the early seat trim, by the way.

one cannot always trust factory material as a positive dating method for tracking changes!

Almost as if to confirm that statement, for the G-Wagen, the 230G with the older M115 V23 engine was allowed to continue in limited production for countries burdened with poor fuel quality, and in 1986, it gave way to the 230G with a 109bhp carburettor version of the M102 unit (the 2299cc M102 V23), which was built in small numbers until 1989. For the record, the chassis codes were the same as those applied to the early 230G variants.

The 300GE van featured in the face-lift photography.

The 240GD short-wheelbase estate, from the same period as the 300GE van. Note the new-style towbar, adopted as an option during the 1982 season and having a 2800kg (6160lb) trailer limit, and the GfG badge on the lower trailing edge of the nearside front wing, which had disappeared well before 1983 dawned.

With injection, the 2.3-litre car was no longer the cheapest. As of April 1982, domestic prices included the manual 240GD cabriolet at DM 38,872, the 230GE cabriolet priced at DM 40,454, the 240GD swb van at DM 41,075, the 240GD swb estate at DM 42,375, the 230GE swb van at DM 42,657, the 300GD cabriolet at DM 42,827, the 230GE swb estate at DM 43,957, the 240GD lwb van at DM 44,522, the 300GD swb van at DM 45,030, the 230GE lwb van at DM 46,104, the 300GD swb estate and 280GE cabriolet at DM 46,330, the 240GD lwb estate at DM 47,629, the 300GD lwb van at DM 48,477, the

A 1983 Model Year 280GE short-wheelbase estate (left) and 300GD long-wheelbase estate featuring wheelarch extensions over alloy wheels, contemporary 'go-faster' stripes, foglights, headlight grilles on the lwb machine, and Recaro sports seats. Note the heavier fender flares on the lwb station wagon – those on the swb car were considered the regular version, whenever they were specified, of course.

The Mercedes-Benz line-up for the start of the 1983 season, with the W123 saloon, estate and coupe, the S-Class saloon (lwb and swb models were available) and coupe (the SEC), the R107 SL, and the Geländewagen, seen here in lwb estate guise.

A 1983 230GE short-wheelbase station wagon being put through its paces on the Mercedes test track.

A minor styling face-lift put forward by Frank Weinhold in February 1983, although the face of the G-Wagen was destined to remain much the same for the rest of its production life.

280GE swb van at DM 48,533, the 230GE lwb estate at DM 49,211, the 280GE swb estate at DM 49,833, the 300GD lwb estate at DM 51,584, the 280GE lwb van at DM 51,980, and the 280GE lwb estate at DM 55,087.

Prices were held over for what was basically the whole of the 1983 season after this, although an all-new compact car, the 190/190E (W201), was announced in November 1982, bringing forth a predecessor to today's C-Class. A diesel-powered 190D was added in 1983, along with a high-performance 16v model, which managed to claim a number of world speed records a few weeks before it was launched.

Export markets

Right-hand drive versions of the G-Wagen became available in 1981, opening up the all-important UK market, and the Australian one in particular, for while British owners could drive a left-hooker without restrictions, lhd was pretty much outlawed Down Under; in fact, the rules on using left-hand drive vehicles in Australia is still very strict to this day.

With Great Britain always taking a large number of Mercedes-Benz passenger cars, making an rhd Geländewagen must have seemed like a dead cert, as one had every right to assume the investment money would soon be recouped going by past experience. However, the Brits are rather proud of Solihull products, which could also be bought significantly cheaper in their home market – even a base Range Rover could match the cost of an swb 300GD, and Land Rovers were a lot less expensive, starting at £8200, which undercut the Toyota Landcruiser by quite some margin.

Anyway, UK sales began in December 1981, with the £13,560 300GD short-wheelbase estate being the entry-level model, and the 280GE version adding £350 to the invoice. The long-wheelbase 300GD station wagon cost £14,300, and again, opting for the six-cylinder petrol engine cost a £350 premium. An automatic gearbox was standard on the early 280GEs, or an £825 extra on the diesel models, while diff locks, PAS and cloth trim were standard on all cars, and tinted glass added to the 280GE's spec sheet. Interestingly, while a single rear door was the norm, a double-door arrangement was listed as an option for British buyers for a year or so.

Prices remained the same at the UK's 99 dealers going into the 1983 season, but the fact that one could buy a 280SE saloon for £15,875 (or a 4.2-litre Jaguar XJ6 for a bit less) put things into perspective – the G-Wagen was an expensive vehicle, and buyers had a right to expect something impressive on opening the door. For pure off-road users, for the price of a Geländewagen, one could buy a basic Land Rover and still have enough change for a Lada Niva or Suzuki SJ (Jimny) to tow behind it. At least the folks back in Stuttgart realised this, and further upgrades, building on those implemented in 1982, were already in the pipeline to try and stave off the Range Rover threat, which in luxury 'Vogue' guise had gone seriously upmarket in a hurry.

Indeed, *Motor* decided the Range Rover was still the car to beat in the upmarket SUV sector: "Even with a three-pointed star on its grille, the G-Wagen cannot challenge the refinement and style that are the keynotes of the Range Rover's long-standing

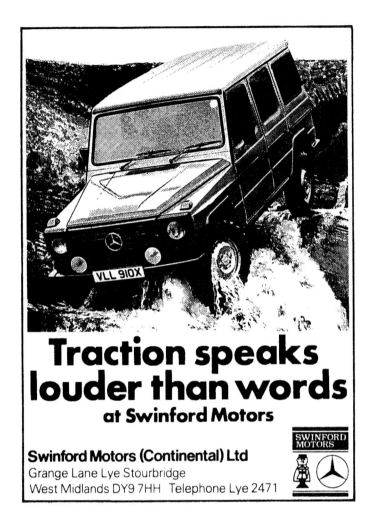

Traction speaks louder than words
at Swinford Motors

Swinford Motors (Continental) Ltd
Grange Lane Lye Stourbridge
West Midlands DY9 7HH Telephone Lye 2471

SWINFORD MOTORS

British advertising from December 1981.

Mercedes-Benz G-series wins Cop-Drive '82.

When you put 100 policemen into 50 four-wheel drive vehicles and ask them to punish said vehicles across 140 miles of roads, rocks and rivers, you have what is called the 'Cop-Drive '82.'

And it's what we call success.

Because 1st place was captured by a Mercedes-Benz 280GE, driven by officers Chris Smith and Ted Stringer, entered by Mercedes-Benz dealer, Bradshaw and Webb Ltd., Chelsea.

And joint 2nd place went to another Mercedes-Benz 280GE, driven by officers John Trafford and Derek Purdy, entered by Mercedes-Benz dealer Drake and Fletcher, Maidstone.

Not bad, considering that of the 50 vehicles entered, only two of them were G's. So if you want a tough four-wheel drive vehicle, your Mercedes-Benz dealer, and a few PC's, can tell you all about it.

Just ask for the one that copped top honours.

Mercedes-Benz

RESULTS (Subject to official confirmation)	THE MERCEDES-BENZ G-SERIES
1st Place: Mercedes-Benz 280GE Drivers: Chris Smith and Ted Stringer 2nd Place: (equal) Mercedes-Benz 280GE Drivers: John Trafford and Derek Purdy	280GE: 2.8 litre petrol injection engine developing 156 DIN/h.p. Available in two and four door versions. 300GD: 3 litre Diesel engine developing 88 DIN/h.p. Available in two and four door versions. Standard equipment on all models includes: Transfer gearbox. Front axle differential lock. Rear axle differential lock. Power steering. Automatic transmission (280GE only).

696

MOTOR SPORT, JUNE 1982

A UK test had clocked the four-door 280GE at 94mph (150kph), so its use in competition was totally justified – a point proven in the 1982 version of the off-road challenge for the British police force. Only two G-Wagens (both 2.8-litre models) were entered amongst the 50 cars, coming first and second.

success. In our minds, the British car is still the ultimate dual-purpose vehicle – one which can tow a hefty horsebox across a muddy field in the morning, and in the evening take the family to the theatre without being in the slightest bit out of place. Its crown remains firmly in place." Notwithstanding, comments passed on superb off-road manners but disappointing on-road performance and utilitarian looks were also being addressed in the background.

Japan was becoming an increasingly important market for Mercedes-Benz passenger vehicles (the truck side of the business was still very weak), and this is illustrated by the fact that the 300GD was offered in the Land of the Rising Sun a month

before the UK. Only the swb 300GD station wagon was listed initially, priced at 7,250,000 yen, which was about the same as the W123 280E saloon, and a significant 2,100,000 yen less than the 280SE. As such, we can see a subtle difference in the car's market positioning in Japan, and, unlike the UK at the time,

there was no stigma attached to diesel either, as the Japanese were already used to the 300TDT estate and 300SD saloons being in the showrooms. One should not lose sight of the fact, however, that one could buy ten of the cheapest Subarus for the same money, or five 1800s with four-wheel drive! Interestingly, by the time the 1983 Model Year was announced, a lwb 300GD estate had been added to the line-up, commanding 8,410,000 yen against 7,200,000 for the existing short-wheelbase model.

Australia eventually got a long-wheelbase 300GD estate in January 1983. Coming with an automatic transmission and fully-loaded with options, it was priced at $39,500, and continued as the only G-Wagen model sold Down Under until the spring of 1985. Just 100 vehicles were imported in the first year, making the G-Wagen a real rarity, and early reports complaining of how slow the car was on the highway (a top speed of 76mph/122kph was recorded in one test, with even minor inclines calling for downchanges) probably kept it that way, too, even though off-road performance was usually highly-praised. Indeed, some even mentioned that the importation was not so much for road users, but a way of tempting the Australian government to plump for the G-Wagen when replacing its military fleet of 2000 4x4 vehicles.

Mention should be made here of the grey market imports making their way into America. Because the Geländewagen wasn't sold through MBNA (presumably due to the fact that the company was struggling to deal with CAFE regulations as things were, without having to try and squeeze a heavy SUV into the line-up), this left a tiny gap for enterprising types like Al Mardikian of Trend Imports, California, to fill. The work carried out by Trend Imports, and other firms like it, allowed US buyers with a minimum of $30,000 to $35,000 to spend to secure a G-Wagen that met all Federal requirements. With MBNA passing over the G-Wagen for some time to come, this was the only option available to Americans wanting an early example of the breed.

The Paris-Dakar victory

The first Paris-Dakar Rally had started in Paris on Boxing Day 1978, finishing in Dakar in the middle of January after about 6000 miles (10,000km) of wild motoring. A Range Rover won

The Paris-Dakar Rally provided the ultimate challenge for adventurous racers during the early 1980s.

the car class in this original '1979' event, lining up alongside motorcycles and trucks. The Paris-Dakar quickly caught the imagination of adventurers and manufacturers alike, and the 1980 event drew in 216 competitors, including the first Mercedes G-Wagen to challenge the deserts. Starting at number 135 in their 240GD, Frederic Harrewyn and Lionel Ligier finished 23rd.

The 1981 rally marked the debut of Jacky Ickx on the Paris-Dakar, driving a works Citroën that he was later forced to

The Ickx/Brasseur Mercedes G-Wagen on the 1982 Paris-Dakar. Ickx's 1983 car looked similar, but carried the race number 142 instead of 154.

Jacky Ickx – one of the most versatile race drivers the world has ever seen. (Courtesy Wikimedia Commons, Gillphoto)

In 1982, things became more serious with regard to the Paris-Dakar marathon, with the Mercedes works providing swb 280GE vans for Jacky Ickx and his film star friend Claude Brasseur, Francois and Jean Migault, and Jean-Pierre Jaussand and Michel Briere. The Jaussand/Briere car finished in third, with Ickx/Brasseur fifth, and private cabriolet models coming eighth and tenth.

More determined than ever, and now with the benefit of experience as well, Ickx was in a different league in the 1983 event. Held from 1-20 January over roughly 7500 miles (12,000km), and with no fewer than 253 cars and trucks plus 132 motorbikes taking part, Ickx and Brasseur drove the number 142 works 280GE (with the engine tuned to pump out 220bhp, and lightweight glassfibre and alloy body panels keeping the car's kerb weight to 1850kg/4070lb despite the extra strengthening and massive fuel tanks), while Jean-Pierre Jaussand and Jean da Silva handled the number 143 car, and Francois Migault teamed up with Michel Gauvain in the number 144 machine. Ickx took the honours in five of the 15 special stages (17 were scheduled, but two were cancelled) to claim a storming victory in the world's most gruelling motorsport event. Although the other two works G-Wagens failed to finish, Mercedes privateers came home in fifth, sixth and eighth.

Ickx went to Porsche for 1984 (Mercedes' Stuttgart neighbour duly claiming the victor's laurels), and there was only one Geländewagen in the top ten – the highly-modified 280GE of Gerard and Frederic Planson, which came ninth. The Mitsubishi Pajero came out ahead of the huge field in 1985, with G-Wagens coming home in seventh, tenth, 11th and 12th. 1986 was disappointing, and marked a turning point in the spirit of the classic rally raid – big budget teams now dominated, with Porsche giving way to Peugeot and Citroën domination, then the Mitsubishi era.

Nonetheless, the G-Wagen continued to feature strongly in this special event, and can be seen regularly in other off-road competitions, from amateur mud-plugging bashes through to deadly serious, international level meetings that demand huge commitment from their entrants. Another book could be written purely on this aspect of the Geländewagen's history, along with the military and tuning angles, but I'm sure you will forgive

abandon – something a long-distance race specialist (including numerous victories in the Le Mans 24-hour classic) couldn't have been happy with! However, he'd caught the bug, and Mercedes-Benz was well represented in amongst the 170 starters in the automobile Class, with 11 of the 60 finishers being Stuttgart models. Bruno Groine and Laurent Nogrette were the top G-Wagen competitors, coming home in fifth with their swb 300GD; a 240GD was ninth, and a 230G tenth.

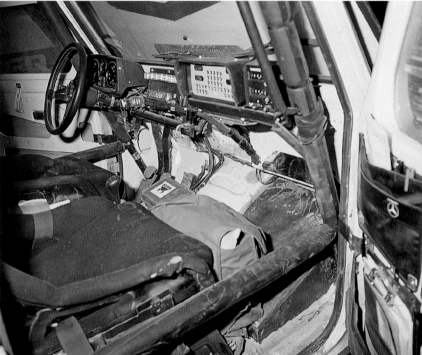

The 1983 Paris-Dakar Rally winner, with its distinctive alloy appendages on the tail to improve aerodynamics, and workmanlike interior; a four-speed manual transmission was linked to the six-cylinder engine.

The works 280GE of Jean-Pierre
Jaussand and Jean da Silva on the 1983
Paris-Dakar. It failed to finish.

The Ickx/Brasseur car having some service work done after another heavy day. The 280GE of Jean-Claude Bouchou and Claude Lebiet can be seen in the background, along with a pair of Mercedes-Benz trucks, which were always successful in the desert.

The almost surreal image of G-Wagens speeding through the desert. Ickx's 1983 winner (nearest the camera) was capable of 116mph, or 185kph.

A specialist vehicle built for the German border guards based on the 280GE lwb station wagon, circa 1983. The regular German police force used a reasonable number of G-Wagens, too, usually finished in green and white.

the author for concentrating on the production models. Before leaving this subject, though, mention should be made of the Peugeot P4 entries. Although they failed to make an impression, the entries did include a couple of cars converted to take the PRV V6 – rare beasts, indeed ...

Progress

As well as an automatic gearbox being made available for the 230GE, a Getrag five-speed manual gearbox was offered on the 230GE, 280GE and 300GD models from March 1983, matched up with the familiar 4.86:1 axle ratio. It was around this time that a rotary switch to operate the three-speed fan blower was borrowed from the saloons. This coincided, thereabouts, with the adoption of a subtly revised dashboard, with softer plastic and a smoother centre section (rather like that found on the original pre-production prototypes) and illuminated rocker switches. Not long after, the optional air-conditioning unit was integrated into the rest of the heating system, instead of being tacked onto the bottom of the central dash stack, and from August 1983, power-assisted steering was added to the 230GE spec sheet, leaving only the 240GD grades with PAS as an option.

On the corporate front, following the death of Gerhard

The W460 dashboard and interior as it looked in 1984.

Prinz, Professor Werner Breitschwerdt stepped up to take on the Chairman's role at the end of 1983, while Dr Rudolf Hörnig took over as head of R&D in May 1984. Catalytic converters became

The Graz factory photographed in the mid-1980s. It kept growing, too, to the point where it was almost three times bigger than it was in 1979.

an option in Germany soon after, while particulate filters were employed on diesel cars, pointing the way for others to follow in a world that suddenly became aware of the 'Green' side of automotive engineering. In addition, the respected 123-series was replaced by a new line of W124 models at the end of 1984, with styling closely resembling that of the W201.

In 1985, the cabriolet version of the G-Wagen was made available with a high-quality fabric top (guided by six gas

The Peugeot P4 was produced in civilian guise in very small numbers from the end of 1985 onwards, with both long- and short-wheelbase versions of the open car being built.

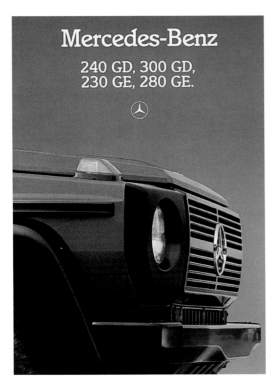

(This page and overleaf) Cover and a few selected pages from the 1986 Model Year catalogue. A lot of its content was already familiar to G-Wagen fans.

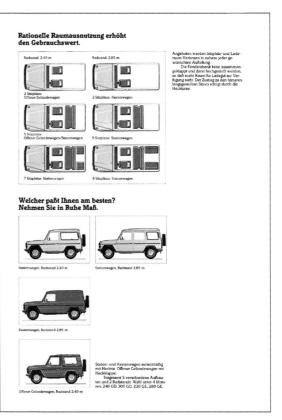

Das Klappverdeck:
Damit wird der Mercedes G schnell zum Cabriolet.

Die vielen praktischen Seiten des Mercedes G lassen sich mit dem besonderen Vergnügen kombinieren, ihn fast im Handumdrehen in ein Cabriolet zu verwandeln.

Das Klappverdeck für alle offenen G-Modelle mit kurzem Radstand macht es dem Fahrer leicht, die Freuden des offenen Fahrens in vollen Zügen zu genießen. Ein paar leichte Handgriffe um es zu öffnen und zu verstauen – und schon erlebt man das Mercedes G-Fahren von seiner schönsten Seite: Man spürt die Sonne und den Fahrtwind auf der Haut. Und wenn einem mal nicht nach Cabrio-Fahren ist, man aber dennoch frische Luft um die Nase haben will: Das Klappverdeck läßt sich auch teilweise öffnen.

Auf die Qualität des Verdecks können Sie sich voll und ganz verlassen: Denn es wird aus dem gleichen widerstandsfähigen Material gefertigt, das sich bei den Mercedes-Benz SL-Modellen seit Jahren bestens bewährt.

Das Klappverdeck für den Mercedes G – wir bieten es ausschließlich in Schwarz an – setzt sich aus vier Teilen zusammen: Dachteil, Heckteil, Seitenteile links und rechts. Damit ergeben sich diese Einsatzmöglichkeiten: Der Mercedes G als ›Targa‹, der Mercedes G mit Dachteil – ohne Heck- und Seitenteile, der Mercedes G mit Dach- und Heckteil – ohne Seitenteile.

springs and made from the same material as that used on the R107 SLs) to replace the rather basic and flimsy canvas one that had been supplied since 1979. It was still a time-consuming job to make the rear compartment weatherproof, but it was a far better arrangement than the original one, and duly became standard in 1987.

When the 1985 Frankfurt Show opened its doors for business, all three mainstream lines – the C-Class, E-Class and S-Class (including the SL) – had been face-lifted, and new technologies, such as ASD (an automatic locking differential), ASR (an early form of traction control) and 4MATIC (an automatic four-wheel

drive system) had been presented to the public. Rightfully proud of its traditional engineering, Daimler-Benz had shown it was capable of moving with the times, taking advantage of the latest electronics wizardry.

The G-Wagen was not forgotten, though, and a number of changes aimed at refining the Geländewagen were announced at the Frankfurt event. Perhaps the easiest thing to spot was the revised cloth on the seats, with a heavier check pattern. This cloth accent was carried over to the door inserts, which were rather more subtle from now on, and also trimmed the optional Recaro sports seats. While the regular seatbacks featured slightly

The landmark 50,000th Geländewagen was produced in 1986.

beefier side bolsters, those found on the Recaros were extremely heavy, with the lower cushion and even the headrests also featuring extra side padding to hold occupants in place that much better. In addition, the front seats were given a greater range of adjustment, while the bench seat in the rear was modified to allow it to fold easier.

Standard fittings on domestic models now included front and rear differential locks, the front skid plate, halogen headlights, a locking fuel cap, tachometer, clock, a lights-on warning chime, central locking, a lockable glovebox, removable carpeting, an improved roofliner, and a front tow hitch. Oddly, the heated rear window and rear wash/wipe remained optional on cars with the single rear door, and while stronger rear seals could still be specified by those who often drove in sandy or dusty environments, they were no longer part of the regular package; this was probably due to the use of two different rear doors (it was still possible to order the double-doors at the back, along with the swivelling spare wheel carrier).

The 250GD cabriolet from the time, with alloy wheels and fender flares.

New options listed in the catalogue included 15-inch five-spoke alloys (previously available through the standalone SA brochure, and combined with fender flares to cover the wider rubber 255/75 employed), an interior upgrade (which we can take to mean wood-style dash trim, although it took a while to filter through), heated front seats, a folding rear seat with a set of three automatic seatbelts for the open car, and a Becker radio with two front speakers. Meanwhile, the self-levelling suspension option was gone, and the auxiliary fuel tank arrangement was now restricted to one 13.5-litre (3.0 imperial gallon) tank only, as fitted as standard on the 280GE.

Incidentally, the short-wheelbase vans failed to make it into the 1986 Model Year line-up, although the long-wheelbase versions continued unabated. Notwithstanding, lwb chassis cab and pick-up variants on the regular 2850mm (112.2in) wheelbase were added soon after to cater for the specialist needs of commercial users. As a result, the G-Wagen could be converted into all manner of vehicles, from coachbuilt motorhomes to rough-and-ready working tools for civilian and military use. That does not imply that special-bodied cars didn't exist before this date, because they did (the ambulances illustrated earlier in the book serve as good examples), it simply made conversion work a lot easier, and opened up the possibility of greater variations on a theme.

Exterior and interior shots of a 280GE fastidiously prepared by Richard Kaan's workshop in Austria (Kaan can be seen holding the bonnet). Fitted with BBS Panzerfelge wheels, it was driven by Ed McCabe and Carolyn Jones in the 1987 Paris-Dakar Rally, but failed to finish after running out of fuel.

By this time, the 280GE had gained EGR and timing tweaks to help it meet new emissions regulations, although it meant a slight drop in power (now quoted at 150bhp/110kW). Not long after, in January 1986, the 230GE swapped its K-Jetronic injection for a more modern KE-Jetronic version combined with electronic ignition, and in the same month, a three-way catalytic converter was offered on the 230GE and 280GE models. Prices increased, of course, with the G-Wagen line-up now ranging from DM 44,403 for the open 240GD all the way up to DM 64,581 for the lwb 280GE station wagon in its native country.

W124-based coupes were introduced at the 1987 Geneva Show, and Edzard Reuter replaced Werner Breitschwerdt in the Chairman's office a few months later. At the same time, at the 1987 Frankfurt Show, new diesel engines were announced for W201 and W124 series cars, and the W126 series was given uprated V8 engines. Things were afoot on the G-Wagen, too ...

Export round-up

In Britain, prices increased a touch for the 1984 season, but the UK Geländewagen range was exactly the same as before, with sales holding steady at around 400 units a year. The 230GE swb estate was added at the end of 1984. Priced at £14,195, it was almost £2500 cheaper than the 300GD lwb version, although still a long way off Land Rover pricing, and only £850 off the three-door Range Rover. Things stayed much the same thereafter. Indeed, other than the higher prices, everything else was unchanged going into the 1987 season.

Over in Japan, things were much the same at the start of the 1984 Model Year, with the 300GD offered in swb and lwb estate guise, and priced virtually the same as before, too. Strangely, though, the G-Wagen was conspicuous by its absence during most of 1984, not returning to the Japanese price lists until early 1985. By then, only the short-wheelbase 300GD station wagon was on offer, priced at 7,600,000 yen, which continued until the end of the 1985. After that, there was another break in the Geländewagen run as far as the Japanese market was concerned, only a longer one this time while Mercedes-Benz Japan was being established, which coincided with the 230GE coming online.

Australia added the three-door 300GD estate to its line-

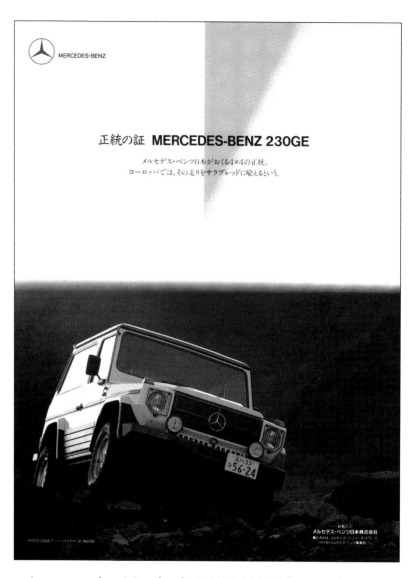

Japanese advertising for the W460 230GE from mid-1987.

up in the spring of 1985, augmenting the existing lwb version. By the start of 1986, the swb variant had gained a manual transmission option, with this model being the new entry-level model Down Under, priced at $61,089. An automatic gearbox added about $1200 to the invoice, while the long-wheelbase estate (4AT only) now commanded a hefty $67,356. The range expanded again in the middle of 1986, however, with both the 230GE and 300GD being made available in swb and lwb estate guise (manual and automatic), while the cabriolet was offered with the 2.3-litre petrol engine as well from this time. These cars were offered again during the 1987 season.

In America, the grey market was picking up, with Dave Holland starting Europa International of Santa Fe to import the Geländewagen in a big way. Unfortunately, Holland, like so many others importing exotic cars from Europe, fell foul of the law passed 1986 that restricted grey imports into the States, and Holland was left for seven years simply servicing the 500 or so G-Wagens that had already made it across the Atlantic. His loyalty to the marque would be rewarded in due course, however ...

An interesting export only G-Wagen came in the form of the 1987 Model Year 200GE, which was built exclusively for the Italian market, where taxes were extremely high on cars with engines displacing more than 2000cc. Powered by the fuel-injected 122bhp (or 118bhp with a 'cat') M102 engine from the 190-series, it could be bought with a manual or automatic transmission, and came with PAS as standard. This 1997cc machine was available as a cabriolet or estate in short-wheelbase format or as a long-wheelbase estate, and was built in fairly limited numbers until 1991.

Another W460 update

The Steyr-Daimler-Puch concern was restructured in 1987, signalling the end of motorcycle production. However, it became more and more involved with other car manufacturers, and in 1990 a deal similar to the one made with Daimler-Benz in the 1970s was struck with Chrysler that led to the Chrysler Voyager being built in Austria. Ironically, in 1994, this partnership (known as Eurostar) resulted in the Jeep Grand Cherokee also being made by SDP. Although the Jeep was a strong rival for the G-Wagen, the Eurostar business was ultimately taken over by DaimlerChrysler in 1999 following the highly-publicised merger of the US and German giants.

Meanwhile, the 1988 Model Year, launched at the 1987 Frankfurt Show, witnessed the last significant batch of changes applied to the W460 G-Wagen, which was now – at last – taken under the wing of the passenger car department. While the extended 3120mm (112.8in) wheelbase chassis cab version was made available from this time, the regular models became far

Cover and selected artwork from the domestic 1988 Model Year catalogue.

Der Mercedes unter den Geländewagen.

G-Modell von Mercedes-Benz – das heißt vor allem: großer Spaß am Fahren, aktives Vergnügen – selbst dort, wo es nicht als unvergleichbar wird. „G" eine faszinierende Formel für Individualismus und Kühem – aber auch für eine außergewöhnliche Nutzleistung unter härtesten und schwierigsten Bedingungen. Mercedes-Qualität – das bedeutet bei diesem Fahrzeug zuerst einmal:

Das gleiche gilt für die Qualität des Fahrzeugs selbst: Mercedes-Robustheit z.B. durch den lange- und vielwidrungsordnen Stahlrahmen, durch die Dauerleistungsfähigkeit der Triebwerke – und durch die Widerstandsfähigkeit der Materialien. Zuverlässigkeit aller Funktionen – Spitzenwerte – auch für Spitzenbelastung.

Bis zu neun Personen finden Platz im Mercedes-G. In seinem bis zu 2,05 m² fassenden Laderaum (bei umgeklappter Sitzbank) kann er bis zu 840 kg Zuladung befördern. Als Zugmaschine angelassen, ist er sogar in der Lage, bis zu 4.000 kg Anhängerlast mit auf die Reise zu nehmen: den Pferde-Transporter, den Bootsanhänger, den Wohnwagen. Auch ein durchdachtes Programm für Dachtransport ist selbstverständlich – vom attraktiven Gepäckcontainer über

die Skibox bis zum Kajakträger. Der Mercedes-G muß seine technische Übertriebenheit und Zuverlässigkeit längst nicht mehr in extrem harten, gekämaktären Wettbewerben beweisen. Er ist ihm hier und am Polarkreis war er schon zu Hause, ganz vor oder der Öffentlichkeit vorgestellt wurde. Und das Gesamtzeige in der Rallye Paris–Dakar erbracht bereits, bevor es üblich war, den Erfolg durch großen Begeisterungsanklang abzuzeichnen. In jedem Fall gut aufgehoben sind Sie mit dem G-Modell auch durch die Mercedes-Qualität der Betreuung. Wo immer Sie mit ihm fahren, was immer Ihnen begegnet – weltweit stehen die über 5.000 Service-Stationen mit dem Stern bereit. Mit enga-

gierten und geschulten Fachleuten. Und vor allem: mit allen wichtigen Ersatzteilen – gerade auch für das G-Modell. Ein herragender Hintergrund für Leute, die beim Fahren nicht anstecken sind.

Die in diesem Katalog enthaltenen Aussagen über die Grundausstattung, über gesetzliche, rechtliche und steuerliche Vorschriften und Auswirkungen beziehen sich nur für die Bundesrepublik Deutschland. Gültigkeit. Die Abbildungen enthalten auch Sonderausstattungen, die nicht zum serienmäßigen Lieferumfang gehören.

Frischer Wind auf schnellstem Wege.

G-Modelle sind zuerst einmal Fahrzeuge von größtem Einsatz: Deshalb gehört zu vielseitigen Programm von Sonderausstattungen und Zubehör dazu. Zur individuellen Steigerung des Nutzens und der Fahrfreude. Er ist also in folgenden Ausführungen lieferbar:
○ Als Normal-Ausführung mit Plane
○ In Sonderausstattungen

Für den offenen „G" gibt es mit Wunsch: eine Hardtop – oder das Cabriolet-Klappverdeck – zusätzlich bzw. anstelle der serienmäßigen Plane. Erleichterung des serienmäßigen Schutzsplitter über den Baumschleuss bis zu Aluminium-Felgen mit Breitreifen.

– mit Cabrio-Klappverdeck
– mit Hardtop
– mit Hardtop und Cabriodeck
– mit Hardtop und Gasdeck.

Das Cabrio-Klappverdeck für die komfortablen Porta, auch bei wechselhaftem Klima die schönsten Seiten des offenen Fahrens zu genießen. Mit wenigen Handgriffen ist es größer. Und bevor die ersten Tropfen fallen,

ist es genauso schnell und problemlos wieder geschlossen.

Oft genügt es auch schon, das Dachteil zu schließen. Das Heck und die Seiten (oder nur die Seiten allein) bleiben offen. Ideal zum Beispiel auf der Jagd oder beim Pirschfahren in freie Wildbahn.

Vier starke Typen.

Gleich, welchen Motor Sie wählen – es ist ein Triebwerk mit Stern. Das heißt: ein Musterbeispiel für Leistungspräsenz, Dauerleistungsfestigkeit und Wirtschaftlichkeit.

Vier verschiedene Modelle stehen zur Wahl: das 250 GD und der 300 GD als Diesel. Sowie die beiden Benziner 230 GE und 280 GE.

Kraft, Sparsamkeit und Lebensdauer. Die Diesel-Modelle 250 CD und 300 GD

Die Triebwerke beider Typen in Fünfzylinder-Bauart. Beim 300 GD mit 3 Litern Hubraum. Eine Idealkombination von Zylinderzahl und großem „Atmungsvermögen". Dadurch hohes Drehmoment schon bei niedrigen Drehzahlen. Kraftvoller Durchzug also „von ganz unten heraus". Die typische Elastizität des Drei-Liters – auch für besonders feinfühligen Krafteinsatz im Gelände. Leistung 65 kW (88 PS).

Der neue 250 GD mit Fünfzylinder-Motor und 2,5 Litern Hubraum. Seine beachtliche Leistung erbringt das neue Aggregat mit besonders günstigem Kraftstoffverbrauch. Ruhiger runder Motorlauf, leises Außengeräusch. Spontane Startdynamik und sichere Funktion auch bei extrem niedrigen Temperaturen. Nicht zuletzt durch automatische Anhebung der Leerlaufdrehzahl und thermostatisch gesteuerte Kraftstoff-Vorwärmung. Leistung des neuen Triebwerks: 62 kW (84 PS) bei 4600 U/min. Der 250 CD ist serienmäßig mit 5-Gang-Getriebe ausgerüstet – wobei der 5. Gang als echter Fahrgang ausgelegt ist, mit dem man die Höchstgeschwindigkeit erreicht.

Dynamik und Robustheit: Die Benzin-Modelle 230 GE und 280 GE

Beide Aggregate sind Einspritzmotoren der Spitzenklasse. Hochwertige Mercedes-Technik – hunderttausendfach bewährt und erfolgreich – im Gelände und auf der Straße. Hohes Drehmoment schon bei niedrigen Drehzahlen – der entscheidende Vorteil im Gelände. Hoher Laufkomfort auch bei engagierter Fahrweise sowie bei Straßenfahrt mit hoher Geschwindigkeit, die sprichwörtliche Robustheit von Mercedes auch bei harter Beanspruchung.

Der 2,3-Liter-Motor im 230 GE: Vierzylinder-Einspritzer. Leistung 92 kW (125 PS).

Das 2,8-Liter-Triebwerk im 280 GE: Sechszylinder-Einspritzer. Leistung 110 kW (150 PS).

Der 230 GE auch als schadstoffarmes Fahrzeug.

Der 230 GE wird auf Wunsch auch mit geregeltem Katalysator und Sauerstoff-Sonde geliefert. Ansonsten als sogenannte RÜF-Version, die für den späteren problemlosen Einbau des Katalysators vorbereitet ist.

A modern Edition 35 car (left) with 'Otto' – the nickname given to a travel-stained 1988 300GD by its owner, Gunther Holtorf. Together with his wife, Christine, Holtorf travelled through more than 200 countries on every continent with the blue G-Wagen, covering over half-a-million miles (800,000km) along the way.

Puch G MONTANA
SWISS

Catalogue for the limited edition Puch G 230GE and 280GE Montana, and the 230GE Swiss models of 1988. Small-run specials were becoming increasingly popular by this time, with a 200-off Mercedes 250GD offered with two-tone metallic paintwork, and a 300-off 230GE Classic model built to mark tenth anniversary of the Geländewagen. This latter model had Blue-Black metallic paint, a chrome accent in the rubbing strips, luxurious interior enhancements and the option of a bull-bar.

more high-profile, with a catalogue worthy of a unique road car rather than a quasi-commercial vehicle.

The biggest change was the loss of the 240GD in favour of a new 250GD grade. The 250GD was powered by the distinctly more modern inline-five OM602 D25 sohc unit borrowed from the W201 and new W124 saloon series, albeit de-tuned a touch to suit its rather different application. Sporting an 87.0 x 84.0mm bore and stroke, this gave a displacement of 2497cc, and with Bosch indirect injection and a 22.0:1 compression ratio, the normally-aspirated engine gave 84bhp (62kW) DIN and 114lbft of torque. The 250GD came fitted with a five-speed manual transmission and 6.17 axle ratio as standard (the 300GD continued with 4MT and 5MT gearboxes), with a four-speed automatic as an option, as per the flagship diesel model.

Other changes for the 1988 season included the adoption of the 280GE's larger fuel capacity on the 230GE and 300GD, as well as the new 250GD models; heated screenwasher nozzles were added to the spec sheet as well, along with halogen foglights and a rear foglight, a demister and wash/wipe system for the rear of the estates (optional on the vans), dustproofing for the rear door, child-proof locks, a rheostat for the dash lighting, and a revised brake pad wear indicator. New optional extras included an automatic aerial for the updated radio range, power windows, a two-piece blind for the luggage compartment, tilt adjustment on the driver's seat cushion, and the heated seat option carried over to the Recaro buckets. Not long after, these new options were augmented by armrests for the inside of both front seats.

On the corporate front, 1988 brought with it news of Mercedes-Benz officially returning to motorsport, with a Group A programme, and a prestigious Group C one, building on the success of the Swiss Sauber team. Swapping black paint for silver, the Group C cars were in form from the off in the following season, taking the WSPC title with ease in 1989, and then again in 1990.

End of the original model
Enhancing the marque's new-found sporting image, the technologically-advanced R129 SL was launched at the 1989 Geneva Show, released with a pair of 3-litre straight-sixes and a

The UK G-Wagen brochure from September 1988.

One of the last 280GE models sold in Britain.

5-litre V8. There was also a 190E 2.5-16 Evolution announced at the event, produced as a 500-off homologation special to further the chances of the top Group A racing teams. That was also the month in which new plastic fuel tanks were adopted on the diesel G-Wagens, presumably to prevent the fuel from freezing so easily. These new tanks had a larger, 95-litre (20.9 Imperial gallon) capacity, by the way.

With so many different interests in a wide range of companies, Daimler-Benz AG was restructured in mid-1989, with Professor Werner Niefer named as Chairman of the Board of Management for the Mercedes-Benz AG wing. A face-lifted W124-series was announced soon after, and by the spring of 1990, all Mercedes passenger cars were powered by fuel-injected engines to give cleaner exhaust emissions.

For fans of the Geländewagen, though, the biggest news of

the year came at the 1989 Frankfurt Show, when the 463-series G-Wagen was announced. To avoid confusion, and with the end of the 460-series imminent, we look at the new generation in the next chapter, along with the 460's more direct replacement.

Meanwhile, a catalytic converter was made standard on the 230GE, meaning a slight power reduction (the model now produced 122bhp DIN). The 280GE variants did not appear in the October 1990 price lists, and the 300GD line had gone by the spring of 1991. The remaining W460 models – the 230GE and 250GD – were finally killed off in August 1991, with final prices ranging from DM 58,539 to DM 73,587, which was a far cry from the prices of 1979!

Looking at the main rhd export markets, the UK again continued with its same line-up for 1988 and 1989, with just the prices increased a little. The vehicles were still there at the end of

1990, as it happens, with the 230GE swb estate at £20,600, the 300GD version at £21,000, and the 280GE variant at £22,150. Only the 300GD and 280GE estates were available with lwb bodywork, commanding £23,120 and £24,300, respectively. Options included things like an automatic gearbox at £1267, alloy wheels at £1941, electric windows at £715, Recaro seats at £735, front armrests at £218, magazine nets at £33, rear headrests at £164, occasional seats for the rear compartment at £936, a Becker radio at £642, headlight grilles at £84, a rear step at £27, and metallic paint at £619.

For 1988, Japan had the automatic 230GE cabriolet at 6,200,000 yen, the 230GE station wagon (6,750,000 yen in 4AT swb guise, or 7,600,000 yen in lwb format), and the automatic 300GD lwb estate at 7,800,000 yen – the same as a W124 300E saloon. Things continued exactly the same until the end of 1989, when exchange rates allowed prices to be reduced, and the last few 230GEs were sold in 1991, by which time the five- and six-cylinder machines had already fallen by the wayside.

The Australian story can be summed up very quickly, with no changes to the 230GE- and 300GD-based line-up or its pricing going into 1989, and then the G-Wagen was discontinued not long after. Unfortunately, the 463-series models would not meet the finicky Australian Design Rules due to its novel exhaust system, and the Aussies had to do without the Geländewagen until the 2011 season. Other countries were luckier, as we will discover in the next chapter ...

5

A new chapter

Tiddlers like the Lada and baby Suzuki no longer needed to be considered competition, as the Graz-built car moved upmarket in a big way in 1989 in response to customer demand and market developments. The off-roader distinction was still there, for sure, but the higher price and new-found prestige moved the Mercedes Geländewagen into a category expected of a vehicle carrying a three-pointed star on its nose. Notwithstanding, fresh competition – particularly from the Japanese makers – and the polishing of existing rival models kept G-Wagen sales fairly limited at this stage ...

The 90 and 110 had propelled Land Rover into the modern era in the mid-1980s, with full-time 4WD and a coil spring suspension, and the Range Rover was face-lifted in 1986. Then, ironically, at the 1989 Frankfurt Show – where the updated G-Wagen made its debut – there was the launch of the Land Rover Discovery, the application of the Defender badge on the old cars, and a beefier engine for the Range Rover, helping to keep Solihull products to the fore.

The Y60 Nissan Patrol (which also carried a Ford badge in Australia) was launched in November 1987, along with the all-new Suzuki Escudo/Vitara (also badged as a Chevrolet) in the summer of 1988, giving yet more competition from Japan. The Land Cruiser was evolving, too, with the workmanlike J70 of 1984 being augmented by the more refined J80 that was introduced at the 1989 Tokyo Show. The J80 had the advantage of worldwide sales, and looked far more modern than its predecessor. The original Mitsubishi Pajero soldiered on for a while, but a larger second generation was introduced at the start of 1991, and a new Isuzu Trooper followed a few months later. Isuzu also marketed the MU at this time, along with the Rodeo, which was duly badged as the Passport by Honda.

The traditional Jeep had almost run its course by now, although the Jeep Wrangler (type YJ) still had shades of the original, and was continued when the Jeep brand came under

The 463-series G-Wagen making its debut at the 53rd Frankfurt Show, held on 14-24 September 1989. The car on display was a 300GE model, fitted with optional alloys.

Chrysler ownership in 1987. The SJ Wagoneer was at last replaced in 1991, with a ZJ Grand Cherokee duly augmenting the compact XJ Cherokee that had been introduced in time for the 1984 season. Meanwhile, Ford introduced the compact Bronco II to run alongside the full-size Bronco in March 1983, and the UN46 Explorer was about to break cover as the new Geländewagen was being announced; an updated Chevy Suburban (also badged as a Holden) was on its way, too.

The Land Rover Discovery that was also launched at the 1989 IAA. The five-door version looked much better.

Faced with this onslaught of fresh SUVs, when even Lamborghini had a go with the LM002, let's see how the folks in Stuttgart responded via the new 463-series G-Wagen ...

The 463-series models

At first glance, one could be easily forgiven for not noticing the difference between a W460 and a W463 model. Indeed, for regular customers, this could be classed more as a face-lift than a full model change, as even half of the old engine line-up was carried over, along with all the main body components, and the change in chassis code was only really known by brand anoraks. Ultimately, it was down to detailing on the exterior, some drivetrain refinements to improve on-road driving dynamics, and some rather more drastic changes to the cockpit to make it more inviting.

Starting with the coachwork, thanks to input from Bruno Sacco and his team of stylists in Stuttgart, the front grille and headlight surrounds were now finished in body colour rather than flat black. The grille gained new evenly-spaced slats, without the vertical bar in the centre, and a fresh dressing piece

underneath to neaten the appearance between the grille and bumper. The light housings were also new, squared off with the headlights set deeper within them, and again, dressing pieces beneath them to finish the area above the bumper and around to the wheelarch – as such, the front-end lost its signature angled wingline, but the car looked a lot better for it. Of course, cars with black paintwork made the latter a tad difficult to pick up, but the difference between gloss paint and a matt finish is still there if you look hard enough, and there's no mistaking the fresh shapes involved. The changes to the front face were completed by a deeper bumper blade, finished in silk black, with softer corner profiles, integrated foglights and a centrally-mounted number plate instead of the towing hitch; Puch models received a larger badge on the nose, too.

All in all, the car looked a lot more substantial without adding much to the width, for the only extra bulk was accounted for by the narrow wheelarch extensions that used to be optional, but were now fitted as standard, painted in the same black as the bumpers. For the record, the new bodywork increased the car's width to 1760mm (69.3in) – an increase of 60mm (2.4in)

The four-page preliminary brochure produced to introduce the W463 model, printed in August 1989.

compared to the standard 460-series body. The body length was altered by around 50mm (2.0in) due to the bigger bumpers, although the fixed spare wheel arrangement was perhaps the same amount narrower than the old swivelling carrier setup. Notwithstanding, for those that had the fatter 255/75 tyres fitted to the alloy rims to contend with, an extra 210mm (8.3in) was added on top of the additional bumper bulk, due to the spare wheel.

Rounding off the changes to the side view, there were air vents cut into the top of the nearside front wing, close to the A-post and just under the bonnet line, and new, smaller mirrors with power adjustment and heater elements to keep them clear in poor weather. There was also a peak of the exhaust tailpipe, which now exited on the nearside, just ahead of the rear wheel, and a fuel filler cap on the offside rear wing, meaning an end to the exposed fuel cap. Of course, a new fuel tank was needed, due to the neck being in a different position, and the opportunity was taken to increase the capacity to 96 litres (21.1 Imperial gallons) for all cars at the same time – a fraction more than

A very early cabriolet displaying all the styling updates applied to the W463 models. The first pre-production models had been built in June and July 1989.

it said in the early paperwork. For those who required it, the fuel filler lid could be tied into the central locking for a small additional charge.

Around the back, there was a new bumper blade to suit the one at the front, with an integral foglight and reversing light inset on either side, and a recess for the number plate, which was lit by sunken lights. The double-door option was gone, with the exterior face-lift completed by revised rear mudflaps, and larger rear combination light units, ribbed like those of the saloons to keep them cleaner for longer. In addition, while the 'Mercedes-Benz' badge adopted on single-door cars in the past was carried over, the model grade badge on the nearside (in line with the central rubbing strip) was a new thing, signalling the end of the old badging system seen below the door mirrors.

Cutaway drawing of the W463 in swb station wagon guise, allowing us to see the side exhaust arrangement, the revised driveline, and the way the fuel tank capacity was increased. Note the lack of a rear anti-roll bar on this home market car – it would be quite some time before domestic vehicles were given one.

While the changes to the bodywork were purely cosmetic, those applied to the car's mechanical components were a great deal more far-reaching. With regard to the engine line-up, the 230GE was powered by the existing four-cylinder M102 E23 unit, rated at 122bhp (90kW) due to its newly-adopted catalytic converter, while the 250GD kept its OM602 D25 straight-five, although the use of direct-injection helped boost power up to 94bhp (69kW). Not long after the regular line-up started rolling off the line, the export-only 200GE was continued as well, employing the familiar M102 E20 lump for motive power. This left the new 300GE, which replaced the 280GE, and a revised version of the 300GD, with an old designation but a fresh engine lurking beneath the bonnet.

The 300GE used the M103 E30 six-cylinder engine borrowed from the W124 saloons, albeit slightly de-tuned. With an 88.5 x 80.2mm bore and stroke, this gave a capacity of 2960cc, while a combination of a 9.2:1 compression ratio and indirect Bosch

KE-Jetronic injection produced 170bhp DIN (125kW) plus 173lbft of torque. Not only was the cat-equipped 12v sohc 300GE unit more powerful and fuel efficient (and therefore cleaner, too), it was also significantly lighter than its predecessor.

The new 300GD also employed an sohc power-unit shared with the W124s, this one being an OM603 D30 straight-six. This 2996cc engine (87.0 x 84.0mm) had a 22:1 c/r and indirect-injection to give 113bhp (83kW) and 141lbft of torque, and was both smoother and more powerful than the old OM617 unit. Like all of the other powerplants used in the 463-series G-Wagens, it featured a rerouted exhaust that exited on the nearside, aft of what is the driver's door on left-hand drive models.

All cars came with a five-speed manual transmission as standard, with a four-speed automatic gearbox as an option on the two petrol-engined machines and the 300GD. A 5.29:1 final-drive ratio was the norm at the front and rear axles (4.86:1 on the 300GE), but, as with the 460s, there was another set of gearing ratios to consider, too – that of the transfer box, which was a major component amongst the mechanical differences that set the W460 and W463 apart. To summarise the difference between the two G-Wagen types, one can simply say that the older W460 came with a part-time four-wheel drive system, while the newer W463 was given a permanent, full-time one.

In their basic layout, the two drive systems looked much the same, but, while the power coming from the engine was still taken through a gearbox (MT or AT) to a dual-range central transfer box, the 463-series did away with the mechanical diff locks and their levers. Instead, with the new car, a bevel-gear differential was tacked onto the latest VG150 transfer box, and drive, with a 50:50 torque split, was taken from this – the angle of the propshaft was still similar up front, but the rear one was now offset as well.

The full-time setup's advantages were improved on-road handling, a reduction in transmission noise, and an end to the conflict the old system created with ABS – a safety feature that Daimler-Benz was very proud of, and one that it was desperate to incorporate into the G-Wagen's specifications. The off-road credentials were still strong, though, for the engineers provided the W463 with diff locks for all three differentials, electro-hydraulically-operated in sequence via a group of dashboard

Testing the new car's ABS system.

switches. The latest transfer box had a high ratio of 1.05:1 and a low ratio of 2.16:1, by the way, and a simplified selector lever.

Other than some minor tweaks to the spring and damper rates, as well as the rubber link bushes, the front suspension was carried over from the W460. The rear suspension was also much the same, although some markets gained an anti-roll bar in addition to the tuning that had been applied up front. This endowed the car with a flatter cornering attitude at the cost of a reduction in suspension movement in severe off-road scenarios. Notwithstanding, the differential locks made up for the lack of articulation, even if a wheel was completely off the ground. It should be noted that the rear sway bar was not fitted in Germany as standard, although it could be fitted on request. The only other chassis change, other than the use of wider 6J steel rims and a revised steering ratio, was the adoption of anti-lock brakes, initially listed as an option on home market cars. Incidentally,

Short- and long-wheelbase estates from 1990. As it happens, despite the late 1989 public debut, the press launch (held in the south of France) didn't take place until March 1990, and full-scale production of the W463 models would only start in the following month.

It seems wasteful, but it has to be done – an early swb wagon taking part in a crash test. As with all Mercedes-Benz models, the safety programme didn't end as soon as a car's type approval had been rubber-stamped, with this particular test being conducted in 1990.

the ABS system could be switched off manually (on some surfaces, such as gravel roads, stopping distances are actually shorter if the wheels are allowed to lock up), or switched itself off as soon as one of the differentials was locked.

The interior was also completely overhauled to give the W463 the kind of ambience one expects of a Mercedes-Benz passenger car, as opposed to a commercial vehicle, for, if one is to be perfectly honest, that is the category that a lot of the early W460s fell into. While the basic W460 layout was carried over, detail work and the careful use of attractive materials gave the new G-Wagen interior a more luxurious feel, making it a truly pleasant place to be.

Using a domestic car for reference, starting with the dashboard, the top roll was a familiar shape, but it was bulked up a bit to allow the rotary light switch to sit to the left of the instrument binnacle. Within the subtly redesigned pod was a new set of three gauges, with a central speedometer, a tachometer to the right with a clock below, and the familiar combination

meter for fuel level, coolant temperature and oil pressure off to the left. Other than those for the indicators, the bank of warning lights was arranged in a line underneath the gauge pack, as per the contemporary saloons, and the grab handle in front of the passenger was less spartan than the original.

Below the dark grey top roll was a narrow piece of full-width Zebrano wood trim, carried over to the door cappings for a few inches on either side, as well as the redesigned centre console. While the old steering wheel and column stalk were retained, along with the ignition barrel, the air vent to the left of the steering column was squared off, as was the matching one at the opposite end of the fascia, and there was a new glovebox, too – its colour-keyed plastic being the same used for all the lower part of the dashboard, centre console and door casings, and looking far more attractive than the harsh painted surfaces of the past.

The central stack was much deeper than before, with the upper half containing a bank of traditional rocker switches

and the all-important diff lock switches trimmed in wood, and the lower section, which housed the HVAC controls, radio slot and oddments box, in black plastic. Moving back, the console between the seats was now integrated with the centre stack, with wood accents breaking up the acres of coloured plastic. There was a cigarette lighter and ashtray closest to the dashboard, the main transmission lever with a stubbier one aft of it for high/low ratio selection, and a car-like handbrake to the left. Between the gearlevers was a gap where various electrical goodies – like the power window lifts, seat heater switches, power mirror control, and even a trip computer – could reside.

In addition to the more supportive and comfortable seats (front and rear) trimmed in a fresh cloth upholstery, better carpeting and improved seatbelts, the door furniture was also changed, combining with new cloth inserts and redesigned door pockets below to help give the Geländewagen an altogether more modern and civilised appearance, easily on a par with the W124 saloons.

A 1990 cabriolet in open guise, and a second one photographed during the same PR shoot with its soft top in place.

For those who wanted to give their G-Wagen an even more luxurious aura, leather trim was made available as a new option, joined by options such as central armrests for the front seats, seat heaters, occasional seats for the rear compartment, leather trim for the steering wheel and gearlevers, air-conditioning, auxiliary heating, power windows, a steel power-operated sunroof, and Becker stereo equipment. The familiar German-made, five-spoke 15-inch alloys were carried over as an alternative to the standard

16-inch steel wheels, and for dealing with the urban jungle – or a real one, for that matter – there was additional underbody protection and a bull-bar, too.

There were no vans produced in the 463-series run, only open cars on the swb chassis, and station wagons in two- and four-door guise. There's not much point in quoting the September 1989 prices, as W463 production didn't begin until April 1990. But for the record, here are the home market prices for all models at the start of 1990: the 250GD cabriolet was priced at DM 60,876, the 230GE cabriolet at DM 61,218, the 300GD cabriolet at DM 63,954, the 250GD swb estate at DM 65,493, the 230GE swb estate at DM 65,835, the 300GD swb estate at DM 68,571, the 300GE cabriolet at DM 69,939, the 250GD lwb estate at DM 72,276, the 230GE lwb estate at DM 72,618, the 300GE swb estate at DM 74,556, the 300GD lwb estate at DM 75,354, and the 300GE lwb estate at DM 81,339. However, other than a couple of price increases (the second taking the flagship 300GE station wagon up to DM 86,298), things remained unchanged for the 1991 season.

In the background, Professor Hartmut Weule took over as the R&D boss in September 1990, and in the following month, closer ties were forged with AMG (the famous tuning company). In addition, the 500E was introduced as the flagship of the W124 range, duly built at the Porsche factory in the Zuffenhausen district of Stuttgart.

The W140 S-Class made its debut at the 1991 Geneva Show, with three-, four-, five- and 6-litre powerplants, the latter being an exotic V12. By the autumn, a large range of AMG models had joined the fray, as well as a four-seater convertible based on the W124 series (officially going on sale in the summer of

One of the very first 350GD Turbo models, seen here in swb station wagon guise, and with optional alloy wheels. Note the 'Turbo' badge on the opposite side of the back door to the regular grade one.

A 1992 Model Year 350GD Turbo long-wheelbase estate with alloys, sunroof and a bull-bar.

Interior of the 350GDT with optional leather trim – a far cry from the driving environment offered by the 1979 G-Wagens.

1992), and a C112 experimental sports car with a gullwing body configuration.

The 1991 Frankfurt Show, which opened in the middle of September, witnessed the launch of the 350GD Turbo – until then, the fastest and most powerful G-Wagen to come directly from the works, easily recognised by the extra vent on the offside front wing (required for the oil cooler) if one couldn't see the badge on the tail.

With a 0-60 time of 16 seconds, the 350GDT was powered by a turbocharged version of the OM603 diesel six, with a new alloy cylinder head that cured the problems encountered with the earlier versions. An 89.0mm bore and 92.4mm stroke gave a cubic capacity of 3449cc, and with indirect Bosch injection and a 22.0:1 c/r, the sohc unit delivered 136bhp (100kW) and a stump-pulling 225lbft of torque.

The turbocharged car was fitted with a four-speed automatic transmission only, with a 4.11:1 front and rear axle ratio, and a

0.87:1 high and 2.16:1 low ratio specified for the transfer box. The braking system of the normally-aspirated machines was considered strong enough for the turbocharged car, with ABS remaining an option at this stage, along with alloy wheels – the 16-inch pressed steel wheels were still the norm, even on this G-Wagen, with things like walnut trim, cruise control, power windows and central locking as standard, and prices ranging from DM 86,412 to DM 93,936.

Although the 350GDT wasn't a direct replacement, it did however signal the imminent end of the rather gutless 250GD. With the W463 unquestionably being a road car, there was no place in the line-up for such a slow beast, and the heavier long-wheelbase machine was last built in December 1991; the final swb variants were built during the summer of 1992. The 3.5-litre car was built with all three 463-series bodies, by the way, with the cabriolet being the lightest at 2115kg (4653lb).

Mercedes officially withdrew from racing at the end of

(This page and overleaf) Long- and short-wheelbase turbocharged estates being put through their paces on- and off-road at the time of the 350GD Turbo's announcement.

1991, but new S-Class coupes were announced at the 1992 Detroit Show in January, and, with an eye on the future, work continued on alternative fuel units. The 600SL kept up the momentum, followed by a revised engine line-up for the W124 and W140 models later in the year. In an unusually unsettled era by Stuttgart's standards, Dr Dieter Zetsche was appointed Chief Engineer in early 1992, with Jürgen Hubbert in charge of the passenger car division. Zetsche took the place of Dr Wolfgang Peter, who'd been head of passenger car development since 1985 but was moved sideways after the W140 project, which, while it had its fans, had run behind schedule and well over-budget. Zetsche would later go on to become the head of Mercedes-Benz, but in the meantime, another Geländewagen line had made it to the marketplace…

The 461-series models

The W461 was basically the true successor to the W460, as it featured the same part-time 4WD system as the original G-Wagen (with a locking front differential moving to the option list), as well as its suspension, 16-inch steel wheels, and somewhat more workmanlike coachwork and interior. The W460 had continued well into 1991, of course, so it wasn't until

(Right and opposite) Catalogue pages showing a fraction of the working vehicle variants that were possible using the W461 as a base car. As before, a Puch version was also sold, sporting the old W460-style badge on the nose, as opposed to the larger 463-series one.

Die freie Entscheidung

Freiheit und Freizeit
Genießen Sie Ihre Freizeit un-
beschwert in Ihrem neuen,
zeitlos schönen Geländewagen
461 von Mercedes-Benz. Erleben Sie, wie schön Freiheit
sein kann. Die Freiheit, sich
richtig zu entscheiden.

3

Eine wirtschaftliche Investition:
MB Geländewagen Baureihe 461

Eine wirtschaftlich vernünftige Entscheidung
Durch langjährige Entwicklungen und die Erfahrungen aus dem Pkw- und Nfz-Bereich entstand ein perfekter Geländewagen der außergewöhnlichen Ansprüchen im Hinblick auf Solidität, Robustheit, Langlebigkeit und Sicherheit standhält und in seinen Verwendungsmöglichkeiten einzigartig ist. Wer jetzt einen täglichen Begleiter mit allen technischen Vorzügen sucht, wird an dem Mercedes-Benz G 461 einfach nicht vorbeifahren können. Mit unübertroffener Geländegängigkeit und bemerkenswertem

Straßenverhalten. Ein Fahrzeug, das Spaß macht und in ernsten Situationen verläßlich reagiert. Die Baureihe 461 ist die gelungene Synthese aus ausgereifter Technik und hoher Wirtschaftlichkeit – die Basis für eine sinnvolle Entscheidung.
Perfektion und durchdachte Details, Vielfalt und Funktionalität, Sicherheit und Zuverlässigkeit zeugen von einer Philosophie, die Mercedes-Benz bei der Entwicklung des G 461 als richtungsweisendes Ziel verfolgt hat: ein Fahrzeug zu schaffen, das strenge ökonomische Anforderungen erfüllt.

Ihr zuverlässiger Partner für jeden Einsatz

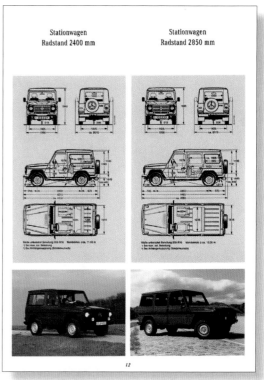

Stationwagen
Radstand 2400 mm

Stationwagen
Radstand 2850 mm

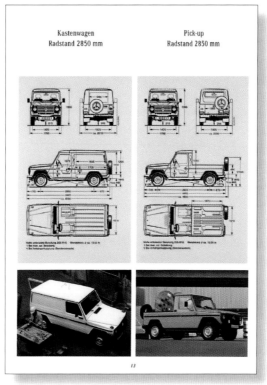

Kastenwagen
Radstand 2850 mm

Pick-up
Radstand 2850 mm

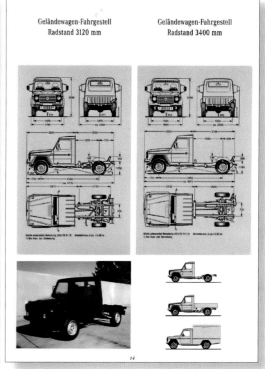

Geländewagen-Fahrgestell
Radstand 3120 mm

Geländewagen-Fahrgestell
Radstand 3400 mm

the spring of 1992 that the newcomer put in an appearance, aimed squarely at commercial, municipal and military users. As such, the interior was very spartan, with a distinct lack of luxury features (even the list of optional extras was short), the old W460 dashboard, and rubber mats on the floor.

The earliest price list applied to the 461-series models was printed in February 1992, covering the five-cylinder 95bhp diesel 290GD cars, with a second one added in May for the four-cylinder 122bhp petrol 230GE variants. Basically, the short-wheelbase chassis estate was offered alongside a long-wheelbase version, a lwb van, and a lwb pick-up, each having an exhaust peeping out from under the rear valance,

Italian advertising from the end of 1990. The 200GE was still built for this particular market.

as per the W460s, in the early days of the breed. There was also the extended 3120mm (112.8in) wheelbase chassis cab model that had been introduced a couple of years earlier, which was ideal for coachbuilders or military use, and by 1993, it had been augmented by an even longer 3400mm (133.8in) wheelbase version; the latter also provided the basis for a model featuring a double-cab (or crew cab) combined with a chassis-only rear-end.

Incidentally, before 1992, the W461 designation had previously been reserved for cars with a 24v electrical system, which were largely used by the military. There was also a W462 as well, but more on that particular angle of the story later.

Export news
As mentioned in the last chapter, the W463 was not sold in Australia until recently, and the Americans had to do without the

A 1991 (92 MY) long-wheelbase 300GE estate, or 300GEL as the UK dealers liked to call them.

Geländewagen for a little while longer, so exports were fairly limited in the early days of the new series.

As usual, Britain provided the largest right-hand drive market, with W463 sales officially beginning in March 1991. The UK market listed the 300GE and 300GD grades; both available in short- and long-wheelbase estate guise, with the 300GDS commanding £29,690, the 300GES £31,980, the 300GDL £32,580, and the flagship lwb 300GEL station wagon £34,870.

PAS and ABS came as standard, along with power windows, power mirrors, central locking, and heated seats. Major options included the 4AT gearbox, metallic paint, a sunroof, alloy wheels, air-conditioning, leather trim, centre armrests up front, stereo equipment, and an outside temperature gauge.

As a road car, *Performance Car* noted that the 102mph (163kph) 300GE was "very much better in every respect. On soaking wet Scottish roads, with a liberal topping of mud in places, the G-Wagen's permanent 4WD made it much better-balanced and more sure-footed than its part-time predecessor. Equally impressive is the long and well-controlled suspension

GELÄNDEWAGEN

半世紀を越え、4WDエンジニアリングのパイオニアであり続けたメルセデスがおくる、4WDの最高峰。
メルセデス・ベンツ ゲレンデヴァーゲン300GE。

GELÄNDEWAGEN 300GE/300GE LONG SOHC L-6 3.0ℓ, 4 SPEED A/T. RIGHT HAND DRIVE.

パワフルでなめらかな走りを生む直列6気筒3.0ℓエンジン、フルタイム4WD、クロスカントリー用に新たに開発されたABS(アンチロック・ブレーキング・システム)、様々な路面状況に応じてたくましい走破性を発揮するディファレンシャルロック・システム…。オールロード4WDの本質を追求した先進テクノロジーを注ぎ込みました。さらに特筆すべきは快適な乗り心地と必要にして充分な機能を最高の品質と素材で仕上げたインテリア。よりパワフルに、より心地よく、そしてよりセーフティに、すべての道を思いのままに愉しんでいただけます。

A page from the Japanese catalogue issued for the 1992 season.

travel that delivers a very supple ride. There's virtually no road noise either, and new mountings have succeeded in isolating engine and transmission noise to a remarkable extent."

The pricing was significantly higher than before, but, armed with a true Range Rover competitor at last, the UK distributor was confident of boosting sales to the 1000 units a year mark by the mid-1990s, by which time a restyled G-Wagen was expected

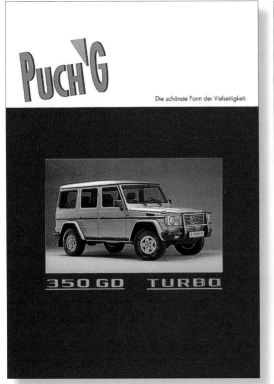

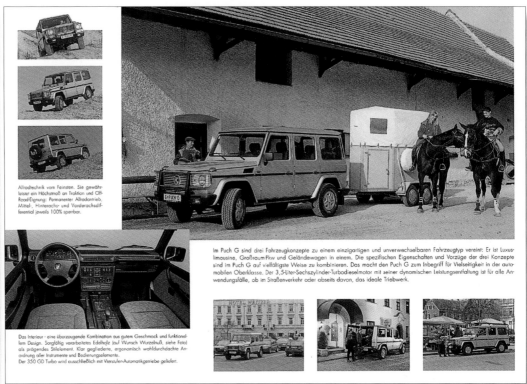

A 1992 German-language brochure for the Puch version of the 350GDT.

to be made available. Well, even though prices were reduced on the four SUV grades slightly for 1993, sales never did quite reach the hoped-for figures (400 units per annum was closer to the mark), and as for the fresh bodywork, although some design proposals were put through, one only needs to look at the current catalogue to see how far things got on that front!

Japan restricted its 1992 Model Year Geländewagen line-up to just the 8,700,000 yen 300GE swb estate, and the 9,600,000 yen 300GE lwb estate. More expensive than the Range Rover by a fair margin, the G-Wagens came in right-hand drive automatic guise only. As far as Japan was concerned, there were no major changes for the 1993 season.

Germany's 1993 season

The 1993 Model Year started quietly, with a new steering wheel and a few more cosmetic options (such as walnut trim in place of the Zebrano interior garnishing pieces, stainless steel running boards on the rocker panel between the wheelarches, and a high-quality spare wheel cover with the outer section finished

Military matters #2

The early military G-Wagen sales may have been disappointing, but, like the DKW Munga before it, the Volkswagen Iltis had become hopelessly outdated, and the larger Mercedes (or Puch on occasion) at last found its rightful place in military circles. The German army moved over to the Geländewagen, Norway increased its stocks, Austria and Switzerland continued their support for the G-Wagen, and places like Holland, Denmark, Singapore, Greenland and Luxembourg joined the fray, pledging allegiance to the Graz-built machine, which was usually given the 'Wolf' name.

More than 12,000 W461-based Wolf vehicles found a new home within the German Federal Army between 1990 and 1998 alone, taking advantage of the full range of body types and chassis options, and usually employing the 250GD, 290GD or 290GDT powerplants and 24V electrical systems. Incidentally, despite its size and weight, the G-Wagen could still be air-dropped when necessary.

From 1992, the G-Wagen was also built under licence in Greece by ELVO SA, with the four-cylinder 240GD-based vehicles – like the Peugeot P4 – carrying the W462 chassis designation. To appease the national interests of the Greek government, these models were supplied as CKD (complete knock down) kits, incidentally, for final assembly at the old Steyr Hellas SA factory in Thessaloniki. It is believed that around 5000 cars have been made in Greece, supplied to the country's army, navy, air force and police force. As well as Indonesia and Malaysia building a fair few 461- and 463-series models in right-hand-drive, Turkey also built a number of W460-based models from CKD kits. Interestingly, the G-Wagen could often be seen on the news during the tense build-up to the Turkish elections held at the end of 2015.

It should be noted that the Geländewagen also plays a strong role in a United Nations (UN) capacity, being used on countless peacekeeping and relief missions. The Peugeot P4 version even appeared on a British Virgin Islands postage stamp in the mid-1990s – a two-door ragtop in its familiar white livery, although the UN has employed all manner of G-Wagen variants over the years, from regular station wagons, through to ambulances and pure military machines.

Early Wolf models pictured in Afghanistan in 2007.

Members of the Greek Special Forces Commando Squadron in the summer of 1996, overseeing the security of the forthcoming Bosnian elections.

ELVO staff at a recent event, speaking with potential clients about the G-Wagen it builds under licence in Greece.

Engine bay of the mighty 1993 500GE.

in body colour), along with the chance to order cruise control on automatic cars.

Spring 1993 witnessed the launch of the DM 178,250 500GE model, based on the long-wheelbase estate and limited to just 500 cars, with 300 reserved for Germany. This was a very special model, with power coming from the fuel-injected M117 241bhp (177kW) 5-litre V8 found in the S-Class saloons and roadsters, and an automatic transmission, cruise control, 16-inch alloy wheels shod with 265/70 rubber, ventilated front disc brakes and ABS coming as standard. Oddly, no front diff lock was offered, but there was no question over luxury appointments, which included a headlight washer system, a bull-bar, stainless running boards, a metal spare wheel cover, power sunroof, air-conditioning, a two-tone leather interior, burr walnut trim (carried over to the gearknobs and handbrake lever), and power seat adjustment with heated seat cushions.

Probably due to the expense involved, only 446 500GEs were built, all in 1993, although sales continued into 1994. However, despite not selling the entire proposed run, the experiment proved that an upmarket approach certainly held appeal amongst connoisseurs of the brand.

Meanwhile, a replacement for the 190 – the W202 C-Class – was launched in mid-1993, bringing with it a new form of model designation. The recently released 600SL became the

The limited edition 500GE, with its special Amethyst-Blue metallic paintwork and two-tone, black and grey leather interior with burr walnut trim. Note also the scalloped five-spoke alloy wheels specified for this model.

SL600 overnight as a result, but it was timely for the new engines adopted on the six-cylinder SLs, and the face-lifted W124s, which were now correctly termed as E-Class models. It was all change in the administration offices, too, with Helmut Werner named as the new Chairman of the Board of Management at Mercedes-Benz AG.

Pure class

"As I wheel the Mercedes-Benz G500 Geländewagen into my neighbourhood and park it in the driveway, one thing is immediately apparent: I have just increased the value of my house and property by more than double ... This thing costs more per pound than fresh swordfish." – Steven Cole Smith injecting a little humour into the proceedings, writing for Car & Driver in 2000.

September 1993 brought with it a concept that duly became the A-Class, new AMG models, and a revised G-Wagen, keeping the off-roader alive and well. Then, in November, the company announced it was taking a stake in Britain's Ilmor Engineering, which signalled a wish to enter the Formula One and Indycar arena.

More S-Class and E-Class variants put in an appearance at the 1994 Geneva Show in March, but it was the Turin Show, which opened a month later, that held the interest of sports car fans, as that was where the SLK prototype made its debut, which ultimately led to a production model being launched in spring 1996. It has to be said, the timing couldn't have been better to announce a sports car. The end of March 1994 had witnessed the company's first involvement in Formula One for four decades, as an engine supplier to the Sauber team at this stage, and a couple of months later, Al Unser Jr won the prestigious Indianapolis 500 in the States with a Penske-Mercedes PC23.

For now, though, let's go back to the start of the 1994 season, and take a look at what was happening with the G-Wagen competitors before taking up the Geländewagen story again ...

The rivals
The SUV market was hotting up, with the Range Rover becoming more luxurious, and joined by the new P38A model in 1994; the two ran alongside each other for a little while. Then the

The 100,000th Geländewagen, a 1994 model, with Dr Dieter Zetsche (later the head of the Daimler empire) smiling in the centre of the picture. By the mid-1990s, two out of every three W463s built were lwb estates, with the cabriolet becoming a rarity, at one in ten; around ten per cent of G-Wagens carried Puch badges at this time.

The Hummer H1 road car (right) pictured with the military vehicle that inspired it.

compact Land Rover Freelander made its debut in time for the 1998 season, and a new version of the Discovery was launched soon after.

The J100 Land Cruiser replaced the J80 model at the start of 1998, both spawning a luxury Lexus variant, and the smaller, shapelier Harrier was launched at a similar time, which also provided the basis for a second Lexus SUV line. The rather more mundane RAV4 (XA10) was introduced in 1994, becoming bigger and bigger as the years passed, and was joined by the Toyota Highlander/Kluger as the new millennium dawned.

The third generation Mitsubishi Pajero (also known as the Shogun or Montero) was released in 1999, with the smaller Pajero iO sold alongside it, while the Isuzu Trooper had fallen by the wayside a couple of years into the new century; at least the second generation MU was there, built from 1998 to 2004, and the short-lived – and now quite rare – VehiCROSS model. At Nissan, the Y60 gave way to the Y61 Patrol in 1997, looking much like its Japanese counterparts; Subaru introduced the Forester in 1997, too, and Suzuki launched a fresh Escudo range in the following year.

Jeep continued to develop its Wrangler, Cherokee and Grand Cherokee ranges, although they all looked rather dated against their Japanese foes, while Ford launched a new Explorer in 1995 and an Expedition soon after as a replacement for the Bronco.

Chevrolet had its Tahoe (GMC Yukon) in the full-size category, and the Suzuki-based Tracker by the end of the 1990s, while Chrysler brought out the truck-based Dodge Durango in 1997.

Other heavyweights included the 1999 Model Year Cadillac Escalade – a badge-engineered Tahoe, brought out in response to Ford's new UN173 Lincoln Navigator (launched in August 1997), but the undoubted star of the era from US soil was the Hummer marque. Based on the military Humvee, it was released in civilian guise in April 1992, powered by a huge V8. The H1 (as it was later called) started something of a boom for He-Man-type SUVs that possibly helped other manufacturers punt their more sensibly proportioned goods – including the boxy Benz – although the Hummer brand was carefully nurtured in the new millennium with vehicles of a more modest size.

Although the likes of Asia's SsangYong and Mahindra were always going to be small fry on the global stage, one of the huge advantages enjoyed by many of these rivals was a strong export market, whereas that for the G-Wagen was weak – while the American market stuttered back online in its own roundabout fashion, others were shrinking and, as we'll find out in the coming pages, even the UK gave up on the Graz-built machine for a time. As US-based journalist Don Schroeder so eloquently put it in 1994: "You might find it in a stream or atop a mountain. But not at the local Mercedes dealer."

The 1994 to 1996 cars

The 1994 season brought with it a number of changes, not least a new numbering system for all the Mercedes-Benz passenger car lines. Starting in the spring of 1993, the compact car line was christened the C-Class, with the intermediate models becoming the E-Class, positioned below the top-flight S-Class machines, and the old-style engine-size-related number followed by a series or body style designation was replaced by a class letter followed by a number. As such, the 200GE became the G200 for the 1994 season, the 230GE the G230, the 300GE the G300, the 300GD the G300 Diesel, and the 350GD Turbo the G350 Turbodiesel.

All G-Wagens gained ABS as standard from September 1993, although the introduction of the G320 at the Frankfurt Show that month threw the future of the G300 into question. Indeed, greater changes were afoot in Stuttgart, with the G200 run ending in March 1994 (the last lwb estate had been built in June 1993, as it happens), the G230 variants being dropped in the middle of 1994, and the G300s and G300 Diesels at the tail-end of summer. All of a sudden, this left just two G-Class models – the G320 and G350 Turbodiesel, both being made available with swb and lwb estate bodywork, as well as with an open cabriolet body.

A driver's-side airbag was fitted as standard from March 1994, with the steering wheel being similar to the one introduced in the previous year, but naturally featuring a new centre pad to house the airbag. With all the commotion surrounding the other G-Wagen grades, full-scale production of the G320 didn't start until two months later, with the cabriolet costing DM 94,300, the short-wheelbase station wagon DM 94,185 (the three-door hardtop variant becoming a new entry-level model in the process), and the long-wheelbase estate DM 101,775; the contemporary G350T line-up started at DM 91,080 at this time, by the way, meaning the diesel engine option was cheaper, although that situation changed after the diesel-powered machine inherited

(Right and overleaf) Cover and selected pages from the domestic catalogue printed in June 1994, in time for what would ultimately be an early 1995 season. The page showing standard and optional equipment is particularly useful.

The latest G-Wagen interior, as of spring 1994, when a driver's-side airbag became standard.

DIE G-KLASSE VON MERCEDES-BENZ
BAUREIHE 463

Das bißchen Freiheit mehr

Das Außergewöhnliche erfahren

Straßen, die an gesteckte Ziele führen. Den eigenen Weg kennen und erfahren, das Leben in seiner schönsten Form genießen. Die Mitternachtssonne am Nordkap und Rush-hour in der City. Ein Straßencafé in Paris und hinter Sanddünen das Meer. Mehr Zeit, seinen Lebensstil zu leben. Noch mehr Möglichkeiten und einfach das bißchen Freiheit mehr.

2

Variationen sehen und erleben

Finden Sie Ihren Typ

Der Mercedes G mit Cabrio-Klappverdeck und festem Überrollbügel ist nach oben ohne Grenzen offen. Und der wendige Station-Wagen zeigt sich von seiner besten Seite. Beide Modelle haben durch ihren kurzen Radstand eine kleine Verkehrsfläche und sind die Parkspezialisten für die Stadt. Oder der praktische Station lang. Als Fahrzeug für die ganze Familie ist er ganz schön einladend. In Kombination mit den zwei Motoren haben Sie also die Wahl zwischen sechs Grundmodellen. Aber egal für welchen Typ Sie sich entscheiden, eines haben alle gemeinsam: Fahrspaß pur und ein Entwicklungskonzept, das Funktionalität (Automatik-Getriebe, permanenter Allradantrieb mit 100%-Sperren) und Sicherheit (geländespezifisches ABS, serienmäßiger Fahrer-Airbag), Zuverlässigkeit und Robustheit, Eleganz und das typische zeitlose Erscheinungsbild in sich vereint - der G, ein ausgereifter Klassiker mit modernster Technik.

4

Das beste Gespann – Sie und der G

Der G ist anhänglich

Der Mercedes-Benz Geländewagen ist ein schönes Stück Wertarbeit. Kurze Überhänge und eine aufwendige Fahrwerksabstimmung garantieren die typische Fahrstabilität des G. Es gibt kein Schlingern und Schaukeln, in festen Bahnen erreichen Sie Ihr Ziel sicher und mühelos. In Verbindung mit der Automatik fahren Sie besonnen und dennoch kraftvoll. Sanftes Anbremsen sichert Ihr wertvolles Gut. Ein beruhigendes Gefühl, denn nützlich zu sein ist ihm keine Last. Bis zu 3.500 kg Anhängelast verkraftet er problemlos und läßt sich dabei noch einiges an Gepäck einladen. Sie sind jetzt gespannt? Fahren Sie den G und Sie werden seine Gutmütigkeit zu schätzen wissen. Denn Sie und der G sind das beste Gespann. So bleibt beim Hobby der Spaß und beim Reisen die Freude am Fahren.

5

Technik im Detail

Automatisch überzeugend

Der Mercedes-Benz G fährt mit permanentem Allrad-Antrieb. Die Geländeuntersetzung ist vollsynchronisiert und problemlos während der Fahrt zuschaltbar. Der G ist mit einem komfortablen Automatik-Getriebe ausgestattet. Wenn hohe Zugkräfte gewünscht sind, treten ohne Schaltzeiten keine störenden Zugkraftunterbrechungen auf. Im Stau oder beim Rangieren fahren Sie bequemer und werden automatisch entlastet. Auch bei schwierigen Situationen im Gelände, die Ihre ganze Aufmerksamkeit fordern, bewährt sich dieser unschätzbare Vorteil.

Mit Sicherheit fahren

Das aufwendige Fahrwerk mit starren Achsen, die an Längs- und Querlenkern geführt sind, ausgerüstet mit Teleskopstoßdämpfern und einem Stabilisator an der Vorderachse, sorgt für eine konstante Bodenfreiheit. Für noch bessere Sicherheit hat Mercedes-Benz neben dem serienmäßigen Fahrer-Airbag und den neuen innenbelüfteten und größer dimensionierten Scheibenbremsen zusätzlich ein ABS-System geschaffen, das erstmals den spezifischen Einsatzbedingungen eines Geländewagens voll gerecht wird. Auf der Straße ist es für das Bremsen ein wichtiger Sicherheitsfaktor. Im Gelände, auf lockerem Untergrund, verlängert es aber den Bremsweg. Doch hierfür ist das System manuell abschaltbar. Automatisch abgeschaltet wird es, wenn eine der drei Differentialsperren angewählt ist. Die Anwahl der einzelnen Sperren wird dabei durch eine gelbe, die Aktivierung durch eine rote Kontrolleuchte angezeigt. Alle Sperren sind in einer logischen, dem zunehmenden Traktionsbedarf angepaßten Reihenfolge durch Tipptasten sperrbar (Mitte - hinten - vorne). So werden Fehlentscheidungen sinnvoll ausgeschlossen.

Automatik / Verteilergetriebehebel

Die neue innenbelüftete Scheibenbremse

Angepaßtes 7,5 J x 16-Rad für die größer dimensionierten Scheibenbremsen

ABS- und Differentialsperrenschalter

Infrarotfernbedienbare Zentralverriegelung mit integrierter Wegfahrsperre

Elektrische Sitzverstellung (SA)*

Standheizung (SA)*, auch fernbedienbar

Leuchtweitenregulierung, verhindert das Blenden der Partner im Straßenverkehr bei Fernzuschaltung

Abschleppschutzschalter, verhindert das Auslösen der Alarmanlage, z.B. wenn das Fahrzeug transportiert oder verladen werden soll (SA)*

*(SA) = Sonderausstattung

16

Extrem zuverlässig

Technik, auf die man sich verlassen kann

Die Serientechnik für den Mercedes-Benz Geländewagen überzeugt in jeder Situation durch Robustheit und Langlebigkeit. Selbst bei Fernreisen in einsame Gegenden können Sie dieser Zuverlässigkeit beruhigt vertrauen.

Auch im Sporteinsatz sind erfolgreiche, private Rally-Raid-Teams von der extremen Zuverlässigkeit der serienreif erprobten Mercedes-Benz Serien-Aggregate überzeugt.

19

110

A 1995 model G320, readily identified by the lack of a vent on the offside front wing. Oddly, seeing as all the W463s beforehand had sported one, the straight-six G320s didn't have one on the nearside either! Turbocharged cars had a vent on each side, of course.

7.5J x 16 alloys shod with 225/65 rubber as standard, along with the ventilated front discs used on the 500GE, in July 1994.

Looking at the G320 in detail, it was powered by the M104 straight-six with double-overhead camshafts and four valves per pot in its alloy head, and superior induction technology thanks to a microprocessor-controlled injection system with a hot film air mass sensor (HFM). With a 89.9mm bore and 84.0mm stroke in the cast iron block, this gave a capacity of 3199cc, and combined with a 9.2:1 compression ratio, the cat-equipped engine produced 210bhp (155kW) and 221lbft of torque.

Like the turbodiesel model, the G320 came with a four-speed automatic gearbox, with no manual option; the final-drive ratio was different, though, with the petrol-engined car having 4.86:1 axles front and rear, while the diesel continued with a

The 1995 G350 Turbodiesel in long-wheelbase estate guise, with Atik alloy wheels now being a standard fitment (increasing the track by 50mm/2.0in at both ends as a result). Fender flares were normally black, incidentally, but came in body colour on cars with metallic paint.

4.11:1 ratio. The latest aluminium alloy wheels (introduced as a new option for the 1994 season, similar in design to those used on the limited run 500GE) and uprated braking system of the 1995 Model Year G350T were fitted to the G320 from the off, with both cars ultimately hitting the showroom at around the same time.

Standard features for the 1995 season not already mentioned included infra-red remote control central locking with an integrated engine immobiliser (a useful new item), halogen headlights and foglights, headlight adjustment, a laminated front screen, heated washer nozzles, power windows (front), a heated rear screen with wash/wipe facility on estates, heated power mirrors, PAS, front and rear headrests, a split rear seat, Zebrano wood trim, an outside temperature gauge, tachometer, quartz clock, a reading light for the passenger, luggage compartment lighting, and a first aid kit. Major options included alternative 235/85 or 265/70 off-road tyres, headlight washers, running boards for the sides of the car, a metal spare wheel cover, power

Cover and a couple of images unique to the April 1995 catalogue.

The AA Vision SUV concept made its debut at the 1996 Detroit Show, held in January, but was later shipped to Geneva. Interestingly, several stylish off-roaders based on the G-Wagen have been built by private concerns, such as the Sbarro model, and the Heuliez Intruder, which was later modified by OPAC and called the Status Contender XG.

seat adjustment, centre armrests up front, audio equipment, an alarm (available with a tow protection upgrade), a front tow hitch, and a Webasto auxiliary heating system.

By the spring of 1995, tinted glass had been added to the spec sheet, along with a leather-wrapped steering wheel, seatbelt pretensioners, cruise control for the G320, and an integrated aerial for the station wagons (the cabriolet continued with the old wing-mounted antenna). A passenger-side airbag was added in 1996.

In the background

Less than two weeks after the 1994 Paris Salon closed its doors for another couple of years, Mercedes-Benz presented its new Formula One car, launched in partnership with the British McLaren team. The alliance had to wait until March 1997 for its first win, but after that, it was easy to recall the domination of the 'Silver Arrows' of yore, not only in F1, but in the American CART (Indycar) series as well.

June 1995 saw the launch of the twin-headlight W210

E-Class saloon. The fresh front mask design had first been revealed in a concept car displayed at the 1993 Geneva Show, becoming something of a Benz styling signature for a little while.

At the 1995 Frankfurt Show, held in September, the crowds were treated to a series of upgrades for the SL and C-Class, as well as the launch of the E50 AMG saloon. The AMG name was flying high in both the DTM and ITC touring car racing series at this time, the competition programme being treated as a partnership between the Stuttgart and Affalterbach companies, and the success on the tracks was a magnificent marketing tool for all concerned. The two concerns would become closer still in the future, but their relationship, even at this stage, brought forth a range of officially approved tuning parts to allow owners greater individuality.

On the subject of individuality, the first Designo consulting centre opened at the Sindelfingen plant in November 1995. This allowed customers to order cars with special interior and exterior finishes, adding to the enjoyment of purchasing a new car and the years of ownership ahead. Five more centres were planned for Germany, although the Designo name would eventually hold worldwide appeal.

In January 1996, Daimler-Benz got together with its Stuttgart neighbour Porsche to form Car Top Systems Fahrzeugdachsysteme GmbH in Hamburg. The CTS concern would serve both companies well in the development and manufacture of roof systems for their respective open car models.

On the technical front, January 1996 witnessed the beginning of the EURO 2 emissions regulations. Looking further ahead, the even stricter EURO 3 rules came into force in 2000, almost halving CO limits, and calling for a dramatic cut in NOx emissions on petrol engines. Tighter standards were outlined again in the EURO 4 (2005) proposals, and for 2009, when the EURO 5 regulations kicked in, PM emissions were also included on petrol-engined cars with direct-injection. As well as the need to save resources and preserve the Earth's atmosphere, fuel economy was in everyone's interests, of course, with the price of 98 RON fuel increasing by over 30 per cent between 1994 and 2000 in one central European country, and continued to rise thereafter, going up by another 30 per cent on top of that by the time 2009 rolled along.

The AMG Story

The Mercedes brand has always managed to attract the attentions of tuning companies, but few are as synonymous with the Stuttgart maker as AMG of Burgstall, Baden-Württemberg, and later Affalterbach, a few miles to the north-east of Stuttgart.

AMG was officially founded in June 1967 by Hans-Werner Aufrecht (who'd worked for Daimler-Benz, and had been in the competition department building engines in the glory days of the 1950s) and Erhard Melcher. For the first ten years of its history, AMG concentrated on engine and suspension development to further its highly-successful racing programme, but body kits and wheels were added to the firm's catalogue, and ultimately complete cars were built and offered for sale, either in turnkey guise or to the specific requests of customers.

In 1983, AMG developed a four-valve per cylinder head for the V8, leading to signature vehicles like the Hammer, but it also provided the foundation stone for further expansion, not just in Germany, but in places as far afield as America and Japan. The bored-out, 6-litre 32v conversion on the 5-litre V8, around since 1987, would duly provide enthusiasts with the 500GE 6.0 AMG in due course.

The real breakthrough, however, came in October 1990, when AMG secured a deal in which its tuning parts could be sold and fitted via Mercedes-Benz dealerships, and complete cars started filtering through into domestic showrooms by May 1991. In addition, the racing programme was treated as a partnership, with the works DTM cars being prepared by Aufrecht's company.

AMG did a 232bhp version of the 300GE (the 300GE 3.2), as well as the 272bhp G36 AMG, based on the straight-six G320 unit, but bored out to 3606cc. A gaggle of G55 AMGs would follow later on, giving archrival Brabus something to think about. Eventually, on the 1st January 1999, DaimlerChrysler bought a 51 per cent stake in AMG, sealing the relationship once and for all with the foundation of Mercedes-AMG GmbH.

While the 1996 Geneva Show was used to launch a new line of C- and E-Class estates, the 66th Turin Show, held in the following month, was reserved to give the R170 SLK a full share of the limelight. The S-Class coupes were face-lifted two months after the SLK production car was launched, giving rise to a new CL-Class designation.

Export market review

After years of waiting and a huge investment in testing and certification equipment, Dave Holland was able to restart his G-Wagen import business in the States in 1993. Europa International of Santa Fe was declared a quasi-official dealer by MBNA, who still shied away from the big SUV, and stood alone as the only US Geländewagen importer at the time. In 1994, a basic 300GE lwb station wagon would have cost $90,900, but cars leaving the showroom were regularly priced 30 per cent higher after options. So, cheap it was not, but at least Americans were able to buy one again.

For 1995, the 320GE became the base car at Europa, providing buyers with more power and better fuel economy at the same time, although the base price went up to $119,500 – the cost of two high-spec Range Rovers! Exclusivity was guaranteed with only 50 or so fully-loaded cars imported by Holland during the year, but there was no escaping that the price was prohibitive for a lot of folks. Of course, there was a lot of work involved in converting the Benz to meet Federal regulations, and the investment made before importation could restart had to be clawed back through limited sales. The maths does make sense if you think about it, although another $8000 was added to the base price for the 1996 season.

Holland's company continued as sole importer of the G-Wagen, with the G500 duly becoming the weapon of choice to distance the oldtimer from the new M-Class, and by the end of the 1990s, Europa International was listing the swb and lwb estates, as well as the cabriolet – each available for around $130,000, and already attracting a long list of celebrity owners amongst the roughly 150 cars sold per year. Ultimately, with contemporary Porsche 911 prices starting at $65,000, one can see that 'ordinary' buyers would have been few and far between. Things were about to change in a big way Stateside, though...

A UK 300GEL that was registered at the tail-end of summer 1993.

The UK market was still ticking over, with the same four cars listed in 1993 being carried over for the 1994 season. Prices were reduced again, making the entry-level diesel-engined G300 £27,406 – about the same as an E300 saloon, and in touch with Mitsubishi Shogun (aka Pajero) pricing. Things stayed much the same for 1995, but the car had already become a special order item and only the petrol models were sold in the 1996 Model Year – the swb estate commanding £39,000, and the lwb version £42,500.

Having moved around 5000 cars since British imports started, Mercedes-Benz UK officially stopped sales at the end of 1996, although the last time the SUV appeared in price lists was March 1997. However, a few specialists, such as Caversham, Automotive Technik (ATL) and others, including an official MBUK dealer, continued to import a mix of rhd and lhd G-Wagens in limited numbers for those who simply couldn't live with anything else.

Australia was still out of the game, leaving Japan as the only other major rhd market. For 1994, Japan listed the same two cars as the 1993 Model Year, although the prices were lowered, in line with most of the other Mercedes-Benz Japan cars that

Two pieces of Japanese advertising – one from 1996 (right) showing the G320 long-wheelbase estate, and the second from four years later.

particular season. The 3-litre petrol-engined models were reduced once more before being replaced by the G320 range in 1995. For the 1996 Model Year, Japanese buyers could opt for the G320 swb estate at 7,500,000 yen, the lwb version for 1,000,000 yen more, or the G320 cabriolet at 7,800,000 yen. There was also an AMG G36 station wagon at 10,300,000 yen (or 11,300,000 yen in long-wheelbase guise), which was well into SL territory on the pricing front.

There was no change whatsoever going into 1998, but at the end of the year, the G320s were joined by the equivalent G500s and a G55 AMG long-wheelbase estate, the latter commanding a hefty 15,600,000 yen, which was almost exactly the same money as a Ferrari F355! This seven model line-up took the G-Wagen into the new millennium as far as the Japanese market was concerned. We'll come to the G55 AMG in a little while, but first something a little bit more mundane.

The 461-series

While the W463 line continued ever onwards on its path towards the upper echelons of the SUV market, the W461 was also developing, although not quite at the same pace. The 230GE line was discontinued in 1996, with the last cars built in August that year, while the end of 1997 saw the replacement of the normally-aspirated 290GD for a turbocharged version – the 290GD Turbodiesel. Note that the old designations were retained on the 461-series models, as they were not officially classed as passenger cars, rather they were sold as commercial vehicles. Indeed, the revised interior was lifted from the Sprinter van!

Powered by the 120bhp (88kW) OM602 DE29 straight-five unit borrowed from the E-Class, the 290GDT was a lot more spritely than its predecessors, although it looked just the same, with a different intercooler to that used on the saloons being employed to allow the old front bumper to be retained. Under the skin was much the same, too, except disc brakes were specified all-round – not to keep the power in check, as the old disc/drum system could handle 120bhp with ease, but because of the desire to reduce maintenance costs for end-users. Running costs were reduced further by the new engine (hooked up to a four-speed automatic transmission as standard), with its direct-injection enhancing fuel economy no end.

With the turbocharged W461s, there was still no vent on the nearside wing, but one was added on the offside, which is an unusual combination. Available as a short-wheelbase estate, a long-wheelbase estate and a long-wheelbase van (the pick-up variant was dropped), as well as in chassis only format, the 461-series fell by the wayside for a while as far as the civilian market was concerned, with production of the W461 290GDT ultimately ending in December 2001, although – like the strict 290GD, as it happens – a few were built beyond this date for military users. The 461-type G-Wagen would be revived in the future, however, with the later cars featuring a side exhaust like the W463s.

Short- and long-wheelbase W461 estates sporting turbodiesel power.

A 290GDT chassis playing host to a flatbed rear, which has then had a framework attached to it for a tarp cover.

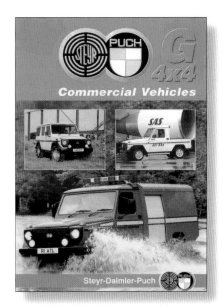

The Puch W461 catalogue from 1998. Note the new badge on the nose – it was a small single Puch roundel on the earlier 461-series models. The pick-up wasn't sold at this time, by the way, even though it is illustrated.

The 1997 Model Year

There was no Frankfurt Show in 1996, but the 1997 Model Year changes were introduced in September 1996 nonetheless, illustrated in an all-new catalogue printed two months earlier. The main identifying feature was a new front bumper with vents cut into the centre to feed the turbodiesel's intercooler, although the same bumper blade was also used on the NA petrol-engined car. As before, the G320 was identified by its lack of vents on both sides of the bonnet.

There were big changes under the bonnet, though, at least on the diesel-powered car, for the 3.5-litre engine was dropped in July, replaced on the line by a 3-litre OM606 D30LA unit, thus giving birth to the new G300 Turbodiesel model. This straight-six had the same bore and stroke as the old OM603 D30 lump used in the 300GD, so its 2996cc displacement was a familiar one. With a 22:1 c/r, combined an exhaust-driven turbocharger, an intercooler, indirect-injection and a revised emissions set-up, the dohc 4v per cylinder unit was able to deliver a healthy 177bhp (130kW) and 243lbft of torque.

The diesel model gained a lightweight electronically-

DIE G-KLASSE VON MERCEDES-BENZ
G 320 UND G 300 TURBODIESEL

Cover of the July 1996 (1997 MY) catalogue.

An odd picture perhaps, but, thanks to the colouring, this fire vehicle based on the 1997 G320 perfectly highlights the revised front bumper styling.

The turbocharged 3-litre OM606 engine.

controlled five-speed automatic gearbox with torque converter lock-up and cruise control at this time, too, employing the same 4.86:1 axle ratios as the G320. There were no other changes mechanically, apart from EBV (electronic brake force distribution) for the G300TD, although headlight washers were added to the spec sheet on both cars, as were a pair of armrests between the front seats, a 12V socket in the rear compartment and puddle lights for all doors; the clock was changed to a digital one (meaning the look of the tachometer changed, too), along with the oddometers, and power windows were made standard for all windows. The cloth trim was also revised, changing from a particularly staid, lightly ribbed monotone fabric that had been with the W463s since their birth to a dazzling geometric pattern; thankfully, most cars are trimmed in the optional leather, as – unless it was the black version – its modernity was a little at odds with the traditional wood inserts.

As for home market pricing, the G320 short-wheelbase station wagon was listed at DM 99,107, the long-wheelbase version at DM 107,775, and the cabriolet (still with a manual top this stage of the proceedings, incidentally) at DM 100,682.

A useful interior shot showing the G300TD model, identified by the gearshift for the 5AT transmission. Note also the digital array under the speedometer, the optional air-conditioning unit, and the passenger-side airbag in the top roll. Although this car has walnut veneer, Zebrano wood was still classed as the norm, by the way.

The rear compartment of the 1997 G-Wagen with cloth trim, seen here with the optional occasional seating.

The G300 Turbodiesel cabriolet, with its different badging style compared to the estates due to the spare wheel location. The colour-keyed steel spare wheel cover was still an option, incidentally.

A couple of publicity shots of the 1997 Model Year G300TD in long-wheelbase station wagon guise.

The diesel-powered short-wheelbase estate dressed up with running boards and a bull-bar, although the spare wheel cover is the latest standard item.

A final image from the 1997 season photography session, with the lwb G300TD estate looking at home on the quayside.

The turbodiesel model – cleaner and more frugal than ever before – was almost identical to the petrol-engined machines in terms of price, with the swb estate at DM 99,912, the lwb estate at DM 107,812, and the open car listed at DM 101,487. A CD-changer was offered as a new option at this time, by the way, along with a lumber support upgrade for the front seats.

In the background, the sporty two-door CLK coupe (C208) was announced at the 1997 Detroit Show; the tin-top version was duly joined by a convertible model in March 1998, by which time a homologation special had been built to compete in the

FIA GT Championships – a series the model would quickly go on to dominate.

As it happens, Klaus-Dieter Vöhringer had taken the place of Hartmut Weule as head of the R&D section at about the same time as the CLK coupe was unveiled, while the E280 and E320 models that made their debut in Amsterdam in February 1997 were the first vehicles to make use of the all-new M112 V6 engines featuring three valves per cylinder and twin ignition. A new generation of 4MATIC was also announced, with permanent four-wheel drive. In the following month, it was the turn of the

new A-Class to take a bow in Geneva, as the Mercedes car range blossomed at a staggering rate.

The business was restructured again in April 1997, when Mercedes-Benz AG merged into Daimler-Benz AG. More importantly, the new vee-engine plant in Bad Cannstatt (touted as the "factory of the future") was officially opened at the same time, allowing the production of M112 V6 and M113 V8 units in an efficient and eco-friendly manner. The one-millionth engine was built there just three years later.

A couple of weeks later, at the International Off-Road Vehicle Show in Munich, a new power top was announced for the Geländewagen. Designed by Car Top Systems (CTS), cars with the latest hood were easy enough to spot, as a triangular section was added aft of the B-post for the electro-hydraulically controlled top to mate up with. The mechanism added around DM 10,000 to the base price when it was introduced on production models in June that year, but it could open or close in around 30 seconds at the touch of a single button, and the reduced fabric area made the vehicle a lot quieter and therefore more refined.

Equally noteworthy, May 1997 saw the release of yet another new vehicle range, this time launched in the shape of the 163-series M-Class SUV, which featured the second generation 4MATIC drivetrain and an independent suspension mounted on a strong ladder frame, and was initially built in America. A few months later, the 1997 Tokyo Show played host to the debut of the Maybach luxury saloon concept vehicle; it would eventually go into production, thus reviving a treasured name from the past, in mid-2002. More things were happening on the G-Wagen front, though ...

The launch of the new US-built W163 M-Class came in May 1997, which coincided with the official opening of the Alabama plant, seen in this picture. From mid-1999, the M-Class was also built at the SDP factory at Graz.

The 1998 season

Even though things looked much the same at first glance, the 1990s had witnessed a relentless barrage of revisions made to the G-Wagen, and the 1998 Model Year saw even more applied. The biggest change by far was the dropping of the straight-six

The first M-Class model was the ML320, like the one in this 1998 US advert. Then, hot on its heels came the V8-engined ML430, which was on display at the 1998 Detroit Show, followed by an ML230, with diesel and AMG variants joining the line-up in 1999. The car was duly face-lifted in the autumn of 2001.

The M112 engine.

G320 in favour of a V6-powered version, the swap-over taking place in September 1997.

The M112 V6s signified an important advance, with their all-aluminium alloy construction (rather than the alloy head and cast iron block arrangement of the straight-sixes) saving a lot of weight. In a world first, even the cylinder liners were made of light alloy with a high silicon content allowing a good compromise between reducing weight and friction, whilst maintaining long-term service and reliability levels.

The M112 units were unusual in having three valves per cylinder instead of four: their operation being designed in such a way as to allow the use of a single overhead camshaft per bank. From a technical standpoint, the single exhaust valve reduced heat loss in the exhaust gases, thus making the catalytic converter heat up quicker, and work in its most efficient operating band more of the time. Another interesting feature was the dual ignition, with two coils and two sparkplugs per cylinder.

To enhance engine flexibility, the sequential port fuel-injection took advantage of variable length intake manifold technology, with the manifold structure being cast in magnesium

125

alloy as part of the weight saving programme. Indeed, the intelligent selection of lightweight materials throughout the powerplant made the new V6s 25 per cent lighter than their straight-six predecessors. All told, the new specification promised a ten per cent fuel saving, faster warm-up times and significantly lower emission values, while a balance shaft reduced first and second order vibration.

Although the configuration was quite different, the bore and stroke dimensions were carried over on the 3.2-litre unit, meaning a cubic capacity of 3199cc. Even the 10.0:1 compression ratio was retained, although power increased slightly to 215bhp (158kW), with maximum torque listed at 221lbft at 2800rpm. A five-speed ECT automatic gearbox was the only option, paired up with the familiar 4.86:1 axle ratios.

The equally familiar 16-inch alloys were called for duty once more as well, but the braking system was uprated on the G320 to incorporate EBV and discs on all four corners; the G300TD inherited the same system at the end of 1997 to make life easier on the production line. This same train of thought was later applied to the bodywork, too, with the G320 finally getting a pair of front wing vents midway through 1998, while all station wagons gained a high-mount brakelight, and fender flares were now painted in body colour regardless of the paint being metallic or not.

Inside, officially, the wood trim was changed to 'G-Line Anthracite' inserts in place of the old Zebrano ones, although most people opted for the walnut veneer, and it seems like Mercedes-Benz Japan, for instance, ordered walnut as a matter of course. For those wanting something extra special, one could order the steering wheel and gear selector in a wood/leather combination, and things like mobile phones and radios with integrated navigation systems were becoming the norm, albeit still expensive options at this time. Meanwhile, air-conditioning was made standard for all cars, along with the Assyst active maintenance monitor, and rear speakers were something new for the station wagons.

At the end of April, just as the German VAT rate increased from 15 to 16 per cent, the company unveiled the G500 at the 1998 International Off-Road Vehicle Show in Munich. Available with all three bodies (with prices starting at DM 128,180),

this new flagship model was propelled by a 5-litre M113 powerplant, which was basically an M112 unit with two extra cylinders tacked on. As such, being a modular engine, most of the technical features were the same as the new V6s, apart from the lack of a balance shaft, as one wasn't needed on a V8. Indeed, even the 84.0mm stroke of the 3.2-litre unit was shared, although the 97.0mm bore was completely different; combined with eight cylinders, the displacement was 4966cc as a result. The resulting 296bhp (218kW) and 336lbft of torque was fed through a five-speed automatic gearbox, with the front and rear axles sporting a 4.36:1 final-drive ratio and a diff lock at both ends.

Prices for the V6-engined G320 started at DM 100,625. The cabriolet was the lightest of the three models, but still tipped the scales at 2175kg (4785lb).

The tasteful interior of the G500. Domestic sales of the high-speed V8 model began in June 1998.

Front and rear views of the G500 in lwb estate form, with optional running boards but the 'correct' wheel and tyre combination for the model. Note the new indicator lenses.

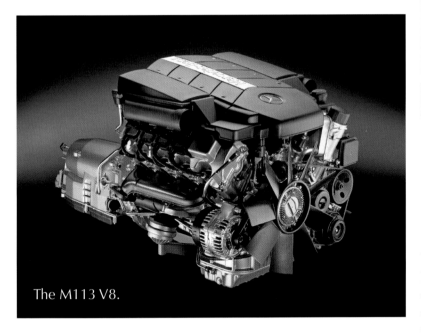

The M113 V8.

As well as being powerful (something the uprated front brakes confirmed), the G500 was also extremely luxurious. Building on the regular specification, the G500 added standard features like metallic paint, 18-inch five-spoke wheels shod with 265/60 rubber, chrome slats in the front grille, clear indicator lights at both ends, 'V8' emblems on the front wings, illuminated treadplates, leather and walnut trim (including a wood/leather steering wheel and gearshift), heated seats with power adjustment, velour carpets, map nets on the seats, and a radio/cassette player. Not much was left on the option list, of course, but reversing sensors were listed as a new item, along with darkened rear windows and heated rear seats.

Corporate happenings

The company opened its third Advanced Design Studio outside Germany in February 1998, this time in Como, Italy. The others had been established in Irvine (CA) in the States in 1991, and in Yokohama, Japan, during the following year. Things were happening at Steyr-Daimler-Puch, too, for in 1998, Canada's Magna International Inc bought a majority shareholding in SDP, the Board having approved the acquisition at the tail-end of March that year. Magna Steyr would be formed as a result, but G-Wagen production would continue in Graz along the same lines as before.

Meanwhile, the first of the 'smart' microcars were presented shortly after in the spring of 1998, although it's probably fair to say that younger folks were more interested in the face-lifted SL range, announced at the Turin Show that April. Then, in the following month, the highly-publicised merger between America's Chrysler Corporation and Daimler-Benz AG resulted in a new company called DaimlerChrysler AG being formed (see sidebar for details).

The W220 S-Class was launched at the 1998 Paris Salon, with the company's huge new proving grounds at Papenburg opening for business at around the same time. With the workforce now standing at over 440,000 people, passenger car production had hit a staggering 947,517 units in 1998.

The 1999 Detroit Show was selected as the venue to present the 5.4-litre supercharged Vision SLR coupe concept, suitably impressing the crowds gathered before it. A couple of months later, in Geneva, the new CL-Class (C215) was unveiled, along with the CLK55 AMG – one of many AMG machines launched in 1999, following the restructuring of the AMG concern made earlier in the year. Incidentally, Bruno Sacco retired as head of styling at about this time, with his old right-hand man, Peter Pfeiffer, duly taking his place in April 1999.

A face-lifted E-Class (W210) was presented in July 1999, with the CLK updated in the following month. The relentless pace of development continued with a roadster version of the V8-powered Vision SLR being displayed at the 1999 Frankfurt Show. New engines were announced for the S-Class at the same time, making the most of the latest in diesel technology, and before the year came to an end, the AMG range expanded once more, just after the celebrations surrounding Mercedes-Benz winning another F1 driver's title with Mika Hakkinen were starting to die down.

Annual passenger car production passed the one-million mark for the first time ever in 1999, which was a significant achievement for the Stuttgart company. The figure rose to 1,161,601 units in the following year, proving it was no fluke, partly thanks to the success of the new W203 C-Class, launched in March 2000. The G-Wagen was also playing its part in boosting sales, too!

Yet more G variants

A limited edition model was announced on the first day of March 1999 to commemorate the 20th anniversary of the Geländewagen, called the G500 Classic. The Classic package was actually available on all three bodies, with special aubergine-coloured paintwork (carried over to the bumpers and door mirrors), chrome inserts in the side rubbing strips, a two-tone Nappa leather interior, walnut trim, a multi-function

The limited edition G500 'Classic,' with a close-up of the coachwork and a view of the distinctive black and purple interior. Even more exclusive, however, was the Neiman Marcus limited edition featured in the US company's 2000 Christmas catalogue. Built up by Europa, only 15 were available, with special trim and upholstery, and a rather hefty $160,000 price tag.

steering wheel, instruments that were slightly different (with the gauges being given a more retro look and a larger display area), and special badging. The car actually started something of a trend, for the colour-keyed mirrors were adopted on the regular 2000 MY vehicles, as well as the steering wheel and dashboard that had made their debut in the Classic model.

In the following month, AMG announced a bevy of tuned Mercedes models, including the G55 AMG. With production starting in July 1999, the AMG car had an enlarged version of the M113 unit, stroked to give 5439cc and 354bhp (260kW). The engine and exhaust system cost about DM 37,000 at this time, but the AMG variant was not yet classed as a catalogue model.

Something else not readily found in the catalogues was the G-Guard series, introduced in 1999 to meet the call for an ex-works armoured vehicle. Based on the lwb G500 station wagon, the factory offered varying levels of protection, from run-flat tyres to bulletproof glass and coachwork. Thankfully, after all this activity, things settled down on the G-Wagen front, for the 2000 Paris Salon had something special in store for Geländewagen fans ...

A typical G55 AMG model from the time. Not all AMGs were as flashy – some of the 6-litre conversions the author has seen are very tame, with just a badge on the tail and the twin exhausts giving an indication of something special.

The heart of any AMG conversion. This is the contemporary 5.4-litre V8 engine, although several tuned power-units were created over the years.

The prototype G500 Guard and its unique interior designed to protect and ensconce VIPs. Private companies had been offering armoured cars based on the G-Wagen for many years before, of course.

A 2000 Model Year V8-engined cabriolet making light work of an icy road. The power top was always black.

7

Further evolution

Gorden Wagener, Daimler AG's Head of Design, once said: "The more perfect the form, the more timeless it appears." This is definitely true of the G-Wagen, which looks more at home on the road now than it did three decades ago. Now, finally, it has earned its place as an automotive icon, in much the same way as the Porsche 911, Jaguar E-type and Volkswagen Beetle.

As the market share for full-size sports utility vehicles has grown year-on-year, so has the competition. But, rather like the revival of the lightweight sports car (LWS), the swelling of the ranks has increased awareness, and thanks to this and MBNA taking on the Graz-built SUV, G-Wagen sales are now thriving like never before. The car's presence and the way that celebrities (real ones from the expected Sylvester Stallone, Floyd Mayweather and Arnold Schwarzenegger to the rather more unexpected fans like Hilary Duff, Diane Keaton and Elle MacPherson, and high-profile wannabes that want to be in with the in-crowd alike) have taken to it in a big way in recent years has helped it overcome the fact that its basic bodyshell hasn't changed since 1979!

Despite strong rumours of production ending in 2005 after journalists caught wind of the forthcoming full-size X164 GL SUV project, it's fair to say that 20-odd years after launch, the Geländewagen finally came of age with the announcement of the 2001 Model Year changes. The Puch badge was dropped at the same time, making the G-Wagen exclusive to the prestigious Mercedes-Benz brand as soon as the last of the pre-face-lift G320, G500 and G300TD cars rolled off the line in November 2000.

A new era

The Frankfurt Show, usually a showcase for the German manufacturers, was a low-key affair for Mercedes in 2000, as it

Reason to celebrate: A face-lifted V8 model from 2001 was the 150,000th G-Wagen built – the last chapter had started with a picture of car number 100,000, so sales were certainly picking up, when normally it would be a very hard job indeed selling a vehicle that had been running for so long virtually unchanged ...

was reserved for commercial vehicles. But when the 2000 Paris Salon opened up for business on the 30 September, fans of the marque were treated to the launch of the new C-Class Sports Coupe (C203) and the face-lifted W463 Geländewagen.

The engine bay of the G400 CDI. Unfortunately, there were reliability issues with the earliest V8 engines, although the problems were soon sorted.

Both the V6 G320 and V8 G500 were carried over without mechanical changes, although there were cosmetic upgrades that we'll come to in a moment, and the G500 gained a rear anti-roll bar as standard. The AMG version of the G-Wagen fell into line with the face-lift in spring 2001, a couple of months behind the regular petrol-engined models, but again, there were no revisions made to the leading specifications. However, big changes were outlined for the diesel car, with the old G300 Turbodiesel being replaced by the G400 CDI grade.

The G400 CDI was powered by the twin-turbo OM628 common-rail diesel V8 found in the S-Class. This engine incorporated all the leading-edge technology Stuttgart could muster, with an intercooler, a dohc per bank arrangement to operate four valves per cylinder, and the very latest emissions control equipment. With both the bore and stroke measuring 86.0mm, this gave the all-alloy unit a cubic capacity of 3996cc.

The 2001 Model Year line-up, with a G320 cabriolet nearest the camera, a V8-engined swb estate in the centre, and a six-cylinder lwb estate on the far side.

The new G400 CDI grade, with optional running boards and metal spare wheel cover. The cast alloys are correct, but would come with a black centre cap on the 2001 production models, and stay that way for a couple of seasons.

The compression ratio was set at 18.5:1, with everything combining to deliver 250bhp (184kW) plus a huge 413lbft of torque, the latter available from just 1700rpm. This power was taken through a five-speed automatic transmission, with a 4.11:1 ratio specified for the front and rear axles.

A number of styling and interior revisions were introduced to coincide with the launch of the 2001 MY cars, with chrome inserts in the side rubbing strips and body-coloured bumpers for the V8 machines (colour-keyed mirrors had been adopted on all cars during the previous season), smoked indicator lenses for the G320, and a third brakelight for the cabriolet to bring it into line with the estates. The G400 CDI had all the styling enhancements applied to the G500, such as the chrome grille slats and clear indicator lights, as well as that car's suspension and wheel and tyre combination, with 2001 models featuring a black centre cap on the 18-inch rim. For the G320, the old 16-inch wheels were carried over, but they were now shod with 265/70 rubber. By far the biggest changes were seen inside the car ...

The face-lifted interior was a blend of the old and new – the old G-Wagen dash was still recognisable, both in general layout and the strong top roll and the large grab handle in front of the passenger, but it's fair to say that the car was treated to a distinct move upmarket, bringing it in line with contemporary top-end saloon thinking.

The revised dashboard and instrument cluster of the 2001 MY cars, this being a G500 (the red-line was marked at 4500rpm on the diesel model) with the standard wood/leather steering wheel, and grey trim in this case.

133

Another G500 interior, this time in black. This angle is particularly useful, as it shows the revised centre console and armrest, as well as the new seats, door furniture, handbrake, COMAND unit and grab handle insert (the G320 didn't have the latter piece of trim).

One of the first 2001 Model Year G320 cabriolets, this one having leather trim. Note the extended header rail above the windscreen, the bulge in the centre playing host to the overhead control panel.

Starting with the main instruments, the binnacle was rounder, allowing the sweep of the central semi-circular speedometer plenty of space. Inside the speedo was a huge display area and a bank of warning lights, leaving just a tachometer off to the left, and a fuel gauge to the right – the display and the keys on the multi-function steering wheel covered just about everything else, with electronics taking over analogue meters. To the left of the heavy shroud was an air vent with a small speaker beyond, and to the right, a larger speaker grille and two separate air vents, between which was a new switch panel for the differential controls. Moving further to the right was the passenger-side airbag, grab handle, and another air vent and speaker setup in the corner.

Most of the switchgear to the sides of the power-adjusted steering column was fairly familiar, as was the glovebox on the other side of the car, but the centre stack was completely revised. The remaining old switches that were positioned above the HVAC controls were grouped tighter together, with the heated rear seats batched in with them. Below this was a slot for the Audio 10 radio and an oddments box on the G320 or the COMAND system (a dedicated radio, CD player, telephone

Rear of the G320 cabriolet, with its new – if somewhat ungainly – high-mount rear brakelight sitting above the spare wheel carrier.

The G500 and G400 CDI chassis layout, with a decidedly short-lived rear anti-roll bar setup (previously an option in most countries, including Germany, for those that hardly ever ventured of-road). The change was not publicised, as we'd sadly entered an era in which gadgets took priority in the column inches of catalogues and magazines alike, and it had disappeared again by car number 144226.

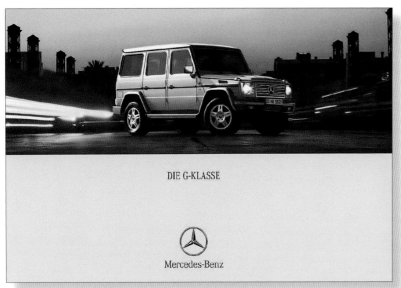

The cover of the German catalogue, printed in November 2000, and a couple of the more dramatic G400 CDI images from within. For the record, a different catalogue had been issued in September, but this one was more realistic, and was duly reprinted with the same cover and suitable amendments in August 2001 and June 2002.

and navi system combination unit, that could also be upgraded with a TV tuner and voice control if the buyer wished) on the V8 machines, and further down again was the automatic air-conditioning controls, the latter being made standard for all cars. At the bottom of the stack was the ashtray and cigarette lighter.

The door furniture was changed to incorporate switch panels for the power seats (complete with a memory function on seat, steering wheel and mirror positions) and power windows, freeing up space aft of the gear selector (now featuring a +/- slot for manual-style shifts) and the redesigned handbrake. By changing the transfer box controls to rocker switches close to the gearbox, this allowed the designers to add a new armrest between the seats, which contained a decent-sized storage compartment and a cupholder.

Front and rear shots of the contemporary G55 AMG.

The OM612 diesel unit.

Inner fittings could be specified in black or grey, with dark grey G-Line wood for the G320, and walnut for the V8 machines. As before, the six-cylinder model had a plain leather steering wheel and gearshift, while the V8 cars had a wood/leather wheel, with the same theme extending to the gearlever and grab handle. The cloth trim was the same as the 1997-style fabric, although leather upholstery was standard on the V8 models – the

seat designs were different, too, as it happens; easily recognised by the new panel shapes and sizes, and leather that was a lot more gathered than before.

Convenience features included automatic light control, an automatic dipping feature on the rearview mirror (surrounded by a new overhead control panel full of switches, from interior light controls to the TELEAID's SOS button), a parking assistance device via sensors on the mirrors, and automatic wiper control, thanks to rain sensors integrated into the wiper units.

One would have thought there was very little else anyone could have wished for, but quite a few options were listed for the G-Wagens, including a green or blue soft top for cabriolet (black was still the norm), a steel spare wheel cover, stainless steel running boards, a bull-bar, a power sunroof for closed cars, reversing sensors, an alarm, a garage door opener integrated into the rearview mirror, a fire extinguisher, a radio/CD upgrade for the G320, a CD-changer, an orthopaedic driver's seat, occasional rear seats (these seats would eventually be outlawed, however, due to seatbelt regulations), tinted rear windows on the estates, a luggage blind, cargo nets, a towbar (a trailer plug socket and wiring was already in place), and mobile phone connection with the TELEAID rescue service.

Domestic pricing at this time saw the G320 swb station wagon at DM 109,581 (equivalent to €56,028), the lwb station wagon at DM 117,976 (€60,320), the G320 cabriolet at DM

Interior of the G270 CDI estate, with the correct steering wheel, seats and wood trim for this grade and the G320 model (the lower red-line on the tachometer shows this to be the diesel machine), although the stereo has been upgraded with a CD player on this particular car. Note also the overhead control panel between the sunvisors.

120, 471 (€61,596), meaning a rise in status for the open model, while both the G400 CDI and G500 short-wheelbase estates came in at DM 138,395 (equivalent to €70,760), the equivalent long-wheelbase estates at DM 146,789 (€75,052), and the G400 CDI and G500 cabriolets at DM 149,284 (€76,328). With the Deutschmark ceasing to be legal tender at the end of 2001, Euro prices will be quoted from now on.

The 2001 Frankfurt Show brought with it yet another G-Wagen update, with the launch of the C270 CDI grade as a new entry-level machine, available in swb or lwb estate guise only. Residing under the bonnet was a straight-five turbocharged OM612 DE27LA common-rail diesel unit with a cubic capacity of 2685cc (88.0 x 88.3mm), borrowed from the 210-series E-Class. With direct-injection and an 18.0:1 compression ratio, it delivered 156bhp (115kW) and a meaty 295lbft of torque.

From the outside, the G270 CDI looked just like the G320, apart from the badging and the black grilles either side of the bonnet, for on the base diesel car there was no vent on the nearside, and the offside one was positioned much closer to the A-post. The interior and equipment levels were much the same as the V6 car, too, with prices starting at €50,228.

Brake Assist (aka BAS) was added for all cars at the same time (the system calculating and applying maximum possible braking pressure in a split second if an emergency stop situation was detected), along with ESP (the Electronic Stability Programme – an evolution of the earlier ASR setup that used the ABS sensors to determine the onset of oversteer or understeer, selectively reducing engine torque or applying one of the rear brakes to bring the car back into control) and the 4ETS electronic traction control system that used the same sensors to detect wheelspin; selecting the low range in the transfer box automatically switched off these driver aids. Oddly, the V8 cars lost their rear anti-roll bar again – it wasn't even listed as an option now.

2002 saw the 354bhp (260kW) AMG lwb station wagon

taken in as part of the official Mercedes-Benz production programme (a very good move considering US G-Wagen imports were just starting up via MBNA), with build figures now listed separately. As well as the regular conversions on swb cars, there was also a limited run 6258cc AMG machine, powered by a 444bhp (270kW) V12, as well as an extended wheelbase XXL Pullman model.

Cars built for the 2003 season onwards inherited new door mirrors with integrated indicator repeater units, which act as a good dating feature as there was little else to report – for once, specifications had just about settled down! However, the AMG cars started adopting rounded exhaust pipes and heavier wheelarch flares that would ultimately cover the new 18-inch wheels and tyres, and a Harman/Kardon sound system was listed as a fresh option.

2004 saw the introduction of side window airbags on the long-wheelbase estates as an option, and a three-point seatbelt arrangement for the centre of the rear bench (the swb cars, including the cabriolet, officially became four-seaters at the same time). There were also a few minor chassis and suspension tweaks, and the option of some attractive new 18-inch six-spoke alloys.

Next up, the G55 AMG Kompressor lwb estate was announced in February 2004, just ahead of its public debut at the Geneva Show. The first prototype had been built in October 2003, as it happens, although the first production models – taking the place of the 354bhp NA car – only started rolling off the lines in June 2004, priced at €108,228.

The handbuilt supercharged engine was based on the old M113 unit used in the earlier G55 AMG model from 1999 onward, but forced induction added a whole new dimension to the motor, as well as 122 more horses. With the same 97.0mm bore as the regular 5-litre lump, the longer 92.0mm stroke gave a larger displacement of 5439cc. Most of the other details were the same as the other contemporary M113 engines, except for the adoption of reinforced bearings, a lower 9.0:1 compression ratio, the helical-screw IHI supercharger, mounted in the vee between the two-cylinder heads, a modified sump, and an air-to-water intercooler. According to the catalogue, the new M113 E55ML engine developed a healthy 476bhp (350kW) and 516lbft

The 2002 AMG XXL Pullman model.

The Baur G-Cabrio XL from the same era, with a power roof on an extended G-Wagen body. Like the regular cabriolet, it featured a full-length soft top, so while it looked like a landaulette, the car was, in fact, a convertible.

of torque – a staggering figure that only the 6.7-litre Bentley could better. Naturally, not all of this power was required all the time, so the ECU was hooked up to an electromagnetic clutch

A G320 lwb station wagon in doctor's clothing. Note the stubby aerial on the roof – something generally adopted by the tin-top cars after the 1998 MY face-lift, although it's not a perfect distinguishing feature, as some cars have it, others don't ...

History in the making: a Mercedes W461 model pictured on The New Silk Road at the end of 2003.

A G400 CDI cabriolet with the optional 18-inch alloys introduced in time for the 2004 season. The tonneau cover seen here was also an option.

A very early G55 AMG Kompressor model, complete with the latest five-spoke alloy wheels, and stainless running boards, which were made part of the supercharged car's package. This new AMG offering could achieve a governed top speed of 130mph (208kph) and dismiss the 0-60 dash in 5.6 seconds!

The swb version of the C270 CDI estate from the same time, also sporting the six-spoke RL6 alloy wheels.

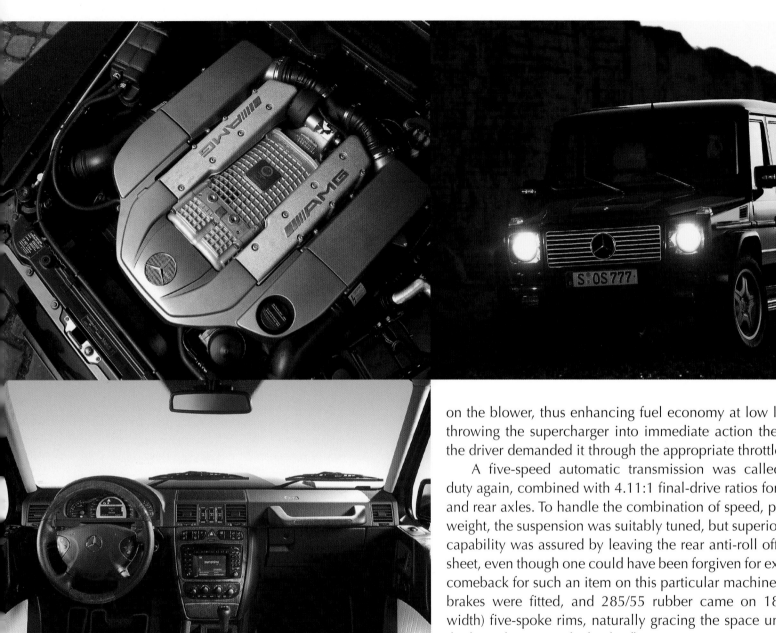

Three pictures released at the time of the G55 AMG Kompressor's announcement, with shots of the engine, the tasteful interior, and a supercharged car in a suitable environment.

on the blower, thus enhancing fuel economy at low loads, but throwing the supercharger into immediate action the moment the driver demanded it through the appropriate throttle action.

A five-speed automatic transmission was called out for duty again, combined with 4.11:1 final-drive ratios for the front and rear axles. To handle the combination of speed, power and weight, the suspension was suitably tuned, but superior off-road capability was assured by leaving the rear anti-roll off the spec sheet, even though one could have been forgiven for expecting a comeback for such an item on this particular machine. Uprated brakes were fitted, and 285/55 rubber came on 18-inch (9J width) five-spoke rims, naturally gracing the space underneath the latest heavyweight fender flares.

Running boards were standard on the supercharged model, and other features like a silver-painted raditor grille, polished waistline moulding inserts and special badging quickly allowed the car to stand out from the crowd. Inside, Designo leather and wood trim parts were employed, as well as stainless treadplates with an illuminated 'AMG' logo, and an AMG instrument panel.

The G-Wagen's silver anniversary was marked by the

250-off Limited Edition model (also known as the Classic 25 outside Germany). Announced in the middle of 2004, this lwb V8 estate (the G500 or G400 CDI could be specified as the base car) featured special 18-inch alloy wheels with five heavy spokes that looked like a modern version of the 1989 alloy rim, black or silver paintwork, a silver-coloured grille, darkened rear windows, an attractive dark wood and black Nappa leather interior, dedicated illuminated treadplates, and special badging. This is a very rare beast indeed ...

Business survey

Not long after the face-lifted G-Wagen's launch, the company withdrew from the US CART racing scene in order to concentrate its efforts on Formula One and touring cars – motorsport arenas in which the Mercedes-Benz marque was enjoying great success. McLaren-Mercedes had won the F1 constructors' title in 1998, with Mika Hakkinen taking the drivers' crown for the UK-based team in 1998 and 1999, while Bernd Schneider was winning everything in sight with the Mercedes CLK in the high-profile German DTM series.

Then, in January, visitors to the 2001 Detroit Show witnessed the official public launch of a couple of new C-Class models and the rapid SLK32 AMG. The all-new R230 SL was announced at the end of July 2001 in readiness for the 2002 Model Year. By adopting the vario-roof design that had made its debut on the R170 SLK, this was the first SL to move away from a traditional

The Models

It's like a candy store for grownups.

THERE'S A FLAVOR for everyone in the 2001 Mercedes-Benz family. In fact, we've never offered more ways to provide you with the exact Mercedes of your dreams. There are 28 distinct models. Powered by eight different engines. In ten particular body styles. There are sedans and cabriolets. Sport utility vehicles. Coupes. Roadsters. Even coupes that can turn into roadsters. And every one of them is a celebration of the Mercedes-Benz tradition: unsurpassed luxury, fine craftsmanship, brilliant engineering, leading-edge style – and truly exceptional value.

C-CLASS Totally redesigned for 2001, the new C could just be the perfect V-6 powered complement to your fun-packed life – with loads of features at an amazingly low price.

SLK-CLASS It's a coupe. It's a roadster. It's both, with a clever retractable hardtop. Choose supercharged-4 or V-6 power, 6-speed stick or 5-speed automatic – and open it up.

CLK-CLASS Lusciously styled in either coupe or cabriolet form, both can be powered by a V-6 or a V-8. Then there's the new CLK55 AMG – the quickest Mercedes ever offered.

E-CLASS There's a reason it's the best-selling import luxury car: it's stylish, refined, secure, powerful, a sedan or a wagon, rear wheel or all-wheel drive, a lot for the money.

S-CLASS "The introduction of an S-Class," Car and Driver said of the 2000 model, "always heralds a new era in technology." For 2001, the S-Class heralds a new era in power too.

SL-CLASS The Mercedes-Benz SL is the ultimate sports GT – a siren song of extraordinary poise, power and panache that won't leave you alone until you get behind the wheel.

CL-CLASS It brought genuine active suspension to the world. The only body structure of its kind too. And the 2001 CL-Class adds new V-12 smoothness and AMG-bred thunder.

M-CLASS Thanks to some of the most rugged construction and sophisticated engineering, the M-Class isn't afraid to venture anywhere – even if it takes a road to get there.

The by now extensive – and still growing – Mercedes-Benz line-up as seen in the US range brochure for the 2001 season. For 2002, there would be another, somewhat familiar SUV, muscling in on the picture Stateside ...

soft top (with separate hardtop) configuration. As well as the debut of the G270 CDI, a face-lifted version of the M-Class was launched at the 2001 Frankfurt Show, along with a gaggle of AMGs – the latter's supercharged engine duly going on to win several awards.

At the end of 2001, with annual car production reaching almost one-and-a-quarter million units, a small ceremony was held at the Sindelfingen plant to commemorate the production of 20,000,000 passenger cars at the plant since the cessation of hostilities in WWII. Not long after, in January 2002, the new W211 E-Class made its debut at the Brussels Show. A couple of weeks later, the company announced the new M271 four-cylinder engine incorporating a number of advanced technologies pointing the way towards the future, with supercharging, intercooling, four valves per cylinder, adjustable camshaft positioning, and Lanchester-type balance shafts being part of the specification. One of the first applications was the C209-type CLK, launched at the Geneva Show; a drophead version followed a year further down the line.

July 2002 saw the sales of DaimlerChrysler's interest in the Eurostar factory in Graz, allowing Magna International to continue building Jeep and Chrysler products, although the M-series contract was cut in the process, meaning it was built exclusively in Alabama soon after. At least the G-Wagen continued to be built in its birthplace.

The 2002 Paris Salon witnessed the launch of face-lifted versions of the W220 S-Class and C215 CL models, as well as new C- and E-Class variants, and a fresh six-cylinder R230 SL model – the SL350. Unlike the early postwar years, when model ranges were few and stayed much the same for decades, there was seemingly no let-up in the stream of new vehicles.

Dr Thomas Weber took over responsibility for R&D on the first day of 2003, while the 2003 Detroit Show, which opened on 11 January, witnessed the launch of the twelve-cylinder SL600 model, as well as that of the E-Class estate.

September 2003 saw the announcement of the 7G-Tronic automatic gearbox, a 7AT unit developed in-house to give better performance and improved economy at the same time. It was first seen on the eight-cylinder cars, but eventually spread to other lines. Hardly pausing for breath, Mercedes displayed the SLR McLaren, Vision CLS study vehicle (eventually launched as the supremely elegant CLS production car in March 2004), a four-door 'smart' model, and a bi-fuel version of the E-Class at the 2003 Frankfurt Show. The bi-fuel car was a sign of the times, although the Stuttgart maker was in fact experimenting with all sorts of 'Green' technology behind the scenes, ranging from fuel cell vehicles to conventional EVs, through to diesel-based hybrids.

Just before Christmas 2003, the company introduced a new clear coat paint using advanced nanotechnology to help prevent coachwork scratches. The E, S, CL, SL and SLK ranges were the first to employ this new paint, although it spread to the other model lines soon after. At the same time, a new four-cam 3.5-litre V6 (M272) engine was presented to the press. Using four-valve per cylinder technology, it was first seen in the new R171 SLK, launched at the 2004 Geneva Show. As it happens, the Swiss event – the 74th to be held – also witnessed the first appearance of the supremely elegant C219 CLS-Class, and a face-lifted version of the 203-series C-Class.

Following on from the launch of the SLR McLaren, the 612bhp SL65 AMG with its award-winning twin-turbo V12 engine made its debut at the 2004 New York Show, which opened in mid-April that year.

The export scene

The last chapter saw the franchised UK and Australian importers turn their backs on the G-Wagen, but things were looking up for the American market, and sales in Japan continued at a steady pace. Indeed, Japan has become an excellent source for secondhand cars in today's marketplace.

Anyway, the big news during the early part of the new millennium was that MBNA would start importing the W463 Geländewagen from October 2001. The G500 lwb station wagon was the only model listed initially, and while it was heavier, smaller in most respects, slower and more expensive than the more mainstream M-Class models, it did at least provide exclusivity (with only 1500 earmarked for the 2002 season, and 200 of those reserved for celebrity users), as well as real off-road talent. The biggest fly in the ointment was the price – at $73,145, it was still a lot of money, but it was also around $55,000 less

The 2002 Model Year G500 for the US market, readily distinguished by its lighting arrangements. Only the lwb station wagon was sold through MBNA in the States.

than Europa had been selling them for, and that doubtless left a fair few unhappy punters in the equation, especially seeing as the MBNA car came with all the regular G500 goodies plus a nine-speaker sound system hooked up to the COMAND unit, complete with CD-changer and a navi system as standard.

For 2003, MBNA decided to import 300 G55 AMG models, at just over $90,000 apiece. Things continued much the same for 2004, although the orthopaedic seats were added to the spec sheet, along with reversing sensors to warn the driver of close objects and the Harman/Kardon audio upgrade. US prices for the 2004 Model Year stood at $76,870 for the G500, and $93,420 for the G55 AMG model.

Japan had the choice of seven models going into the 2001 season, with the G320 and G500 available with swb and lwb estate bodies, as well as cabriolet coachwork; there was also the G55 AMG long-wheelbase station wagon. However, by the end of spring, the open car had been dropped, and the G500 was only listed in lwb guise. For 2002, this left the G320 swb estate at 7,900,000 yen, the lwb version at 8,900,000 yen, the G500L station wagon at 10,500,000 yen, and the AMG car at 13,800,000 yen; all came with left-hand drive at this stage.

As the 2002 Model Year progressed, the price of the lwb machines increased by 300,000 yen, while the swb model went

The North American-spec G55 AMG for the 2004 season.

up by 400,000 yen, at a time when the Range Rover Vogue was just under 10,000,000 yen. Things stayed the same then until the spring of 2004, when only a slight increase was applied to the range – the cheapest G-Wagen was now 8,715,000 yen, while the ML350 was only 5,775,000 yen, and also available in right-hand drive.

Military Matters #3

The G-Wagen was basking in its newfound popularity in showrooms at this time, and also found favour in new and existing military circles. The German army took delivery of another large order for an open ESK Wolf with rear seats early in 2000, and this was developed into the lightly armoured LIV or AGF Serval that entered service in 2004. The LAPV Enok is a more heavily armoured closed variant that began its military career in 2008, with over 300 built so far.

Another interesting variant emerged in 2006, this being the limited run Panhard built for the French Special Forces. It was based on the Greenline W461 with full-time 4WD and a G270 CDI engine, although since 2008 the Panhard PVP (aka the A4 AVL) is now considered France's replacement for the old P4. There is also a Force Trax model built in India, adding to the number of nameplates used on the military machines. In fact, we should mention here that Force Motors (previously known as Bajaj Tempo) have been building an SUV based on G-Wagen technology since the late-1990s, although the bodies are locally built.

Across the Atlantic, Canada ordered well over 1000 cars, which could have their light armour removed depending on the mission scenario. In addition, the US Marine Corps ordered 150 G-Wagens to replace its ageing Desert Patrol Vehicle line, and the company received another commission for almost 400 cars to be used by the US military based in Europe.

Switzerland began renewing its Puch fleet with G300 CDI models recently, and Algeria has started building CKD machines. Meanwhile, nations as far flung as Finland, Sweden, Poland, Hungary, Bulgaria, countries born out of the former Yugoslavia, Egypt, Saudi Arabia, Kuwait, Iraq, Mexico and Indonesia have all created fleets of G-Wagens for military use. Even Russia has a few, and they can often be seen as escort vehicles for the President and Prime Minister. Australia has also fallen under the Geländewagen's spell, its government eventually taking delivery of more than 2000 vehicles of varying types, including a number of rare 6x6 models, with a pair of driven axles at the rear.

The ESK Wolf in a Rheinmetall AG press shot.

Canadian Land Forces Command soldiers pictured in convoy in the US during a joint-exercise conducted in 2008.

G-Wagon 280 CDI 4x4.
Mercedes-Benz Military Vehicles.

Cover of a catalogue produced in 2008 to promote military sales, this particular one featuring the 3-litre V6-engined car. In military vehicles, the 270GD, 280GD and 340GD had given way to the G270 CDI, G280 CDI and the G300 CDI chassis in the new millennium.

Just a small selection of the Geländewagen-based vehicles supplied to Australia's ADF recently. The 6x6 models have been made available to the public via AMG, although it should be noted that a few specialist twin-axle conversions exist on the W460 chassis.

Rivalry abounds

Those thinking of buying a luxury SUV had more choice than ever at the start of the new century. The all-new Range Rover was launched for 2002 under Ford management. Then, the Discovery 3 was duly released in April 2004, followed by the Range Rover Sport, and the Freelander 2 and face-lifted Defender in time for the 2007 Model Year. By now, 4,000,000 Land Rovers had been built, proving the UK company was right to have faith in the SUV all those years ago.

Closer to home, Volkswagen and Porsche joined forces to create the VW Touareg and Porsche Cayenne, which also provided the basis for the 2006 MY Audi Q7. A remarkable evolution has been witnessed with these cars, featuring a breathtaking range of engines and grades, from lowly five-cylinder diesels to turbocharged V8s and even a 6-litre W12. BMW also entered the ring, first via the US-built 2000 Model Year X5, and then the 2004 Model Year X3, made by Magna Steyr in Graz.

The Porsche Cayenne, launched as a 2003 model, offered the G-Wagen some serious competition. This is the turbocharged V8 model.

A fourth generation Mitsubishi Pajero in five-door guise.

At Toyota, the J100 Land Cruiser (and its Lexus LX equivalent) were replaced by the J200-series in 2007, while in the meantime, the Prado – which had previously been nothing much more than a marketing name – had gained a unique body and a Lexus equivalent (the GX line); there was also an FJ Cruiser, based on the Prado floorpan, although sales are now almost at an end. The second generation Harrier was released in 2003 (also sold as a Lexus RX model), and the new Highlander/Kluger made its debut at the 2007 Chicago Show.

The fourth generation Mitsubishi Pajero (aka the Montero or Shogun) made its debut at the 2006 Paris Salon, sold in three- and five-door estate format, and since 2001, was now joined by the smaller Airtrek (or Outlander). The second generation – making its way into the 2006 Model Year programme – dropped the Airtrek moniker completely, and received a number of awards. The Delica took on more of an SUV image, too, although it was still an MPV in reality.

While the Patrol (Safari) kept going, gaining an Armada and Infiniti QX56 variant along the way, Nissan launched the Xterra at the turn of the century, basically as a replacement for the little Terrano. However, the latter kept going until 2006, and only then did the second generation Xterra (the N50 of 2004) have

the showroom to itself. The compact X-Trail was released in late-2000, being renewed in 2007, and the full-size Murano took a bow as a 2003 model, with a new generation already being fielded by the tail-end of 2007. There was also a sporty Infiniti FX for 2003, and a fresh Pathfinder line for the 2004 season, which, like its predecessor, was also available in Infiniti guise.

While Isuzu dropped out of the passenger car business, Honda got in on the act with the CR-V of 1997 vintage, but the all-new 2002 models were more successful, and became an attractive proposition after the 2005 face-lift. The launch of the third generation (2007 MY) saw the CR-V come of age, and gain Acura badging at the same time. The HR-V was another line, sold from 1998, but allowed to die off before being revived in 2014 as the rather small Vezel (the HR-V name was used in export markets). The Element was new for the 2003 season, but only lasted until 2011, although the similar-looking second generation Pilot continued the concept.

At Mazda, the Hiroshima firm introduced its full-size CX-9 and slightly smaller CX-7 in 2006; Daihatsu continued with its small kei SUV, as did Suzuki, with the Jimny taking on a cult status. Meanwhile, the Escudo (Vitara) was given a new lease of life for 2006, and the second generation Subaru Forester (launched in 2002) was superseded by a third, made ready for the 2008 season. There was also the 2006 MY Tribeca, which was more of an SUV in looks than the Outback, but this had gone by the spring of 2014.

Over in the States, the Hummer H1 was joined by the equally huge H2 in 2002, and then the H3 for the 2006 Model Year. The latter, with straight-five or V8 power, was built by General Motors, but the Hummer brand ran out of steam in May 2010. As it happens, the Mercury marque was killed-off by Ford soon after, bringing an end to cars like the Mountaineer and Mariner.

On the subject of Ford, the second generation Expedition was launched at the Detroit Show in 2002 with big V8s under the bonnet, running alongside the 2000 MY Excursion, and spawning the second generation Lincoln Navigator. However, the timing was wrong for such beasts, and the Excursion was quickly dropped, along with a short-lived Lincoln Aviator model. Meanwhile, the 2001 Ford Escape (or Maverick) provided the basis for the Mazda Tribute, as well as the Mercury Mariner we've already mentioned, with the second generation being launched at the 2006 LA Show. There was also a fresh Explorer model for 2002, with a far more modern replacement for the 2006 season, and the all-new 2007 Edge, which duly spawned a Lincoln MKX variant. We shouldn't forget the Ford Australia-made Territory either ...

General Motors continued with the Cadillac Escalade, replacing the original with a new generation classed as a 2002 model, and available in two wheelbase lengths. This gave way to the GMT900 version for 2007, with hybrid drivetrains soon making their way into the line-up. There was also a Cadillac SRX by this time, too. The GM men continued fielding the Chevrolet Suburban, as well as the Tahoe (and the equivalent GMC Yukon), with the early 2007 Model Year refit bringing modernity to the nameplate as well as a hybrid power alternative. As for new lines, there was a Chevrolet TrailBlazer, the Chevy Equinox debuted in 2004 (the Pontiac Torrent being available as a badge-engineered version), and the GMC Acadia went on sale in December 2006, while Buick had the short-lived Rainier, which was replaced by the Enclave in mid-2007.

The Jeep Wrangler was updated via the JK model that took a bow at the 2006 Detroit Show, not long after the new WK Grand Cherokee was launched. The compact Patriot and Compass models also joined the Jeep line-up, while the second generation Dodge Durango was launched as a 2004 model, with a short-lived Chrysler Aspen version joining it for 2007.

Even Sweden entered the fray, with the Volvo XC90 being launched at the 2002 Detroit Show. But what's the point of all this column space on other cars, you may ask? Well, when we started tracking the history of the G-Wagen, there were literally just a handful of SUVs on the market. These sections on the competition help put things into perspective, illustrating the trends, and, not least, the sheer number of new machines helps to confirm that the SUV had come of age as a breed. It also shows that while others were moving forward at a rapid pace, stylistically in particular, the Geländewagen stayed true to its roots, and you'll find there are now as many buying it for its retro looks as the badge on the nose.

Refresher course

Having just looked at rivals, interestingly, one of the strongest was fielded from within, for the new W164 M-Class SUV was launched at the 2005 Detroit Show. Like its predecessor, it was built in the Alabama plant, but the body was bigger all-round in its latest form. Notwithstanding, the move to a unit construction (or monocoque) shell saved a lot of weight, so the extra bulk was cancelled out, albeit at the cost of off-road capability. In fact, this was one of the most telling points in terms of buyer profiles – the modern SUV had become more focused on image and practicality than mud-plugging finesse. A range of V6 and V8 petrol and diesel engines were offered, along with an AMG V8. The 4MATIC drivetrain was there from the off, and air suspension was listed as a separate option.

The second generation M-Class (W164), that was introduced at the 2005 Detroit Show. Sales began in the Spring.

With all the recent activity on new model lines, and the numerous changes applied to the G-Wagen itself during the previous months, not surprisingly, there were no major revisions for the W463 line-up for the 2005 season, although in the spring of that year, another 18-inch wheel came online with five spokes and a ribbed rim – a number of catalogue illustrations show this alloy wheel as standard fare on the G400 CDI and

The 2006 Model Year G500 in lwb estate guise. This car has the Ashtaroth wheels, which had become an accessory in Germany by this time.

G500, although the old 18-inch Ashtaroth and the later optional six-spoke alloys continued to run alongside it, which can make things confusing.

Actually, it should be noted that a key decision was made on the future of the series at this time. Dr Zetsche (head of the Mercedes brand then, but about to move up the management ladder) announced in November 2005 that production would continue, and at the Austrian factory, too, silencing the rumour mill once and for all. With around 185,000 cars already built, Magna Steyr's boss, Manfred Remmel, noted: "The decision to continue the production of the G-Class is not only of great economic relevance, but also of historical relevance. This classic off-roader is inseparably connected with the identity of our plant in Graz."

Meanwhile, the 2006 Model Year G-Wagens featured a maintenance-free particulate filter on all diesel grades. February 2006 saw the European announcement of the Grand Edition long-wheelbase station wagon, which was available with V8 petrol or V8 diesel power, and a special Allanite Grey Magno paint finish if customers wanted it. Natural leather trim combined with a silk wood trim to give the interior a unique aura, while dedicated treadplates and badging, plus a set of five-spoke alloys, finished off the €86,536 package. Then, from July 2006, in a bid to stave off the perceived threat from Porsche Cayenne catalogue figures, engine output in the G55 AMG Kompressor model was uprated to 500bhp (368kW), thanks to a black box tweak that had already been applied to cars such as the Benz SL a couple of years earlier. Bigger changes were afoot, though ...

For the 2007 season proper, the two existing G270 CDI and G400 CDI grades were replaced by a single G320 CDI one.

Exterior and interior of the Grand
Edition of spring 2006 vintage.

A Mercedes-Benz Guard model, with the rail above the windscreen being a quick identifying feature, and a detail shot of the bullet-proof glass. The G-Class version of the factory's special protection series had been introduced in 1999, offering B4, B6 and B7 levels of security, the latter being able to fend off bullets from the world's most powerful rifles.

Mercedes-Benz UK registered this supercharged car in 2006 for publicity and to test the water with regard to importation. *Auto Express* noted: "Curiously, a spell behind the wheel of the G-Wagen is great fun. Few cars have such character, or road presence. The roar of the exhausts brings almost any high street to a complete stop, while the acceleration is amazing. But it's only enjoyable in small doses – as a long-term prospect, this G-Wagen is just too extreme."

The G55 AMG Kompressor model gained some extra horses under the bonnet in the summer of 2006.

Detail shot of the AMG car's front wing, giving a good view of the extended wheelarch flares, the standard Style II wheels for the time, and the subdued badging.

Engine bay of the G320 CDI grade.

As it happens, a few 270s were built in 2007 to clear orders in-hand, although the 400 run finished in 2006, as full-scale production of the G320 CDI officially began in September 2006 – two-and-a-half months after the car's initial announcement, and five months after the first prototypes were built.

The G320 CDI was powered by the all-alloy OM642 DE30LA V6 dohc turbo-diesel, with four valves per cylinder and common-rail direct-injection. With an 83.0mm bore and 92.0mm stroke, the resulting cubic capacity was 2987cc, and combined with a 17.7:1 compression ratio, this gave 224bhp (165kW) and a massive 398lbft of torque. The unit was hooked up to a seven-speed 7G-Tronic automatic transmission, with 4.38 axles specified at the front and rear, and the dual-range transfer box in the middle. In high ratio, with its new 16-inch wheels (basically smaller replicas of the familiar Ashtaroth rim found on the pre-2005 G500s), the 2445kg (5379lb), G320 CDI long-wheelbase estate was capable of 111mph (177kph).

Regarding the newcomer, the G320 CDI swb estate was priced at €64,148 on introduction, with the long-wheelbase station wagon at €69,020, and the cabriolet at €69,948; the AMG model was listed at €113,332 at this time. As a matter of interest, German VAT increased from 16 to 19 per cent on the first day of 2007, which naturally necessitated a new price list.

According to the official factory records filed with the VDA, production of the G320 ended in 2006, too, although it's not really surprising, as build numbers were always small – at the end of the day, someone paying the kind of money asked for a basic G-Wagen shouldn't be worrying about a few extra pennies on fuel, and it's also just as likely that, in the real world, fuel consumption on the 5-litre model probably wasn't all that much different, given the power-to-weight ratios involved. (This was especially true at this stage of the proceedings, as the 2007 G500s inherited the electronically-controlled 7G-Tronic gearbox found on the V6 diesel model; the AMG variant retained its old five-speed unit.)

Anyway, all 2007 MY machines gained improved seat cushions, and more powerful xenon headlights and oval-shaped foglights that followed the road, although both sets of lights sat in the old housings, so one had to look carefully to spot the difference – the new foglights were, perhaps, the easiest thing to zoom in on, as their surround was now body colour rather than black. Scratch-resistant nano-particle paints and a hard-wearing synthetic Artico leather upholstery package (matched with plastic floor coverings) were available for those who used their cars in the harsh environments for which they were ultimately intended.

Various views of the new G320 CDI model, including the car's interior. Note the vents on both sides of the front wings, and the new 16-inch alloy wheels employed on this grade only, shod with 265/70 rubber.

corners, one for oil pressure and the other for fuel, and again with chrome outer accent rings; as before, the AMG model had unique gauges, with white centres on the two main dials and sportier graphics for the calibrations.

The centre stack was redesigned at the same time, with squared-off switchgear (all the same buttons, just with a different appearance), a new COMAND APS unit to allow a bigger screen for the navigation system (fitted as standard on the G500 and G55 AMG Kompressor models – the G320 CDI had an Audio 20 radio/CD unit), and fresh HVAC controls to match. There was also a 12V socket added to the passenger footwell, as we had well and truly entered the age of mobile electrical gadgets, and heated seats became a no-cost option (NCO) on the base car.

On the subject of options, new items included a reversing camera for vehicle's fitted with the COMAND head unit, a tyre pressure monitor with information displayed in the screen between the speedometer and tachometer, a sports exhaust (like that fitted to the AMG car) for the G500 lwb estate model, and

From April 2007, the Geländewagen range was treated to a mild face-lift that included new LED-style tail-light clusters, and a revised interior design. The driver was confronted by a new multi-function steering wheel and a new gauge pack, with a speedo and tachometer either side of the display screen, both finished with a chrome bezel. Smaller gauges were added in the

Close-up of the xenon headlights fitted to all 2007 MY G-Wagens.

The back of a G320 CDI providing us with a clear view of the rear light clusters introduced in the spring of 2007.

The revised steering wheel and fascia on a G320 CDI with the optional wood/leather trim upgrade (standard on the V8 cars, but the diesel model's wheel was usually all-leather). Note the latest centre console design, and the 12V socket to the right of it.

some fresh upholstery choices, including the Artico synthetic leather we mentioned earlier and Cognac leather to go with the existing Black and Grey hide shades. As usual, more changes were in store, but for now, let's look at what was happening outside Germany ...

The export markets

The US market was picking up nicely on the back of SUV fever and a bubbly atmosphere that supported luxury purchases, even if they were really beyond reach. The G500 was priced at $78,900 in 2005, with the AMG car at $101,400; both were sold in long-wheelbase station wagon guise only, and both came fully-loaded with just about everything that Mercedes had to offer.

A 2008 Model Year G320 CDI lwb estate.

As such, options were few and far between Stateside, and apart from a voice control system for the COMAND unit and a set of navigation CDs, the only other things available were a pair of Designo packages, priced at $6525 on the G500 and $5150 on the G55 AMG Kompressor model. The Designo Espresso Edition featured Mocha Black paint, contrasting black and brown Nappa leather trim with a touch of dark grey added for effect, maple wood pieces, and special carpeting. The Designo Silver Edition was much the same, apart from its silver paint and black and charcoal trim.

The marketing folks in North America decided to base the 2006 G-Wagen on the Grand Edition package, so the five-spoke alloy wheels seen on the European limited run model were adopted, even before German buyers had the chance to see them! Things continued much the same in the States for the 2007 season, although for 2008, MBNA added the rear camera and tyre pressure monitor to the spec sheet, as well as the TeleAid feature. By now, the G500 stood at $86,200, with the G55 AMG $109,900, although prices went up by $2000 in the spring of 2008.

Another diesel model showing its high level of off-road capability.

Cover from the American G-Class catalogue for the 2005 season, featuring the G500 model for its theme.

Japanese press picture showing the 2008 Model Year G500 with the five-spoke alloy wheels introduced as standard on the non-AMG V8 cars in the spring of 2005. Generally speaking, Japan followed Germany's lead on its choice of alloy wheels.

Front and rear views of the 2008 G500 for the US market.

Great Britain and Australia were still out of the game, of course, but the same four estates continued in Japan (the swb G320, lwb G320, lwb G500 and the AMG machine), with prices now ranging from 8,967,000 yen to 16,065,000 yen for 2005 and 2006. Indeed, not until the spring of 2007 were there any significant changes, when a new two-car line-up was adopted, as per America, and reflecting the loss of the G320 in the European market. The G500 was now 12,100,000 yen (about the same as the GL550 4MATIC), while the AMG model commanded 16,500,000 yen, although prices had increased by around four per cent by the same time the following year.

Company news

The W164 M-Class made its European debut at the 2005 Geneva Show, lining up alongside a face-lifted C209 CLK series, a new B-Class, and the Maybach 57S. This was certainly a busy period for the company, as a few weeks later, the new R-Class was launched at the New York Show in the States – like the B-Class, this model had first been shown as a concept car at the 2004 Paris Salon.

The Mercedes-Benz stand at the 2005 Frankfurt Show had a lot of exhibits focusing on hybrid technology and the AMG brand, especially seeing as the latter had only just unveiled its new 6.2-litre M156 V8 engine at the time. This high-revving 510bhp NA unit started finding its way into cars – including the ML63 AMG – during the autumn, and duly went on to win several awards. The show also witnessed the public debut of the all-new W221 S-Class, featuring all manner of leading edge technologies, along with a new M273 32v V8, and a special feature to celebrate ten years of Designo customizing.

Jürgen Schrempp stepped down as Chairman of the Board of Management at DaimlerChrysler AG at the end of 2005, with Dr Dieter Zetsche taking his place at the helm from the first day of 2006. Shortly after Zetsche took up his new position, the new GL-Class full-size SUV was launched at the 2006 Detroit Show, along with the eco-friendly BlueTec diesel powertrain.

The Alabama-built X164 GL was actually touted by many as the replacement for the W463, but we only need walk into a Mercedes showroom to learn this was not the case. Anyway, this was a bigger machine than the M-Class, albeit based on

The Mercedes-Benz GL-Class further extended the marque's growing SUV line-up.

the same technology, with a pair of petrol engines and a pair of diesels offered initially, all linked to a 4MATIC drivetrain.

2006 Geneva Show premieres included the CLS63 AMG and CLK63 AMG models, as well as a face-lifted version of the R230 SL. In the following month, the face-lifted 211-series E-Class made its debut in New York, and the season was rounded off nicely with the handbuilt 150-off Mercedes-Benz SLR McLaren 722 Edition going on sale in July 2006. A few days later, the AMG Performance Studio opened for business, providing greater individuality for customers, as well as marketing limited run models.

The new C216-series CL made its public debut at the 2006 Paris Salon, where the S63 AMG and CL63 AMG models also made quite a splash. Soon after, in November, when the Maybach 62S was launched, the 25,000,000th postwar Mercedes car was built.

Another Popemobile was delivered to the Vatican at the end of 2007: this one, with special open coachwork, was based on the G500 chassis.

The 2007 Detroit Show, which opened in the middle of January, witnessed the Vision GL420 BlueTec concept taking a bow, along with the launch of the new 204-series C-Class. Variants followed quickly, with a string of four-wheel drive models arriving in the summer, and a line of estates later in the year. Meanwhile, soon after the New York Show, where a number of exclusive AMG products made their debut, plans were laid on the table to terminate the uneasy Chrysler partnership. A deal was ultimately concluded in early August, with the Chrysler contingent leaving the boardroom in Stuttgart with immediate effect. On 4 October, shareholders agreed to the renaming of the company – it becoming known as Daimler AG. The final ties

between the German and American firms were severed once and for all in the spring of 2009.

Meanwhile, the SLR McLaren Roadster had been launched in July 2007, taking the place of the coupe version in the showrooms and the Woking production facilities. But it was the first couple of months of 2008 that represented a really busy period for the executives in charge of the Mercedes-Benz brand. At the end of January, the face-lifted SLK made its debut at the Detroit Show, taking centre stage alongside a pair of GLK concept cars. As the US show was coming to an end, the CLC-Class was launched at the Mercedes-Benz Fashion Week in Berlin, taking the place of the earlier C-Class coupe models.

The Vision GLK Freeside concept car at the 2008 Detroit Show.

The production version of the GLK-Class, which was perfectly capable of earning its SUV badge with the so-called Off-Road Package option.

In the following month, the Maybach Landaulet (first shown as a prototype in November 2007) was launched, and then, from 6-16 March, everyone was full of smiles at the Geneva Show – with face-lifted versions of the R230-series SL and C219-series CLS coming online, plus a European debut for the SLK and a GLK Hybrid concept, there was plenty to be cheerful about. The SL63 AMG took a bow with an advanced seven-speed gearbox aimed at increasing driving pleasure, while four-wheel drive systems and the Blue Efficiency direct-injection system also made a splash in Switzerland.

It was somewhat ironic that just as the new Mercedes look was launched, Peter Pfeiffer, the man behind it, retired as head of styling, handing over the reins to Gorden Wagener – born in Essen in September 1968, he was one of the youngest design chiefs ever appointed in the motor industry.

Anyway, following the conclusion of the Geneva Show, three BlueTec SUV lines (the ML320 BlueTec, GL320 BlueTec and a revised 164-series M-Class) were displayed at the New York Show, and April 2008 – the same month as the A- and B-Class models were launched – saw the official launch of the GLK-Class at the Beijing Show. Going on sale in the autumn,

the X204 GLK estate filled the gap created by the M-Class going bigger, although it's perhaps fairer to categorise the vehicle as a CUV rather than a pure SUV. In reality, from a sales point of view, this was a good move, although a special package allowed the car to be transformed into a more serious off-roader, and it was a lot closer than the R-Class ever was when it came to legitimately being able to don an SUV moniker. There was still one car with SUV credentials that no-one was able to question – the G-Wagen – and it continued to be developed against the odds. The next chapter takes up the story at the start of the 2009 Model Year ...

Another new era

After three-and-a-half decades, and a somewhat rocky start to life, the G-Wagen's following is stronger than ever. Although a few still get used hard, as they were meant to, today, they are the choice of Hollywood's finest and Arabian royalty rather than those needing an off-road tool; seen in prominent roles as diverse as just about every rap video known to mankind to the funeral processions of North Korea's Kim Jong-il, and Singapore's Lee Kuan Yew.

By 2008, the SUV was king – we only need look at the next section in this chapter and compare it to an earlier one on the Geländewagen's competitors to see that. Then, all of a sudden, things began to go dreadfully wrong. The financial crisis, caused largely by easy credit but symbolised by the Lehman Shock, sent shares crashing at the tail-end of 2008, and sales of luxury goods were put on hold after the ensuing credit squeeze. But this wasn't the only problem. In 1999, with petrol at $1.20 a gallon in the US, no-one cared about alternative fuels and EVs, and average prices were even lower two years later. In 2004, the $2.00 gallon arrived, but when it shot up to $3.00 the following year in the wake of Hurricane Katrina, sales of large SUVs blipped immediately. When petrol hit $4.00 a gallon in 2008, there were scores of recorded instances of folks in the States – and elsewhere – simply abandoning their big SUVs and other costly-to-run cars at the side of the road, or dropping them off on dealer forecourts to take anything they could get for them. Political pressure brought the cost of fuel back down to $1.60 a gallon before the end of the year, as America's auto-makers had all invested heavily in keeping its gas-guzzler mentality alive (cornering a market in the process through slick advertising and gasoline prices that had been kept artificially low), and stagnant sales was the last thing the economy needed. However, a lot of damage had been done by this double-whammy attack on large, expensive vehicles, that's for sure ...

The 200,000th G-Wagen built was a 2009 Model Year car. At this time, domestic sales still accounted for almost a third of production, with one in five G-Class models finding their way to America (the USA and United Arab Emirates provided the largest market for AMG variants). Meanwhile, thanks to Europe's love affair with CI engines, 40 per cent of cars built had diesel power.

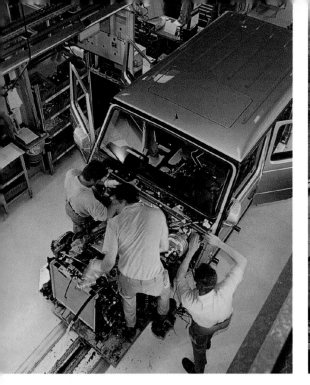

Contemporary G-Wagen production, and a view of the Graz factory. Amazingly, given the way things have moved on in engineering circles in recent years, the car's panels are created still using the original stamping tools from 1979, and there's an almost handmade approach to the build-up, with 6400 spot welds and lengthy seam welding holding the 870 steel body components together. Rustproofing and painting the body is followed by its mating to the separate chassis, before assembly of the interior, and so on. Each vehicle takes around ten days to complete before a PDI test.

The rival camps

Following its sale to Tata in 2008, Land Rover continued to release new models, including the new Discovery (aka LR4), the sporting Range Rover Evoque, and the L405 Range Rover, which made its debut at the 2012 Paris Salon. More recently, the Land Rover Discovery Sport has kept the brand in the headlines. Volvo put a new XC90 into production in 2014, and at the 2015 Frankfurt Show, we witnessed the launch of the Jaguar F-Pace and Bentley Bentayga, while Maserati have promised the Levante, bringing more prestige to the SUV/CUV market sector ...

Meanwhile, amongst the German giants, the second generation Porsche Cayenne was launched at the 2010 Geneva Show, with more diesels and even a hybrid range coming online eventually, which was definitely a sign of the times. The VW version was released at roughly the same time, but the loss of the W12 engine was another sign of the times perhaps, while the Audi Q7 took on the more exotic powerplants, including a

The 2016 Bentley Bentayga.

162

500bhp (368kW) twelve. A second generation Q7 was launched recently, the big SUV by this time being augmented by the smaller Q5 and Q3 models. Volkswagen's compact SUV was called the Tiguan (related to the Q3), and Porsche released the Q5-based Macan at the end of 2013. At BMW, a new X5 was released in 2006, followed by the sporty X6, while the 2010 MY X1 filled the entry-level, and the second generation X3 was launched at the 2010 Paris Salon (but now made in America rather than Austria). More recently, the third generation (type F15) X5 made its debut at the 2013 Frankfurt Show, the X4 took a bow at the 2014 New York Show, and a new X6 (F16) was released at the tail-end of 2014.

At Toyota, the J200 Land Cruiser and its Lexus LX stablemate continued thanks to a few mild face-lifts, while the next generation Prado was introduced for the 2010 season, along with the Lexus GX460 clone. Just before that, the third generation Harrier (and its equivalent Lexus RX models) had been introduced, with hybrids duly coming on line, while the XU50 Highlander made its international debut at the 2013 New York Show. Mitsubishi's Pajero continued much the same, other than a mild face-lift, but the third generation Outlander made its debut at the 2012 Geneva Show, taking on hybrid technology as the seasons passed, while the RVR (or ASX) lingered in the background, moving from basic estate to a crossover vehicle in 2010.

The 2015 model Cadillac Escalade making its debut at a specially-staged event in New York at the tail-end of 2013.

Nissan launched a second generation Infiniti FX at the 2008 Geneva Show, which is now called the QX70. It also released a new Patrol (Safari) in 2010 and a new R52 Pathfinder a couple of years later, with the luxury grades both carrying Infiniti badging in certain markets (the QX80 and the QX60, which replaced the JX). While the end of the Xterra was recorded on one hand, the new X-Trail was released at the end of 2013, and the third generation Murano made its debut at the 2014 New York Show, with production of the latter based in America. Honda launched the attractive Crosstour in 2009, then a new CR-V for 2012, along with an Acura MDX, and a fresh Pilot model at the 2015 Chicago Show.

Subaru announced its fourth generation Forester in 2012, and the XV Crosstrek as an alternative to the Outback; the crossover (CUV) Exiga should provide another SUV line in due course. The Mazda CX-7 disappeared in 2012, although the CX-9 continues, being joined by the 2013 Model Year CX-5. Recently, a slightly smaller Escudo was launched to run alongside the face-lifted original, for those with less serious off-road needs. For those wanting something smaller still, there was always the SX4 S-Cross, or even the Suzuki Jimny or Daihatsu Terios.

Compared to the kei-cars, greater threats to the G-Wagen were now being posed by the likes of the Chinese BYD range and Korea's SsangYong Rexton and Actyon Sports, or the Kia Sorento, while India's Mahindra (which had started out building Jeeps under licence, with the Thar being the current incarnation) had cars like the XUV500, as well as the older Scorpio and Bolero lines, and Tata its Safari.

At Ford, the third generation Expedition (U324, or U326 in Lincoln Navigator guise) had been introduced for 2007, again with V8 power, although a 2015 MY face-lift saw a move towards a more economical V6 for the Ford. The compact Kuga was another sign that the Americans were at last walking away from gas-guzzlers, with this model actually becoming the third generation Ford Escape in 2012, which was also the basis for the Lincoln MKC. The fifth generation Explorer (U502) was released in July 2010, and there was a new Edge (and Lincoln MKX sister car) for 2015. The MKT and MKC rounded off the Lincoln SUV line-up.

General Motors introduced a new range of Buick CUVs with SUV looks to join the Rainier, along with an attractive new Cadillac SRX for 2010, and the fourth generation Cadillac Escalade, which went on sale in the spring of 2014. There was also a Chevrolet Traverse for 2009, based on the GMC Acadia platform, a second generation Equinox (also badged as a GMC Terrain, which replaced the Pontiac Torrent), a new TrailBlazer, a 12th generation Chevrolet Suburban, and a new Chevy Tahoe (aka GMC Yukon), sold as an early 2015 model.

Chrysler gave the Dodge Durango a new identity in 2010, basing it on the fourth generation Jeep Grand Cherokee, which had made its debut at the 2009 New York Show. Meanwhile, the Jeep Wrangler is still going strong, along with the Patriot and Compass, and the small Renegade is a recent addition to the line, brought about by Chrysler's links with Fiat of Italy.

Never before had there been such a wide range of SUVs to choose from, yet the G-Wagen soldiered on, garnering sales despite the financial woes of the world, and as if it still had nothing more than the Range Rover and the odd 'Yank Tank' to compete against. The success of the German oldtimer will doubtless confuse marketing students for many decades to come!

The 2009 MY face-lift

The next phase in the evolution of the Geländewagen can be pegged at summer 2008, for at the end of May, the Stuttgart firm announced its 2009 Model Year changes. Falling into line with the other Mercedes road cars, the radiator grille was simplified somewhat, with the multiple horizontal slats being replaced by three bolder ones on all cars. In addition, the G500 gained a new set of 18-inch RM7 alloy wheels, featuring five double spokes, during the face-lift. Inside, the audio units, now featuring a built-in CD-changer and telephone keypad, were further upgraded with a hands-free system for mobile phones and an external music storage device interface, allowing the steering wheel buttons to be used on iPods and so on; the rear interior lighting was modified, too, allowing reading lights for rear passengers.

On the mechanical front, it was again the G500 that benefited the most, inheriting a brand new M273 V8 that delivered 387bhp (285kW) and 391lbft of torque. The M273 had first been presented to the press in June 2005, and made

A face-lifted G500 with the new grille
design shared by all 2009 MY cars
(albeit in body colour on the non-AMG
models), and the latest 18-inch RM7
alloys fitted to the NA V8 machine, the
7.5J rim playing host to 265/60 rubber.
As it happens, the 18-inch Ashtaroth
wheels were still available as an
accessory, as were the 16-inch Atik rims.

A cutaway drawing of the M273 V8 with a 7G-Tronic automatic transmission tacked onto the back.

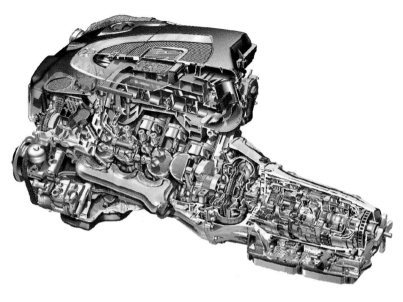

its debut in the W221 S-Class that was introduced at the 2005 Frankfurt Show. When used in the G-Class application, the 32v four-cam unit featured a 98.0mm bore and a 90.5mm stroke to give 5461cc, and a 10.0:1 compression ratio. But it was the addition of variable valve timing that made this engine special, bringing forth huge increases in output that were way beyond what would have been possible through the larger displacement on its own. Indeed, to put things into perspective, the 24v M113 engine was pumping out 60bhp per litre in the G-Wagen, while its 32v counterpart was delivering 71bhp per litre. Despite this, the meaty section of the torque curve continued for longer, and fuel economy was basically unchanged – largely thanks to the 7G-Tronic gearbox. For the record, the G500 was specified with 4.38:1 axles at the front and rear (the same as the contemporary AMG model), with the familiar 0.87:1 and 2.16:1 cogs in the central transfer box.

The domestic price list for 2009 saw the short-wheelbase G320 CDI estate at €68,425, the long-wheelbase version at €73,542, and the cabriolet at €74,494. The G500 equivalents were listed at €86,156, €91,392 and €92,344, respectively.

The 2009 Model Year AMG car, with its chrome grille and new 19-inch alloy wheel design.

The W463-based Edition 30 model.

The AMG model didn't escape the face-lift, incidentally, gaining a fraction more power (507bhp/373kW) and the same three-bar grille design, but with chrome-plating rather than a body colour finish, along with new extra-wide 19-inch five-spoke alloys fitted with 275/55 all-weather tyres. It also sported a Hill Start Assist feature, to prevent the vehicle rolling backwards if the driver failed to properly time the use of the handbrake. The flagship car was priced at €121,618 and, as before, came in long-wheelbase estate guise only. Sales of the face-lifted cars, as per the other two G-Wagen grades, started in September 2008.

In the middle of February 2009, the company announced a pair of vehicles to celebrate the 30th anniversary of the Geländewagen – the Edition 30 and the Edition 30 PUR, both based on the long-wheelbase estate body, but with the latter in the W461 series rather than the W463 camp. The W463-type Edition 30 was distinguished by its Designo Platinum Black paintwork, five-spoke alloy wheels (similar in design to those used on the 2004 Classic 25), commemorative badging on the wings, and Designo interior trim, combining chablis-coloured leather and anthracite poplar wood. Please refer to the 'Workers' sidebar, overleaf, for details on the Edition 30 PUR model.

The Workers

The W461-series had been allowed to fall by the wayside when the 290GDT run came to an end in late-2001, although, as we mentioned earlier, a few were still being built to special order for governments, although mainly for military use.

From October 2002, the company started offering a W461 Worker range in certain markets, now using the same full-time 4WD system as the W463s. Power was provided by the 156bhp OM612 diesel unit used in the G270 CDI grade, although the line-up was limited, with models like the short-wheelbase estate not listed. At the same time, the military machines adopted the Greenline moniker, although these, too, had the OM612 powerplant and permanent all-wheel drive. Production averaged around 400 cars a year after an initial flurry of orders (1138 were built in 2004), although sales dropped off rapidly in 2007, with 200 cars per annum being closer to the norm and the numbers still falling.

As it happens, 2007 witnessed an engine transplant on the W461s, with the 183bhp (135kW) 3-litre 24v V6 common-rail diesel (the turbocharged unit being borrowed from the Sprinter van) creating the G280 CDI Worker and also, from spring 2009, the Edition 30 PUR based on the long-wheelbase station wagon. The latter brought the W461 into private hands, with special off-road tyres on 16-inch alloys, flexible fender flares, lamp protection, a front tow hitch, a two-piece rear door, and even a walk-on bonnet available for this adventurer's companion. It came with four individual seats, trimmed in fabric or manmade leather, rubber floormats, waterproofed switchgear, and an auxiliary heater to augment the manual air-conditioning unit.

The G300 CDI Professional has been sold to regular customers since its 2010 introduction, being powered by the same de-tuned 2987cc all-alloy OM642 DE30LA (red) engine as the G280 CDI, but suitably modified to allow it to meet the stricter EURO 5 emissions regulations. Actually, the two lwb estates were sold alongside each other for a while, with the G280 CDI listed in lhd and rhd,

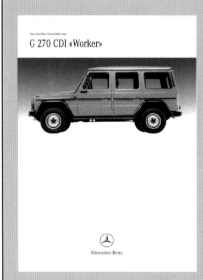

Catalogue for the G270 CDI Worker model.

plus EURO 4 certification only, and the cleaner G300 CDI in left-hand drive guise only; both came with a five-speed automatic gearbox and 225/75 tyres on 16-inch rims. The other variants, sold and taxed as commercial vehicles rather than private cars, were sold purely in G300 CDI format.

After W461 sales almost stalled completely in 2009 (with just 48 cars built), at least the 300-off Edition 30 PUR model and strong military sales kept momentum going for the series, despite a reduction in the amount of body types. Only the G300 CDI was kept in Europe for 2011, although it wasn't until 2013 that the last one was actually built, by which time lwb estate prices started at €56,100, plus €8500 for those wishing to add the Edition PUR upgrade.

Due to the engine's failure to meet 2014 emissions regulations, the end of the W461 run was announced at the end of December 2013. These cars have not been included in the appendices, by the way, due to their strictly commercial vehicle nature and purpose, and the fact that military and civilian build numbers were batched together after 2010. Hopefully, the figures included in this sidebar should suffice.

The G300 CDI Professional model, characterised by its snorkel intake combined with the side exhaust found on the G280 CDI cars.

Exterior and interior shots of the Edition 30 PUR model in its two off-road guises. The individual seats and wood decking on the luggage compartment floor are standard features on this special machine.

The Professional model's fascia in its most basic form. Later cars had a 'Professional' badge added to the glovebox face.

There was another announcement made in February 2009, and that was the huge decision to keep the G-Wagen in production at Magna-Steyr until 2015. A few months later, in mid-2009, it was noted that improvements had been made to the seats, improving comfort and lateral support for both the driver and the front and rear passengers. Fresh black or grey fabric upholstery (far plainer than before, with a light checkered pattern on the inserts) was now augmented by the option of black, grey or chestnut leather, as well as Designo black or red hides. A leather-trimmed dashboard (standard on the AMG grade), Designo piano black lacquer wood trim, the so-called climatised multi-contour seats and an ambient interior lighting package were new options placed on the table, with Designo blue pearl stone trim also becoming available soon after the 2010 season started. As for the exterior, a couple of new paint shades were listed, and it was now possible to have an AMG-style chrome grille on regular cars via the €730 Chrome Package (SA code ZD6), which also added a few chrome accent pieces on the car's interior appointments. In addition, the spare wheel cover could be ordered with a metal three-pointed star badge rather than an illustration of one.

A new badge appeared on the tail of the diesel model as soon as the 2010 season started, although it was otherwise the same car as it was when it wore a G320 CDI nameplate.

The limited run Edition 79 G55 AMG model standing alongside the SLS AMG that was also on display in Dubai at the end of 2009.

After September 2009, the G320 CDI moniker was dropped in favour of a G350 CDI nameplate, although there was no change in vehicle specification, so it does seem odd to go to all this trouble, especially as a newcomer was waiting in the wings with a similar-sounding name.

In the meantime, an unusual G-Wagen was introduced at the Dubai Motor Show in December – the Edition 79 G55 AMG Kompressor model, which was limited to 79 units and aimed specifically at the Middle East market. It featured Designo Magno Allanite paintwork, a bull-bar with a hefty guard underneath, carbon-style side trim, and a titanium finish on the wheels.

Inside was a black-and-sand two-tone interior with carbonfibre trim components, and a plaque bearing the limited edition build number.

The 2010 Geneva show

Diesel technology moved on in leaps and bounds in the new millennium. Despite having been around on petrol units since 1976, Bosch's closed-loop lambda sensor became available for diesel engines for the first time in 2002. The system basically measures oxygen content in the exhaust gas to inform the engine's ECU of combustion conditions. The ECU can then adjust induction settings to improve fuel consumption and give the lowest possible emissions in relation to engine load.

Bosch was also at the forefront of piezo-electric injector development, giving birth to the third generation of the common-rail diesel injection system. Launched in May 2003, the finer control offered by injector nozzle needles switched by fast- and direct-acting piezo crystals or PZT ceramics in an electrical field (as opposed to a traditional magnetic coil), reduced pre-exhaust emissions by as much as 20 per cent.

Another huge advance in cleaning up diesel emissions is selective catalytic reduction. The selective catalytic reduction (SCR) system has actually been around for quite some time, having been patented by the Englehard Corporation of America in 1957. This used ammonia as a reducing agent, converting NOx emissions into nitrogen and water, but was restricted mainly to industrial use because of logistics.

SCR development continued, however, and eventually, the system was refined for use on diesel engines, first in maritime and rail applications, and then trucks. Some manufacturers chose metals as catalysts, including precious metals, while others went down the ceramics route in a bid to enhance sustainability and durability. Many, however, chose to stick with ammonia, and the use of urea (also known as carbamide) is now the common alternative, as it's easier and safer to store and handle than ammonia. An interesting bonus is that carbon dioxide is combined with ammonia in the creation of urea, thus making good use of CO2 emissions, and balancing the CO2 created when urea is liquefied by adding water to this otherwise solid organic compound.

In 2004, Mercedes-Benz announced that it would be introducing a urea-based SCR system for its larger passenger cars – a scaled-down version of that already in use on its commercial vehicles. Depending on the engine size and overall vehicle weight, the modular set-up, marketed under the BlueTec moniker, could be tailored to reduce costs and best suit packaging restraints.

Combined with the testing of SunDiesel biomass synthetic fuel, this was part of Mercedes' long-term plan to comply with EU standards and America's 2007 regulations, and was aimed more at the reduction of NOx gases than PM – the German company,

Display version of the BlueTec engine employed in the G-Wagen.

A second filler allows users to add DEF fluid (or AdBlue) for the BlueTec system. One tank of urea fluid was good for around 7500 miles (12,000km), and helped the diesel car clear the EURO 5 regulations with ease.

along with others in the automotive business, was already fairly confident that particulate matter could be controlled without much effort, mainly thanks to new injectors prompting better combustion, and modifications to the exhaust system, including enhanced filtering.

The key components in the Mercedes SCR system are a diesel oxidation catalyst (often shortened to DOC, this is a precious metal catalyst that converts carbon monoxide and hydrocarbons into carbon dioxide and water), an NOx Absorber Catalyst (or NAC) that firstly traps and then removes oxides of nitrogen as it regenerates with a richer mixture and gives off a measured release of ammonia in the process, a PM filter of some sort, and an SCR cat that treats exhaust gases that have had ammonia (or urea fluid) mixed with them to cause a chemical reaction, converting any remaining NOx gases into harmless nitrogen and water. Generally, depending on the application, the urea fluid (or DEF, standing for Diesel Exhaust Fluid, which is called 'AdBlue' in Mercedes blurb) is stored in a container in the luggage compartment and injected into the exhaust stream just before the SCR unit; in this case, the NAC component is not required.

Launched via the 2007 MY W211-series E320 BlueTec turbodiesel model in America, the BlueTec system spread to other lines, with the use of the more expensive AdBlue injection set-up on the larger GL-, M- and R-Class SUVs more than halving NOx levels. March 2010 finally saw the system adopted on the G-Wagen, when the G350 BlueTec made its debut at the Geneva Show, although sales didn't actually begin until the middle of the year.

The leading specifications were carried over on the V6 diesel, although power output was reduced a touch, down to 211bhp (155kW) – a loss of around six per cent. However, the 398lbft torque figure remain unchanged, as did the use of a 7G-Tronic gearbox, combined with 4.38:1 axles at the front and rear. It should be noted that while the G350 BlueTec replaced the G350 CDI in Germany in June 2010, the older model was still built in small numbers until 2012. The BlueTec car was available with all three body options, incidentally, with prices ranging from €74,839 to €81,146.

By now, official price lists were running to 24 pages, with

Only the badge on the tail gave the game away from the outside ... This BlueTec car has the optional RL6 alloys, when the old 16-inch rims off the G350 CDI were still considered standard fare.

seven pages packed full of options and another two pages of dealer accessories. It is therefore impossible to describe a 'standard' car at this stage in the proceedings, as virtually every vehicle coming down the line at Graz was unique. One interesting thing picked up in the June 2010 price list, though, was the move from RM7 to the similar-looking RM9 alloys for the G500 – a €1547 option on the V6 model, which was a fairly new thing to offer, as for many years, at least on the G-Wagen, certain wheels were reserved for certain grades, and the only option was the RL6 six-spoke rim or an earlier design bought as an accessory.

Moving on, May 2011 saw the announcement of the swb BA3 Final Edition station wagon and the lwb Edition Select estate. The short-wheelbase car (with V6 diesel or G500 power) was an elegant way to mark the imminent end of the three-door estate, while the G500-based five-door model was a little more brutal.

The BA3 Final Edition came with metallic paint (still an extra on the six-cylinder car, but standard on the V8s), the ZD6 package of chrome goodies, wider AMG wheelarches in body colour to cover a set of 18-inch RM9 alloys, running boards, a metal spare wheel cover, chrome inserts on the side protection mouldings (something not normally found on the V6s), a power sunroof, rear mudflaps, a chrome rear sill cover, the ambient lighting package, burr walnut trim, climatised multi-contour

The attractive BA3 Final Edition of 2011 vintage, with BA3 standing for Bauausführung Typ 3. The swb estate body was discontinued in time for the 2012 season, although the cabriolet continued.

front seats trimmed in black leather, velour carpets, and special badging. It was priced at €90,511 in G350 BlueTec guise, or €100,686 if the petrol engine was chosen.

The Edition Select was sold as a €6735 package, as it happens (code ZQ6), featuring black paint on the bumpers, AMG-style wheelarches and mirrors to give a good contrast to the Designo Mystic White, Palladium Silver or Thulite Red coachwork, although an all-over Obsidian Black finish was also available. The wheels found on the BA3 car were called out for service again, but painted black to distance them from the standard G500 fare (a natural finish was possible, however), while other features included a sports exhaust system, the ZD6 chrome package, a heavy sumpguard, running boards, a metal spare wheel cover, carbon-style inserts for the side mouldings, illuminated treadplates, active headrests designed to withstand the worst of accidents, two-tone Designo leather trim (all-black upholstery was listed as a no-cost option), piano black wood accents, the Harman/Kardon sound system, and, of course, special mats and badging.

The Edition Select package for the G500 lwb estate. The RM9 wheels seen here had become standard on the G500 in mid-2010, by the way, albeit sporting a natural aluminium finish on mainstream vehicles.

The contemporary special protection Guard model.

Other than offering a carbon package (SA code ZG6) in the spring of 2012, things in Stuttgart were finally quiet for five minutes. Needless to say, the silence would soon be broken, and by some new noises, too ...

Export analysis

While christening a car with a 3-litre engine a 320 and then a 350 was just as strange as leaving the G500 moniker untouched when the capacity of the V8 was increased, at least America had the idea of making a new G550 badge for the 2009 normally-aspirated eight-cylinder model. In other respects, though – at least for a little while – US cars fell into line with those of the domestic market, albeit fitted with virtually everything the company had to offer as standard.

The 2009 model G550 stood at $100,250, which was quite a jump over the price of the old G500, although the G55 AMG was only a fraction more than before, at $119,450. With climatised front seats added as a new item, plus an Alcantara headliner for the AMG model, there were no major options to speak of. Given the level of standard equipment, that's hardly surprising ...

For 2010, the convenience features list got even longer, with a heated wood/leather steering wheel, as well as the chrome package, and also a sports exhaust for the G550. By the way, in US cars, the G550 had burr walnut trim, while the AMGs had a maple version; leather came in black, chestnut/black or grey/black, although the latter was swapped for a lighter Designo Porcelain-and-black combination on the G55 AMG, and the chestnut shade was replaced by a light brown.

Interestingly, MBNA decided to keep the old RM7 wheels for 2011, and 2012, too, although the Edition Select did have the 'correct' RM9 wheels, which were made available as an option on regular showroom models.

Exterior and interior views of the G550 for the US 2009 season, with the correct wheels for the model. Note the body-coloured grille at the front, and the different badge used in America on the tail. Also, one can just spot the compass reading in the dashboard display between the speedo and tachometer – a truly useful feature that would have been unthinkable in 1979, and even 1989!

The 2010 G55 AMG model for America, seen here in standard trim. Note the different gauges on the AMG machine.

Across the Pacific, Japan also went for the fresh G550 moniker, with sales starting in March 2009. The G550 lwb estate (lhd) was 13,270,000 yen, and its AMG stablemate 17,400,000 yen. This was when the top Range Rover was 14,550,000 yen, and a Lincoln Navigator could be bought for 8,900,000 yen. Prices increased a touch in the spring of 2010, but then held steady into the 2012 season, when the Edition Select went on sale, along with a five-off Mastermind Limited based on

the AMG car. This 20,000,000 yen machine was blacked out virtually everywhere and featured skull and crossbone motifs on the seat's headrests, so, even though it was listed by the official distributors, it was hardly a mainstream product.

As it happens, and probably thanks to huge military orders from the government, the Australian G-Wagen market was reborn at the 2010 Sydney Show, held in October. The G350 BlueTec five-door estate was announced at $136,261, with the G55

A 2012 Model Year G550 driver having fun in the States. The wheels seen here were an option in America, unless one bought the Edition Select car.

The G350 BlueTec model for the Australian market.

The AMG car in Australia-spec guise. The G-Wagen was actually the perfect machine to handle the vast and unforgiving outback.

AMG Kompressor model commanding $178,569. By the 2012 season, these prices had gone up by around 20 per cent, but at least the iconic SUV was available again.

Business round-up

Although diesel power was taking a leading position in Daimler AG marketing at the time, July 2008 witnessed the debut of the 670bhp twin-turbo V12 SL65 AMG Black Series at Hockenheim, which was every bit as wild as the new 650bhp SLR McLaren Roadster 722S launched at the Paris Salon that year. The timing was good for this type of vehicle, as McLaren-Mercedes pilot Lewis Hamilton was crowned world champion soon after following a nail-biting finale to the 2008 F1 season. The New Year saw the release of the last of the 199-series SLR models – the 75-off SLR Stirling Moss roadster. In reality, though, it was the appearance of the more conventional GLK (X204), and the launch of the new 212-series E-Class

An interesting series of pictures showing a fully-loaded G350 BlueTec model imported into the UK, although actual sales were still not being processed at this stage. British fans of the G-Wagen wouldn't have too long to wait for a comeback, though. This car has Designo trim, by the way, as well as the optional six-spoke alloys. Note also the EM7 package, which brought a monitor screen to the back of each front seat headrest.

A G320 CDI model acting as a press and service crew vehicle in the 2009 Dakar Rally – the famous marathon once won by the Geländewagen.

at the 2009 Detroit Show that mattered more to most people, with electric cars looking good for the future.

The 2009 Geneva Show saw the C207 E-Class Coupe take a bow, along with the Maybach Zeppelin, and a new line of 'smart' microcar variants. Not long after, the E63 AMG, plus face-lifted versions of the GL-Class and ML450 Hybrid, were launched at the New York Show in April 2009, while the face-lifted S-Class (W221) was displayed at the Shanghai event in the same month.

While the one-millionth M-Class was rolling off the line, the sporting image craved by the Mercedes-Benz marketing men (bubbling over on the G-Wagen, which would have seemed very unlikely only a few years earlier) was further enhanced in September 2009 when the new 197-series SLS AMG model made its debut alongside the E-Class estate, a plug-in hybrid version of the S-Class and a fuel cell version of the B-Class at the Frankfurt Show. The stunning SLS had an all-alloy gullwing

The tuning business was in full swing by now, riding on the wave of enthusiasm generated by the big SUV. Here, we see a Brabus V12 model from 2009 (left), and an ART AS55K from the same year: the latter built as a one-off for a Saudi prince.

body, and was powered by a 571bhp, 6.2-litre V8.

As it happens, Mercedes power had been chosen by no fewer than three F1 teams for the 2009 season. Jenson Button was duly crowned world champion in his Brawn-Mercedes BGP001, with Brawn also taking the constructors' title. This prompted Daimler AG to take a 75 per cent stake in Brawn to secure the team for a new works F1 effort starting in 2010. At the same time, AMG-Mercedes was classed as DTM champion, keeping the Stuttgart brand firmly in the motorsport spotlight.

Soon after the E-Class convertible (207-series) was announced in Detroit, the new 571bhp AMG M157 twin-turbo 5.5 litre V8 was presented to the press at the AMG head office, in March 2010.

A G500 won the prestigious 2010 Off-Road Challenge, held in November.

A few days later, in Geneva, the F800 research vehicle took a bow, and the 'MercedesSport' brand was launched to allow buyers greater scope for individuality. The Swiss event also witnessed students from the King Saud University in Saudi Arabia display their Gazal-1 SUV based on the G-Wagen. The car had much softer lines, although its heritage was still obvious.

There was no let up in the pace, as the Mercedes range continued to expand. The new R-Class made its debut at the New York Show, along with the SLS AMG GT3 for race enthusiasts. The face-lifted Maybach and a lwb version of the E-Class followed, and in May, the M276 (V6) and M278 (V8) power-units were presented to the press in Stuttgart. Featuring advanced direct-injection and ignition control, as well as a stop-start facility to enhance fuel consumption, they delivered more power and more torque, yet could boast an average of 23 per cent better fuel efficiency. Their debut came in the new CL-Class (216-series), released in July in conjunction with the seven-speed 7G-Tronic Plus gearbox, and the C218 CLS, launched at the Paris Salon later in the year. There was also a great deal of activity on zero-emissions vehicles, with the E-Cell concept being another area of green technology to augment the F-Cell, LPG and advanced diesel systems being fielded by the company.

Having fallen to just over a million cars built in 2009, along with 425,000 trucks, Mercedes production picked up in again 2010, increasing to 1,312,456 units, as well as more than 625,000 commercials. There was more success in the DTM series, too, with Mercedes gaining its third consecutive manufacturers' title, and Paul di Resti claiming the spoils in the 2010 drivers' category.

In January 2011, Mercedes' boss Dieter Zetsche was on hand to present the new C-Class saloons and estates and the R172 SLK, with its launch slated for March 2011. Lining up alongside the new C-Class Coupe at Geneva, the R172 featured such novel ideas as the Magic Sky Control glass roof, and there was even a diesel version released in time for the 2012 season.

The Concept A-Class was the highlight of the Shanghai Motor Show, although the same month also saw the launch of the E63 AMG. Not long after, the third generation W166 M-Class was announced, with a line of four- and six-cylinder engines to get things rolling. Naturally, the SUV was displayed at the 2011

The third generation M-Class, which duly won the coveted Golden Steering Wheel award. An AMG version was added to the line-up in November 2011.

The Mercedes-Benz GL350 BlueTec 4MATIC of 2012 vintage. The flagship GL63 AMG model went on sale in November that year, having made its debut at the Moscow Automobile Salon.

A face-lifted car from the spring of 2012, with the new lighting arrangements and revised door mirrors giving an ideal dating feature. This is a G350 BlueTec model, by the way.

Frankfurt Show, where the SLS AMG Roadster, SLK55 AMG and B-Class models made their debut. The F125 concept car was also on hand at the IAA to give a glimpse of the future.

The new R231 SL was announced in November 2011, making its proper debut a couple of months later at the 2012 Detroit Show alongside a pair of E-Class hybrids (sales began in March). The new A-Class followed at Geneva, where the 'smart' brand was also making a splash, and the GLK SUV gained a face-lift soon after. The relentless pace was kept up via the launch of the new GL-Class (Type X166) at the 2012 New York Show in April. A diesel six and petrol eight were offered with this luxury SUV initially, but things were afoot with its big brother – again!

Another reprieve

The growing importance of the Chinese market can be gauged by the fact that the marketing folks in Stuttgart chose to launch the new G-Class at the 2012 Beijing Show, which opened on 23 April. This amazing machine just kept going, just like the R107 SL had in an era that now seems long ago – the G-Wagen and the boxy SL stood as timeless icons, while everything around them was changing rapidly. But the W463 was still with us, and still going strong. Indeed, 2011 had marked the best sales of the line in six years, with AMG models accounting for 40 per cent of the cars moved.

The latest Geländewagen was treated to an exterior and

Dr Thomas Weber, head of R&D, with the G63 AMG at the time of its introduction in China. The V8 machine was readily distinguished by its unique radiator grille design and its attractive five-spoke alloys. Although the author is no big fan of oversized wheels, the 20-inch rims certainly helped make the car look a lot more lithe – it had always appeared a touch on the heavy side with smaller wheels.

The same diesel car, but this angle gives us a clear view of the PA3 kit and the latest alloy wheels, which carried the RL5 code. These five-spoke rims would later be made the standard wheel contained in the Sport Package, but for now, they were a stand-alone option.

Surely the rarest ex-works G-Wagen badge of them all ...

A G65 AMG at speed. Note that the netting in the air dam intakes was black, the same as that used in the G63. Only the netting on the radiator was silvered.

The redesigned interior. This is a G500 with the optional Exklusiv Package (the leather dashboard trim is a telltale component in this picture, although it also included the upgraded PA1 climatised seating, with multi-contour control), Designo leather and piano black lacquer trim, and the chrome package.

interior face-lift, as well as a new AMG engine line-up, so Daimler AG's commitment to the big SUV was beyond question. Dieter Zetsche, the company's Chairman, stated: "Our G-Class has been a force to be reckoned with for the last 33 years. In its latest evolutionary stage, it offers state-of-the-art, powerful engines, a further improved range of luxurious appointments and the very latest safety features, as well, of course, as its now legendary off-road capabilities. At the same time, the design remains true to its down-to-earth, unmistakable style."

On the styling side of things, new LED running lights were added to the bottom of the headlight enclosures, and the door mirrors were redesigned to bring them into line with the other Mercedes passenger car models on offer at the time.

The basic V6 and V8 machines (ie the non-AMG models) had the same three-slat radiator grille as before, finished in body colour as standard. However, the ZD6 chrome package was still available, bringing a chrome-plated grille and chrome interior accent pieces. The €1725 PA3 kit was still listed, too, bringing with it a set of running boards and a metal spare wheel cover (both the ZD6 and PA3 options were already standard on the AMG cars, of course). A new package introduced at this time was the PA5 Sport Package, which built on the PA3 one with the addition of AMG wheelarch extensions and a titanium grey finish on the RM9 alloys; the G500 also got a sports exhaust, making up for the fact that this wheel design was already being used on the V8 machine.

On the subject of alloy wheels, the diesel car continued with its familiar 16-inch RL3 five-spoke rims, and the G500 retained its RM9 wheels, too. The RL6 wheel continued as an option, joined by a fresh two-tone five-spoke wheel that used the 'RL5' moniker; it was also possible to specify the G500 wheels on the diesel car for €1226, and the Atik and Ashtaroth designs were still there in the accessories listing.

As for the AMG cars, a new radiator grille was adopted with two chrome slats sitting close together; the G65 came with silver netting behind, while that on the G63 had a plain black finish. Below this was a new bumper assembly styled to look like an aggressive air dam, with three large air intakes separated by vertical chrome bars. Finishing the upgrade, the G63 came with new 9.5J x 20 R10 alloys with five open spokes (showing off the latest red brake calipers nicely) and 275/50 rubber, while the G65 gained wheels that were similar to the old five-spoke design, but these RM1 rims had a 20-inch diameter. A black version of the latter was available as an option on both AMG grades, also coming with 275/50 tyres to fill the AMG model's flared arches.

Inside, there was a new four-spoke multi-function steering wheel, and beyond that, the minor gauges were moved from the outer edges of the instrument cluster to being inset on the speedo and tachometer faces. By moving these new combination dials outwards, it allowed space for a larger TFT information screen and a gear indicator in-between them; as before, the AMG cars had different meter graphics, but they weren't all that different this time around. Below this, there was a fresh light switch and ignition barrel design to match the sportier tone of the dashboard.

There was also a totally redesigned centre stack, with the air vents and diff lock switches moving downwards to sit above a new COMAND Online control unit (with internet access on top of all the regular audio-visual and navi features) and a bank of switches beneath that in a frame. The free-standing screen for the COMAND unit was now located where the diff locks used to be, in clearer view of the driver than before, while the refreshed HVAC controls sat below the frame. Aft of this was a new gear selector, more switches and a rotary knob for controlling the COMAND system. The view in front of the passenger didn't change much, although there were a few detail changes, especially to the airbag compartment.

Anthracite poplar wood was used in the V6 car, with burr walnut in the G500, and piano black lacquer pieces on the AMGs. The diesel car came with the same cloth as before, but

A G63 AMG that has been upgraded to the V12 model's diamond-embossed trim via the PA6 option. It also sports the optional carbon package.

now in black only (code SP1); leather trim was employed on all the other grades. As well as all the Designo goodies, the PA4 Exklusiv Package was carried over. There was also a PA6 version now, which allowed G63 owners to get the same level of trim as that offered in the G65. The ZG6 AMG carbon package was also new, with the latter available for all cars. Other new options included the door mirror-based Blind-Spot Assist system (EA2), the Parktronic parking aid with a reversing camera (EZ8), and the Distronic Plus adaptive cruise control system that could keep the car a prescribed distance from the vehicle in front (EZ9).

Engine bay of the G350 BlueTec model.

The twin-turbo V8 engine found in the G63 AMG model.

Mechanically, the 211bhp BlueTec diesel engine and the G500/G550's 387bhp V8 continued much as before. The automatic gearbox was basically carried over, too, albeit in updated 7G-Tronic Plus form to enhance refinement and fuel economy. It now came with a normal setting for smooth shifts and an eye on frugality, a sport setting for sharper response, and a manual operation mode via the new E-Select gearlever and paddle shifts behind the steering wheel. In addition, the ESP system was reconfigured across the G-Class range, with a 'Hold' function for easy hill-starts as standard. The big changes were reserved for the AMG line, however. As you will have probably gathered by now, the G55 AMG Kompressor model was replaced by two new grades – the G63 AMG, and the exotic G65 AMG.

The G63 AMG, available in lwb estate guise only, as had been the norm for some time with AMGs, was powered by the twin-turbo M157 DE55LA V8. This all-alloy 32v unit, with a dohc per bank arrangement and variable valve timing, had the same 98.0mm bore and 90.5mm stroke as the M273 engine, so the capacity was also 5461cc. With a 10.0:1 compression ratio and forced induction with intercooling, though, the AMG eight

The exotic V12 used in the G65 AMG station wagon.

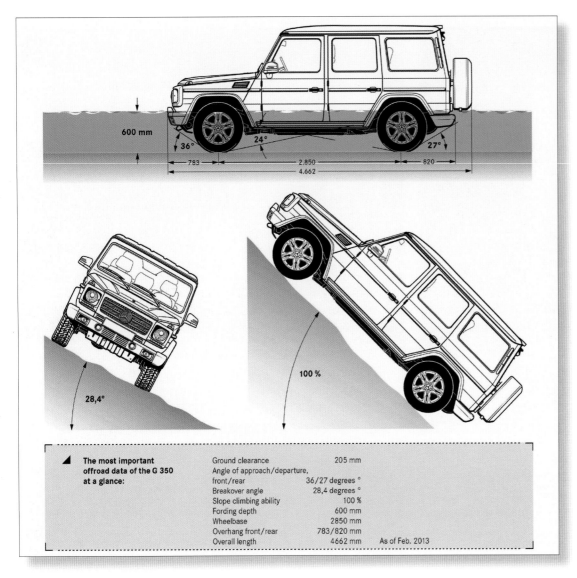

An interesting data sheet. It's worth comparing it with the one at the start of Chapter Four to see the difference between the old swb and the latest lwb models.

▲ The most important offroad data of the G 350 at a glance:		
Ground clearance	205 mm	
Angle of approach/departure, front/rear	36/27 degrees °	
Breakover angle	28,4 degrees °	
Slope climbing ability	100 %	
Fording depth	600 mm	
Wheelbase	2850 mm	
Overhang front/rear	783/820 mm	
Overall length	4662 mm	As of Feb. 2013

developed a healthy 544bhp (400kW) and 561lbft of torque. By the same token, the addition of a stop/start facility and direct-injection aided economy – the new engine was therefore actually better on fuel than the outgoing G55 AMG, despite the increases in power and displacement. The V8 was hooked up to a 7G-Tronic automatic transmission with Speedshift Plus, which had shorter shift times and a sporty double-declutching function, as well as the three operation modes, available through a combination of the E-Select and paddle levers.

The G65 AMG was a real piece of exotica, powered by the all-alloy M279 E60LA V12. This engine was an updated version of the M275 unit, with a sohc per bank arrangement operating three valves per cylinder. The 82.6mm bore and 93.0mm stroke gave a cubic capacity of 5980cc, and combining this with a 9.0:1 c/r and twin-turbochargers released 612bhp (450kW) and 738lbft of torque. Like the G63 model, the V12 AMG car delivered its power through a 7G-Tronic gearbox with Speedshift Plus before being split by the dual-range transfer box, and used a 4.11:1 final-drive ratio on the front and back axles. With all this power and traction on tap, this long-wheelbase estate was capable of dismissing the 0-60 yardstick in 5.3 seconds, before going on to a top speed of 144mph (230kph), although it has

The G63 AMG 6x6 in Dubai. This huge machine was 5870mm (231.1in) long, 2280mm (89.8in) in height, and tipped the scales at an astonishing 3850kg (8470lb)!

The tasteful exterior and interior of the 200-off G500 Final Edition 200 cabriolet of 2013.

to be said that the G63 AMG model wasn't far behind in the performance stakes.

In typical AMG fashion, its engineers developed a complete package, tuning all components to suit the higher power outputs of the latest engines. There were revised spring and damper settings, along with ESP programme tweaks and stronger brakes all-round, as well as the addition of a rear anti-roll bar on the G63 AMG and G65 AMG. None of the other cars had this, and in fact, the G55 AMG Kompressor didn't either, except for limited time when the car was based on a G500 conversion at the start of the new millennium.

Domestic sales began in June 2012, with the full line-up now including just five grades – the G350 BlueTec lwb estate at €85,311, the G500 version at €99,948, the G500 cabriolet at €100,900, the G63 AMG at €137,504, and the G65 AMG at €264,180; the diesel-engined cabriolet had been dropped during the face-lift.

The next big news relating to the G-Wagen came in March 2015, when AMG announced the G63 AMG 6x6 model in Dubai. This featured twin axles at the back, each with its own diff lock, as per the front, an open deck at the rear to give the vehicle

the extra length needed to accommodate the revised drivetrain, and carbonfibre wheelarch extensions covering a truly huge wheel and tyre combination that gave the car amazing ground clearance and something of a Tonka Toy look. It was a deadly serious machine, of course, with a stunning off-road capability, and four individual seats trimmed in the finest Designo leather.

At the time of the car's announcement, there were no firm plans to build a run of the 6x6 models, but the reaction at the show was positive, and a plan was put in motion to build a series of vehicles in the summer of 2013. The last ones were delivered in early-2015, with just over 100 having been built.

The €110,004 Final Edition 200 cabriolet was released in May 2013, when the Sport Package adopted the RL5 wheels as standard with the grey RM9 rim as a no-cost option. This last cabriolet variant (the regular soft top model was no longer listed) came with a beige hood and tonneau cover to contrast with the Designo black paint, the PA3 kit and chrome package, RL5 alloys, an AMG steering wheel, Designo poplar wood trim, two-tone Designo leather trim, and special treadplates and badging. The cabriolet finally disappeared from the price lists a year later, but there were no other major changes on the other grades.

The Edition 35 was announced in September 2014, marking the 35th anniversary of the Geländewagen. Available on the G350 BlueTec and G500 grades, the Edition 35 package brought with it a gloss black finish on the alloy wheels, bumpers, wheelarch extensions, door mirrors and roof to give a strong contrast to the Designo Mystic White or Palladium Silver used for the majority of the coachwork, although Obsidian Black was also available for those wanting to blend in with the crowd a little. The cars also came with the ZD6 and PA5 packages, although the wheel design was not the regular Sport Package rim in this case. Designo leather trim was specified for the interior, in either two-tone black and porcelain, or plain black, although red stitching was applied on the seats, and carried over to the leather dashboard and controls. Multi-contour seats, an AMG steering wheel and piano black lacquered woodwork rounded things off.

The 2015 Geneva Show played host to the G500 4x4² model, which can be summed up as a toned-down, four-wheeled version of the mighty 6x6 special. Powered by the new 422bhp (310kW) AMG 4-litre V8, the design was dominated by the 22-inch wheel and tyre combination covered by carbonfibre wing extensions. The interior appointments were naturally of the highest order, too. The reception received in Switzerland was very positive, prompting Daimler AG to start taking orders for the 4x4² from June, although big changes were in store for the regular line-up as well ...

The Edition 35 model – this particular example being based on the G500 in white. Note the red accent stitching used for the interior, and the optional carbon trim.

The "near-production" 4x4² model that made its debut at the 2015 Geneva Show. Note the vivid colour scheme – something that distances the newcomer from the cars of 1979, in addition to those huge wheels.

The new cars abroad

The new cars were introduced as 2013 Model Year vehicles in the States, with a G550 and G63 AMG making up the range, both in long-wheelbase station wagon guise only. As we have come to expect from MBNA, everything new was added to the spec sheet, so, sure enough, Distronic Plus, Parktronic and the blind-spot assistant packages became standard fitments on the 2013 cars.

The G550 station wagon was priced at $113,905 for 2013, with the G63 AMG estate commanding $134,300. Regarding the NA V8, *Car & Driver* noted: "The G550 couldn't seem more obnoxious around our editorial office's eco-conscious Ann Arbor environs. It's huge, looks like it could eat a Prius, and absolutely stinks of money. But these are classic parts of the G-Wagen experience, an uncommon mixture of old-timey road manners, military-industrial styling, and unexpectedly sprightly acceleration. Taken individually, only the styling and acceleration should appeal, but all together, the refreshed-for-2013 G550 delivers a sense of goodness and satisfaction that has typified the G-Wagen breed for some time."

There were no significant changes for 2014 or 2015, although there was a US-only G550 Night Star Edition released in the spring of 2015, which was basically an Edition 35 model with the addition of a black bonnet. It was limited to just 100 cars.

In Japan, the G55 AMG ran until July 2012, with the fresh twin-turbo V8 and V12 pairing going on sale in the following month alongside the G550 station wagon. Japanese pricing for the 2013 Model Year saw the G550 at 13,400,000 yen, the G63 at 17,800,000 yen, and the G65 at 32,500,000 yen.

April 2013 saw the introduction of the Japan-only G550 Night Edition, with black bodywork, dark grey paint on the RM9 alloys (which produced an 'RM0' code, incidentally), and a cream or red interior with piano black wood trim. A few months later, just in time for the 2014 season, the Japanese importers started bringing in the G350 BlueTec, introduced at 9,980,000 yen, when the existing models ranged from 13,885,000 to 33,428,000 yen.

As it happens, the G63 AMG 6x6 was announced in Japan during April 2014, with five reserved at the princely sum of

Cover of the US catalogue for the 2013 season.

80,000,000 yen apiece. It appeared all over the TV in a publicity campaign par excellence, although it's hard to think of anything more unsuitable for Japanese roads, short of a Sherman tank! Hardly the thing for a country slipping in and out of recession either ...

Sales of the 35th Anniversary Edition cars started in Japan during September 2014. These were distinguished by their special interiors, with a total of 35 G63 AMG versions (with black or matt yellow-olive paint) at 19,500,000 yen each, plus 130 G350 BlueTec models in black, and 70 in white, priced at 10,500,000 yen apiece.

The initial pricing and line-up was much the same in Australia for 2013, but the 2014 season (launched in July 2103) saw the Aussie range including a G350 BlueTec model at $148,145, a G500 at $164,645, and a G63 AMG at $229,725. There were no real changes after that, with only small price increases being apparent.

Britain eventually got back into the G-Wagen market in the middle of October 2012, with the M-Class and GL-Class continuing alongside a pair of face-lifted estate cars. The G350 BlueTec was introduced at £82,945, while the G63 AMG

The 2013 Model Year G550, with a view of the engine bay, the interior (front and rear) and the luggage compartment.

The G63 AMG from the US 2013 season.

A G63 AMG with special paint and the optional alloys used on the V12 model in Europe, duly given the R11 code when finished in black, as seen here.

commanded £123,115; the ML63 AMG was £82,995 at this time, so it was obvious that the oldtimer was aimed at a rather different sector of the market to the other Benz SUVs. Indeed, the top Range Rovers were in the same kind of pricing area as the BlueTec car, but with cars like the five-door Mitsubishi Shogun (aka Pajero) at half the money, it must have been a hard sell to all but the most dedicated followers of fashion. Things were basically unchanged for 2014 and 2015, other than a couple of very small price increases.

Regarding the diesel model, *Autocar* noted: "The modern drivetrain gives the car a surprisingly contemporary flavour. Despite the bluff shape and weight, the G-Wagon has got an impressive turn of speed. It also rides surprisingly well and the body control is remarkably competent."

News from Stuttgart

The elegant CLS Shooting Brake was announced in the summer of 2012, although electric cars were the main theme in Paris. As it happens, the Paris Salon was held in the same month as news broke of a couple of joint engine and transmission projects with

A 2013 Model Year G350 BlueTec in UK trim.

the Renault-Nissan Alliance; the move was expected to bear fruit in 2016.

November 2012 saw the debut of the Ener-G-Force concept, designed by the Advanced Design Studio in California as part of the Los Angeles Design Challenge, which had the theme of a future patrol car for 2025. Gorden Wagener noted: "The Ener-G-Force is the vision of an off-roader that, while reflecting tomorrow's adventures, also invokes the genes of our off-road icon – the G model. Modern and cool, it could also be a clue about a new beginning for the off-road design idiom of Mercedes-Benz."

The face-lifted E-Class made its debut at the 2013 Detroit Show, alongside the all-new compact CLA model. Soon after, they had their European launch at Geneva, when AMG models stole the limelight. AMG was also the focus of attention when the brutal G63 AMG 6x6 was announced, while, at the other end of the scale, electrical power was given priority at the New York Show, and the Concept GLA compact SUV was the highlight on the Mercedes stand in Shanghai.

The new W222 S-Class was announced at a special event in May 2013, with petrol, diesel and hybrid drivetrains, and ultimately went on sale in Europe during the summer; an AMG model followed later in the year, along with a bevy of awards.

The next big event was the launch of the GLA production vehicle at the 2013 Frankfurt Show, allowing the company to field a smaller and more reasonably-priced SUV. In the same month, Tobias Moers took over as the boss of AMG after Ola Källenius became the new head of Sales & Marketing for Mercedes-Benz passenger cars. On the subject of AMG, the SLS AMG Final Edition model was released in November 2013, signalling the end of an era for a classic sports car. As that line ended, though, the new 205-series C-Class made its official debut in Detroit in the New Year, lining up alongside new machines as diverse as the GLA45 AMG and S600, and the new V-Class MPV put in an appearance at a dedicated event in Munich during the same month.

The 2014 Geneva Show marked the launch of the S-Class Coupe line, with the advanced 9G-Tronic automatic transmission being announced at the same time in the E-Class. The Concept Coupe SUV put in an appearance at Auto China in

The presentation of the Ener-G-Force concept, which was later displayed at the 2012 LA Show.

A Brabus B63S-700 Widestar (based on the G63 AMG) in service with the Dubai police force.

Dieter Zetsche, Chairman of the Board of Management of Daimler AG and head of Mercedes-Benz Cars, presenting the GLA model at the 2013 IAA.

Chris Pratt and Bryce Dallas on the set of *Jurassic World* with suitable transport. A 6x6 version of the G-Wagen was also featured in the film.

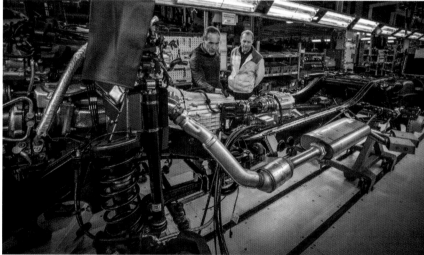

Mike Horn pictured in Graz during a factory tour in April 2015. The Swiss explorer and adventurer made good use of the G-Wagen on many of his expeditions, including a recent one to conquer K2.

Beijing, showing the way forward in modern SUV design, while the introduction of Multibeam LED headlights on the face-lifted CLS model lit the path to follow with a new level of efficiency.

On the small car front, new 'smart' vehicles were released in the summer of 2014, with the announcement of the 4-litre twin-turbo V8 by AMG appeasing power freaks. This unit was duly used in the Mercedes-AMG GT that appeared later in the year, at about the same time as the face-lifted B-Class hit the showrooms, and Lewis Hamilton and Nico Rosberg put the Silver Arrows back on top in the F1 circus after a spell of Red Bull-Renault domination on the tracks; Hamilton picked up the drivers' crown, too. The year was rounded off by the opening of a new R&D centre in China, spawning the presentation of the shapely Vision G-Code concept, and the launch of the Mercedes-Maybach brand, which made better use of the Maybach nameplate in much the same way as Jaguar had used the Daimler and Vanden Plas badges in days gone by.

With the company riding high on its best-ever sales year, the GLE Coupe was launched at the 2015 Detroit Show, and the CLA Shooting Brake went on sale in the early part of the New Year. For racing fans, the Mercedes-AMG GT3 made its debut at the Geneva Show, alongside cars that covered every possible market sector, from the special 4x4 G-Wagon we mentioned earlier in the chapter, through to the Mercedes-Maybach S600 Pullman and 'smart' cabriolet, which came in regular and Brabus guise. It was at this time that the four-door GLE replaced the M-Class, for this was really a face-lift of the W166, with the Coupe giving owners a choice between style and practicality on the same theme, and a new generation of 'smart' vehicles was launched in New York. In a similar vein, the GLK was renamed the GLC with the arrival of the new X205 generation.

Forever young

Just when it looked like the Geländewagen might be reaching the end of its useful production life, the men in Stuttgart gave it yet another reprieve, as a statement released from Graz on 20 October 2014 noted that production would continue at the Magna works through 2022. In fact, insiders probably had a good idea this would happen, as the G-Wagen build area had been modernised quite a bit during 2013 to enhance quality and reduce production time, and the associated costs that come with the latter, of course.

The face-lift announced in 2015 (domestic sales started in June), brought with it a fresh bumper design and wider wheelarch flares for the diesel car and the G500, bringing the pair closer in looks to the AMG models, which were unchanged from a styling point of view. The V6 diesel – renamed the G350d in the overhaul – also gained a new 18-inch alloy wheel design – the RL8 rim, although it has to be said, it looked very similar to the old 16-inch RL3 wheel.

The biggest changes, however, were under the bonnet. Although still employing a 3-litre unit, the G350d's V6 diesel now pumped out 245bhp (180kW), while the G500 inherited a brand new M176 4-litre V8 with twin turbochargers that delivered 422bhp (310kW). The AMG engines gained more power, too (up to 571bhp/420kW and 630bhp/463kW, respectively), allowing the old soldier to continue on its journey as one of the most readily recognizable shapes in the motoring arena.

We could go on, but the story is an ongoing one, and we need to stop somewhere. This seems as good a point as any, and if we get to a second edition stage with this title, we can look in detail at the 2016 Model Year cars and maybe take the story through to probable completion and the end of the G-Wagen series. Deep down, though, I have a feeling that time may never come if the folks in Stuttgart have anything to do with it. This could be an ongoing story for a long while yet ...

The face-lifted 2016 Model Year range, with (from left to right) the G65 AMG, with the optional darker alloys, the G63 AMG, the G350d, and the G500.

Appendix
Model line-up and production figures

Model line-up

The G-Wagen model mix, with the range having had a remarkably long run, is confusing at best, as some lines began in one series and continued into another, while the same basic designation can often be found in two and sometimes three series lines. Add in the lack of short-wheelbase and long-wheelbase differentiation in the model name, and only a limited number of body types being offered on certain grades, and one can be forgiven for not knowing where to start on separation. This listing of the showroom vehicles, with the public sales period for the home market (except on export only models), engine details and factory chassis designation for each variant sold through the mainstream passenger car showrooms, will hopefully serve to make things a lot clearer.

The 460-series models

200GE (1986-1991)
M102 E20 (1997cc)

Swb: cabriolet (460.216), estate (460.236).
Lwb: estate (460.237).

230G (1979-1982)
M115 V23 (2307cc)

Swb: cabriolet (460.210), van (460.220), estate (460.230).
Lwb: van (460.221), estate (460.231).

230GE (1982-1991)
M102 E23 (2299cc)

Swb: cabriolet (460.218), van (460.228), estate (460.238).
Lwb: van (460.229), estate (460.239).

280GE (1979-1990)
M110 E28 (2746cc)

Swb: cabriolet (460.212), van (460.222), estate (460.232).
Lwb: van (460.223), estate (460.233).

240GD (1979-1987)
OM616 D24 (2399cc)

Swb: cabriolet (460.310), van (460.320), estate (460.330).
Lwb: van (460.321), estate (460.331).

250GD (1987-1992)
OM602 D25 (2497cc)

Swb: cabriolet (460.317), estate (460.337).
Lwb: van (460.328), estate (460.338).

300GD (1979-1991)
OM617 D30 (2998cc)

Swb: cabriolet (460.312), van (460.322), estate (460.332).
Lwb: van (460.323), estate (460.333).

The 461-series models

230GE (1992-1996)
M102 E23 (2299cc)

Swb: estate (461.238).
Lwb: van (461.229), estate (461.239), pick-up (461.249).

290GD (1992-1997)
OM602 D29 (2874cc)

Swb: estate (461.337).
Lwb: van (461.328), estate (461.338), pick-up (461.341).

290GDT (1997-2001)
OM602 DE29 (2874cc)

Swb: estate (461.335).
Lwb: van (461.326), estate (461.336).

The 463-series models

200GE/G200 (1990-1993)
M102 E20 (1997cc)

Swb: cabriolet (463.200), estate (463.220).
Lwb: estate (463.221).

230GE/G230 (1990-1994)
M102 E23 (2299cc)

Swb: cabriolet (463.204), estate (463.224).
Lwb: estate (463.225).

300GE/G300 (1990-1994)
M103 E30 (2960cc)

Swb: cabriolet (463.207), estate (463.227).
Lwb: estate (463.228).

G320 (1994-1997)
M104 E32 (3199cc)

Swb: cabriolet (463.208), estate (463.230).
Lwb: estate (463.231).

G320 (1997-2000)
M112 E32 (3199cc)

Swb: cabriolet (463.209), estate (463.232).
Lwb: estate (463.233).

G320 (2001-2006)
M112 E32 (3199cc)

Swb: cabriolet (463.250), estate (463.244).
Lwb: estate (463.245).

500GE (1993-1994)
M117 E50 (4973cc)

Swb: N/A.
Lwb: estate (463.228).
NB. Based on 300GE chassis, so same number.

G500 (1998-2000)
M113 E50 (4966cc)

Swb: cabriolet (463.206), estate (463.240).
Lwb: estate (463.241).

G500 (2000-2008)
M113 E50 (4966cc)

Swb: cabriolet (463.254), estate (463.247).
Lwb: estate (463.248).

G500/G550 (2008-2015)
M273 KE55 (5461cc)

Swb: cabriolet (463.202), estate (463.222).
Lwb: estate (463.236).

G500 (2015-)
M176 DE40AL (3982cc)

Swb: N/A.
Lwb: estate (463.234).

G55 AMG (1999-2001)
M113 E55 (5439cc)

Swb: cabriolet (463.206), estate (463.240).
Lwb: estate (463.241).
NB. Based on G500 chassis, so same numbers.

G55 AMG (2001-2004)
M113 E55 (5439cc)

Swb: cabriolet (463.254), estate (463.247).
Lwb: estate (463.248).
NB. Based on G500 chassis, so same numbers.

G55 AMG Komp. (2004-2012)
M113 E55ML (5439cc)

Swb: N/A.
Lwb: USA estate (463.271), estate (463.270).

G63 AMG (2012-)
M157 DE55LA (5461cc)

Swb: N/A.
Lwb: USA estate (463.273), estate (463.272).

G65 AMG (2012-)
M279 E60LA (5980cc)

Swb: N/A.
Lwb: estate (463.274).

250GD (1990-1992)
OM602 D25 (2497cc)

Swb: cabriolet (463.304), estate (463.324).
Lwb: estate (463.325).

G270 CDI (2001-2007)
OM612 DE27LA (2685cc)

Swb: estate (463.322).
Lwb: estate (463.323).

300GD/G300D (1990-1994)
OM603 D30 (2996cc)

Swb: cabriolet (463.307), estate (463.327).
Lwb: estate (463.328).

G300TD (1996-2000)
OM606 D30LA (2996cc)

Swb: cabriolet (463.308), estate (463.330).
Lwb: estate (463.331).

G320 CDI/G350 CDI (2006-2010)
OM642 DE30LA (2987cc)

Swb: cabriolet (463.303), estate (463.340).
Lwb: USA estate (463.343), estate (463.341).

350GDT/G350T (1992-1996)
OM603 D35A (3449cc)

Swb: cabriolet (463.300), estate (463.320).
Lwb: estate (463.321).

G350 BlueTec (2010-2015)
OM642 DE30LA (2987cc)

Swb: cabriolet (463.306), estate (463.336).
Lwb: estate (463.346).

G350d (2015-)
OM642LS DE30LA (2987cc)

Swb: N/A.
Lwb: estate (463.348).

G400 CDI (2000-2006)
OM628 DE40LA (3996cc)

Swb: cabriolet (463.309), estate (463.332).
Lwb: estate (463.333).

NB. After September 1993, the 200GE became known as the G200, the 230GE as the G230, the 300GE as the G300, the 300GD as the G300 Diesel, and the 350GD Turbo as the G350 Turbo. There was no change in the specifications or chassis codes, it was purely a marketing move to bring the G-Wagen in line with other contemporary Mercedes-Benz models. Also, the late G500 was called the G550 in the United States and Japan, while the G320 CDI was renamed the G350 CDI in 2009.

Production figures

This section of the appendix hopefully gives a definitive guide to production numbers, broken down model-by-model for each calendar year. These are the figures lodged with the VDA in Germany for vehicles built in Graz. They include both civilian and military build numbers, the latter accounting for about five per cent of cars built in the early days, rising to well over half of production from 1992 onward in the case of the 461-series cars; by the new millennium, virtually all 461-series models were produced for either military or specialist working applications. Vehicles built under licence in other countries are not included.

The 460- and 461-series models

	200 GE	230G/ GE	240 GD	250 GD	280 GE	290GD/ GDT	300 GD
1979	-	1044	999	-	401	-	64
1980	-	1347	1799	-	1430	-	2091
1981	-	1739	1260	-	1022	-	2434
1982	-	1090	1340	-	998	-	3138
1983	-	1476	809	-	921	-	2456
1984	-	976	1330	-	1348	-	1878
1985	-	856	2406	-	905	-	2136
1986	147	917	1587	-	897	-	2397
1987	237	838	2169	450	647	-	2027
1988	98	743	1620	998	920	-	1176
1989	124	887	1065	647	392	-	727
1990	2	141	586	3044	106	-	323
1991	2	52	335	3016	1	4	185
1992	-	16	350	3139	-	304	-
1993	-	27	330	2146	-	634	217
1994	-	33	20	1100	-	827	240
1995	-	141	595	886	-	1362	173
1996	-	111	-	674	-	865	-
1997	-	-	-	314	-	1077	-
1998	-	-	-	-	-	1123	-
1999	-	-	-	-	-	1538	-
2000	-	-	-	-	-	1448	-
2001	-	-	-	-	-	755	2
2002	-	-	-	-	-	1243	85
2003	-	-	-	-	-	1008	313
2004	-	-	-	-	-	573	-
2005	-	-	-	-	-	-	-
2006	-	-	-	44	-	-	430
2007	-	-	-	-	-	-	-
2008	-	-	-	-	-	-	-
2009	-	-	-	-	-	-	10
2010	-	-	-	-	-	-	-

	200 GE	230 GE	300 GE	G320	500 GE	G500/ G550	G55 AMG	G63 AMG	G65 AMG
1999	-	-	-	416	-	1637	-	-	-
2000	-	-	-	341	-	2132	-	-	-
2001	-	-	-	396	-	2937	-	-	-
2002	-	-	-	265	-	4900	343	-	-
2003	-	-	-	252	-	2748	928	-	-
2004	-	-	-	236	-	1757	896	-	-
2005	-	-	-	162	-	1664	1493	-	-
2006	-	-	-	77	-	1528	1009	-	-
2007	-	-	1	-	-	1520	1395	-	-
2008	-	-	-	-	-	1290	1968	-	-
2009	-	-	-	-	-	871	1609	-	-
2010	-	-	-	-	-	1749	1832	-	-
2011	-	-	-	-	-	2123	2244	29	1
2012	-	-	-	-	-	3011	261	2532	401
2013	-	-	-	-	-	3137	-	5265	148

Total 200GE (460-series) 610 (for civilian use)

Total 230G/GE (460-series) 12,103 (of which 4138 230Gs and 6884 230GEs were built for civilian use)

Total 230GE (461-series) 331 (for civilian use)

Total 240GD (460-series) 18,600 (of which 7645 were built for civilian use)

Total 250GD (460-series) 16,414 (of which 2051 were built for civilian use)

Total 250GD (461-series) 44 (for military use)

Total 280GE (460-series) 9988 (for civilian use)

Total 290GD/GDT (461-series) 12,761 (of which 3168 290GDs and 1661 290GDTs were built for civilian use)

Total 300GD (460-series) 21,662 (of which 20,415 were built for civilian use)

Total 300GD (461-series) 840 (for military use)

NB. The 230G and 230GE have been batched together, as have the 290GD and 290GDT models. From 2002 onwards, a number of military and working cars were produced using the 461-series designation. These were based on the 270GD, G270 CDI, 280GD, G280 CDI, G300 CDI and 340GD chassis, but because hardly any of these model types were ever made available to the public, they have not been included in the production figures or summaries to avoid confusion.

The 463-series petrol-engined models

	200 GE	230 GE	300 GE	G320	500 GE	G500/ G550	G55 AMG	G63 AMG	G65 AMG
1989	4	6	20	-	-	-	-	-	-
1990	146	188	1487	-	-	-	-	-	-
1991	145	147	1558	-	-	-	-	-	-
1992	89	90	745	-	-	-	-	-	-
1993	6	63	512	-	446	-	-	-	-
1994	3	22	401	799	-	-	-	-	-
1995	-	-	123	1208	-	-	-	-	-
1996	-	-	68	1075	-	-	-	-	-
1997	-	-	24	1143	-	11	-	-	-
1998	-	-	-	753	-	1776	-	-	-

The 463-series diesel-engined models

	250 GD	G270 CDI	300 GD	G300 TD	G320 CDI	350 GDT	G350 BTec	G400 CDI
1989	7	-	21	-	-	-	-	-
1990	136	-	1526	-	-	-	-	-
1991	93	-	1629	-	-	5	-	-
1992	36	-	503	-	-	1417	-	-
1993	-	-	361	-	-	926	-	-
1994	-	-	123	-	-	738	-	-
1995	-	-	-	-	-	916	-	-
1996	-	-	-	753	-	290	-	-
1997	-	-	-	779	-	-	-	-
1998	-	-	-	547	-	-	-	-
1999	-	-	-	386	-	-	-	-
2000	-	-	-	491	-	-	-	14
2001	-	63	-	65	-	-	-	1925
2002	-	1041	-	-	-	-	-	1091
2003	-	786	-	-	-	-	-	689
2004	-	621	-	-	-	-	-	633
2005	-	499	-	-	-	-	-	377
2006	-	365	-	-	-	-	-	246
2007	-	221	-	-	815	-	-	-

	250 GD	G270 CDI	300 GD	G300 TD	G320 CDI	350 GDT	G350 BTec	G400 CD
2008	-	-	-	-	1104	-	-	-
2009	-	-	-	-	795	-	-	-
2010	-	-	-	-	661	-	347	-
2011	-	-	-	-	165	-	1436	-
2012	-	-	-	-	47	-	1429	-
2013	-	-	-	-	-	-	2114	-

Total 200GE/G200 (463-series)   393 (376 swb plus 17 lwb)

Total 230GE/G230 (463-series)   516 (382 swb plus 134 lwb)

Total 250GD (463-series)   272 (241 swb plus 31 lwb)

Total G270 CDI (463-series)   3596 (all models)

Total 300GD/G300D (463-series)   4163 (2547 swb plus 1616 lwb)

Total G300TD (463-series)   3021 (835 swb plus 2186 lwb*)

Total 300GE/G300 (463-series)   4939 (2132 swb plus 2807 lwb*)

Total G320 (463-series)   3781 (1184 swb plus 2597 lwb)

Total G320 V6 (463-series)   1946 (543 swb plus 1403 lwb)

Total G320 2001 on (463-series)   1396 (all models)

Total G320 CDI/G350 CDI (463-series)   3587 (840 swb plus 2747 lwb)

Total 350GDT/G350T (463-series)   4292 (1841 swb plus 2451 lwb)

Total G350 BlueTec (463-series)   5326 (to end of 2013 CY)

Total G400 CDI (463-series)   4975 (all models)

Total 500GE (463-series)   446 (sold in lwb form only)

Total G500/G55 AMG (463-series)   4968 (530 swb plus 4438 lwb)

Total G500 2001-2008 (463-series)   18,390 (all models)

Total G500/G550 2008 on (463-series)   11,433 (to end of 2013 CY)

Total G55 AMG 2002 on (463-series)   1912 (all NA models)

Total G55 AMG Komp. (463-series)   12,066 (all models)

Total G63 AMG (463-series)   7826 (to end of 2013 CY)

Total G65 AMG (463-series)   550 (to end of 2013 CY)

NB. There are a couple of instances where the swb/lwb split in 463-series production figures is not complete, so an estimate has been made based on the percentages of figures that are available. These have been marked with an asterisk. Also, the early AMG build numbers cannot be separated from those of the G500, the car on which the AMG conversions were based; the annual production figures from 2002 on for the G55 AMG include both normally-aspirated and supercharged variants. In addition, while the heading for annual build numbers states G320 CDI, it also includes the rebadged G350 CDI models.

Also from Brian Long and Veloce Publishing –

MERCEDES-BENZ
SL W113 SERIES

1963 to 1971

Brian Long

ISBN: 978-1-845843-04-5 • Hardback
• 25x25cm • £35* UK/$69.95* USA
• 208 pages • 286 colour and b&w pictures

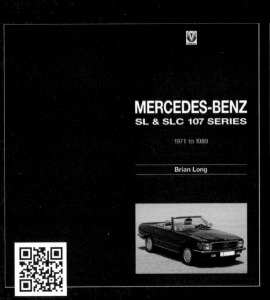

MERCEDES-BENZ
SL & SLC 107 SERIES

1971 to 1989

Brian Long

ISBN: 978-1-845842-99-4 • Hardback
• 25x25cm • £35.00* UK/$69.99* USA
• 208 pages • 355 colour and b&w pictures

MERCEDES-BENZ
SL R129 series

1989 to 2001

Brian Long

ISBN: 978-1-845844-48-6 • Hardback
• 25x25cm • £40* UK/$69.95* USA
• 208 pages • 370 colour and b&w pictures

MERCEDES-BENZ
SL R230 series

2001 to 2011

Brian Long

ISBN: 978-1-845847-47-0
• Hardback • 25x25cm • £50* UK/$80* USA
• 224 pages • 433 colour and b&w pictures

MERCEDES-BENZ
SLK R170 series

1996-2004

Brian Long

ISBN: 978-1-845846-51-0 • Hardback
• 24.8x24.8cm • £45* UK/$75* USA
• 192 pages • 337 colour pictures

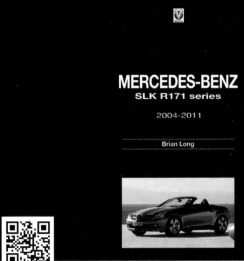

MERCEDES-BENZ
SLK R171 series

2004-2011

Brian Long

ISBN: 978-1-845846-53-4 • Hardback
• 24.8x24.8cm • £45* UK/$75* USA
• 224 pages • 388 colour pictures

These detailed and beautifully illustrated books celebrate several major Mercedes-Benz models, covering a period from 1963 to 2004. Written by a highly regarded motoring writer, with many years' ownership experience behind him, these are the definitive studies of their subjects.

Two Summers

The Mercedes-Benz W 196 R Racing Car

Robert Ackerson

~ Limited Edition of 1500 copies ~

ISBN: 978-1-845847-51-7
Hardback • 25x25cm • £75* UK/$125* USA • 192 pages • 171 colour and b&w pictures

The story of the Mercedes-Benz W 196 R Grand Prix racing car – its development, roots, and magnificent two-year racing career – has enough drama, emotion and excitement to fill a dozen books, but only this volume captures the car's enduring greatness. Hundreds of photos from the Daimler archives, stunning original artwork, and written with authority, reflection and admiration for the W 196 R.

Return to Glory!

The Mercedes-Benz 300 SL Racing Car

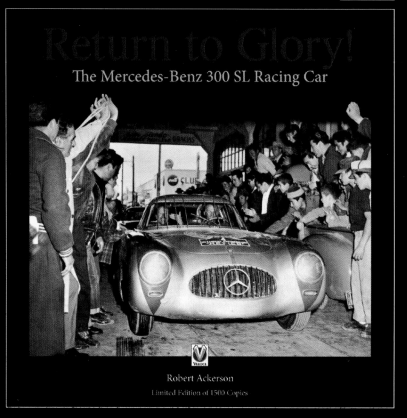

Robert Ackerson

Limited Edition of 1500 Copies

ISBN: 978-1-845846-17-6 • Hardback • 25x25cm • £75* UK/$120* USA • 144 pages • 126 colour and b&w pictures

The 300 SL's 1952 debut was the culmination of a long, difficult road back to racing for Mercedes-Benz after a 13 year break. This book vividly depicts the 300 SL's performance in the five races in which it competed that year, and tells the story of how it became the most successful competition sports car that season. Through dramatic photographs and stirring text, one of the greatest years of sports car racing is brought to life, filled with automobiles prepared by great factory teams, driven by men who were national sporting idols, and raced under gruelling conditions unique to the age.

For more info on Veloce titles, visit our website at www.veloce.co.uk • email: info@veloce.co.uk • Tel: +44(0)1305 260068
* prices subject to change, p&p extra

MERCEDES-BENZ
W123 series

1976-1986

Brian Long

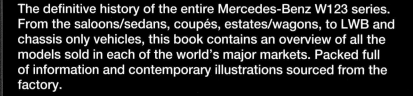

The definitive history of the entire Mercedes-Benz W123 series. From the saloons/sedans, coupés, estates/wagons, to LWB and chassis only vehicles, this book contains an overview of all the models sold in each of the world's major markets. Packed full of information and contemporary illustrations sourced from the factory.

ISBN: 978-1-845847-92-0 • Hardback • 25x25cm • £45* UK/$75* USA
• 192 pages • 321 colour pictures

TRUCKMAKERS™

Colin Peck
Mercedes-Benz
TRUCKS

Combining materials from Mercedes-Benz's official archives with information collected from professionals involved with the marque, this book provides a unique perspective on how the brand developed its products to provide transportation solutions across some of the most diverse operating conditions in the world.

   With rare and previously unpublished photos of working trucks in action, this comprehensive book also features some of the biggest, 'baddest' and most unusual Mercedes-Benz trucks from around the globe.

ISBN: 978-1-845846-43-5 • Paperback
• 19.5x21cm • £15.99* UK/$24.95* USA
• 128 pages • 153 colour and b&w pictures

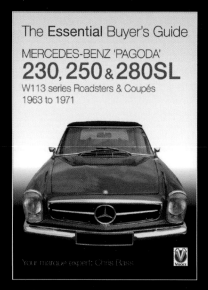

The Essential Buyer's Guide

MERCEDES-BENZ 'PAGODA'
230, 250 & 280SL
W113 series Roadsters & Coupés
1963 to 1971

Your marque expert: Chris Bass

ISBN: 978-1-845841-13-3 • Paperback • 19.5x13.9cm • £9.99* UK/$19.95* USA • 64 pages • 122 colour pictures

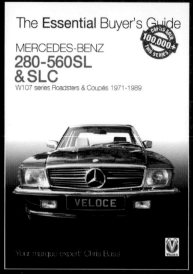

The Essential Buyer's Guide

MERCEDES-BENZ
280-560SL & SLC
W107 series Roadsters & Coupés 1971-1989

Your marque expert: Chris Bass

ISBN: 978-1-845841-07-2 • Paperback • 19.5x13.9cm • £12.99* UK/$19.95* USA • 64 pages • 100 pictures

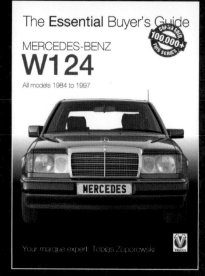

The Essential Buyer's Guide

MERCEDES-BENZ
W124
All models 1984 to 1997

Your marque expert: Tobias Zoporowski

ISBN: 978-1-845848-77-4 Paperback • 19.5x13.9cm • £12.99* UK/$25* USA • 64 pages • 100 pictures

The Essential Buyer's Guide

MERCEDES-BENZ
SL
R129-series 1989 to 2001

Your marque expert: Julian Parish

ISBN: 978-1-845848-98-9 Paperback • 19.5x13.9cm • £12.99* UK/$25* USA • 64 pages • 100 pictures

The Essential Buyer's Guide

MERCEDES-BENZ
SLK
R170 series 1996-2004

Your marque expert: Chris Bass

ISBN: 978-1-845848-08-8 Paperback • 19.5x13.9cm • £12.99* UK/$25.00* USA • 64 pages • 90 pictures

Benefit from the authors' years of ownership experience. These step-by-step guides will help you evaluate any example. With hundreds of photos of what to look for and what to avoid, plus a realistic assessment of running and restoration costs, as well as market values, you're sure to get the right car at the right price!

For more info on Veloce titles, visit our website at www.veloce.co.uk • email: info@veloce.co.uk • Tel: +44(0)1305 260068
* prices subject to change, p&p extra

Index

Mercedes-Benz, as well as Daimler-Benz and Daimler AG, along with their subsidiaries and products, are mentioned throughout the book.